Foreign Trade Regimes and Economic Development: ANATOMY AND CONSEQUENCES OF EXCHANGE CONTROL REGIMES

Foreign Trade Regimes and Economic Development:

A Special Conference Series on Foreign Trade Regimes and Economic Development

VOLUME XI

NATIONAL BUREAU OF ECONOMIC RESEARCH
New York 1978

ANATOMY AND CONSEQUENCES OF EXCHANGE CONTROL REGIMES

by Jagdish Bhagwati

Ballinger Publishing Company • Cambridge, Massachusetts
A Subsidiary of J.B. Lippincott Company

NATIONAL BUREAU OF ECONOMIC RESEARCH

Studies in International Economic Relations

1. Problems of the United States as World Trader and Banker
   Hal B. Lary
2. Price and Quantity Trends in the Foreign Trade of the United States
   Robert E. Lipsey
3. Measuring Transactions Between World Areas *Herbert B. Woolley*
4. Imports of Manufactures from Less Developed Countries *Hal B. Lary*
5. The Responsiveness of Demand Policies to Balance of Payments: Postwar Patterns *Michael Michaely*
6. Price Competitiveness in World Trade *Irving B. Kravis* and *Robert E. Lipsey*
7. Money, Financial Flows, and Credit in the Soviet Union
   George Garvy
8. Foreign Dollar Balances and the International Role of the Dollar
   Raymond F. Mikesell and *J. Herbert Furth*
9. Foreign Trade Regimes and Economic Development: Liberalization Attempts and Consequences *Anne O. Krueger*
10. Anatomy and Consequences of Exchange Control Regimes
    Jagdish N. Bhagwati

This book is printed on recycled paper.

Library of Congress Card Number: 78-18799
ISBN for the series: 0-87014-500-2
ISBN for this volume: 0-88410-487-7

Printed in the United States of America

Relation of the Directors to the Work and Publications of the National Bureau of Economic Research

1. The object of the National Bureau of Economic Research is to ascertain and to present to the public important economic facts and their interpretation in a scientific and impartial manner. The Board of Directors is charged with the responsibility of ensuring that the work of the National Bureau is carried on in strict conformity with this object.

2. The President of the National Bureau shall submit to the Board of Directors, or to its Executive Committee, for their formal adoption all specific proposals for research to be instituted.

3. No research report shall be published by the National Bureau until the President has sent each member of the Board a notice that a manuscript is recommended for publication and that in the President's opinion it is suitable for publication in accordance with the principles of the National Bureau. Such notification will include an abstract or summary of the manuscript's content and a response form for use by those Directors who desire a copy of the manuscript for review. Each manuscript shall contain a summary drawing attention to the nature and treatment of the problem studied, the character of the data and their utilization in the report, and the main conclusions reached.

4. For each manuscript so submitted, a special committee of the Directors (including Directors Emeriti) shall be appointed by majority agreement of the President and Vice Presidents (or by the Executive Committee in case of inability to decide on the part of the President and Vice Presidents), consisting of three Directors selected as nearly as may be one from each general division of the Board. The names of the special manuscript committee shall be stated to each Director when notice of the proposed publication is submitted to him. It shall be the duty of each member of the special manuscript committee to read the manuscript. If each member of the manuscript committee signifies his approval within thirty days of the transmittal of the manuscript, the report may be published. If at the end of that period any member of the manuscript committee withholds his approval, the President shall then notify each member of the Board, requesting approval or disapproval of publication, and thirty days additional shall be granted for this purpose. The manuscript shall then not be published unless at least a majority of the entire Board who shall have voted on the proposal within the time fixed for the receipt of votes shall have approved.

5. No manuscript may be published, though approved by each member of the special manuscript committee, until forty-five days have elapsed from the transmittal of the report in manuscript form. The interval is allowed for the receipt of any memorandum of dissent or reservation, together with a brief statement of his reasons, that any member may wish to express; and such memorandum of dissent or reservation shall be published with the manuscript if he so desires. Publication does not, however, imply that each member of the Board has read the manuscript, or that either members of the Board in general or the special committee have passed on its validity in every detail.

6. Publications of the National Bureau issued for informational purposes concerning the work of the Bureau and its staff, or issued to inform the public of activities of Bureau staff, and volumes issued as a result of various conferences involving the National Bureau shall contain a specific disclaimer noting that such publication has not passed through the normal review procedures required in this resolution. The Executive Committee of the Board is charged with review of all such publications from time to time to ensure that they do not take on the character of formal research reports of the National Bureau, requiring formal Board approval.

7. Unless otherwise determined by the Board or exempted by the terms of paragraph 6, a copy of this resolution shall be printed in each National Bureau publication.

(Resolution adopted October 25, 1926, as revised through September 30, 1974)

Dedication

For

Alex and Rachel

Erlich

Contents

Figures

Tables

Foreword

This volume by Jagdish Bhagwati, together with Anne Krueger's *Foreign Trade Regimes and Economic Development: Liberalization Attempts and Consequences*, published earlier, brings to a conclusion the National Bureau of Economic Research Project on Foreign Trade Regimes and Economic Development, directed by Professors Bhagwati and Krueger. Professor Bhagwati's synthesis volume concentrates on the exchange control regimes themselves, while Professor Krueger's focused on attempts at liberalization. The syntheses draw on the previously published studies of Turkey, Ghana, Israel, Egypt, the Philippines, India, South Korea, Chile, and Colombia, as well as the two studies that were begun but not completed on Brazil and Pakistan. The Project, which began in 1970, is being followed up under the National Bureau's program on International Economic Relations by a study of Alternative Trade Strategies and Employment under Professor Krueger's direction. Both of these studies have been financed under research contracts with the Agency for International Development of the U.S. Department of State.

Perhaps the outstanding point of both syntheses is the conclusion that an export-promoting strategy is superior to an import-substitution strategy for the promotion of economic growth in developing countries. Professor Bhagwati defines export promotion policy as one which removes import bias, and in fact he finds that what are called export promotion policies usually do not involve a bias toward exporting but something closer to neutrality and therefore to a free-trade position.

The very isolation from world markets fostered by an import-substitution strategy leads to "chaotic" incentives, so that the strategy is far from an "ideal" one that might be theoretically constructed. Export-promoting strategy, on the other hand, seems to lead to incentives that are less chaotic—more neutral among industries—and on this ground alone should contribute to economic growth. One reason why export-promotion policies do not involve large biases toward exports is that export subsidies,the main possible source of export bias, are an open cost in national budgets. An import-substitution policy, operating typically through quantitative restrictions, does not involve any budgetary cost for the Treasury, and inadvertent major distortions are therefore much more likely.

Given the way an import-substitution regime actually works, including the fact that it typically operates largely through physical measures (quotas) rather than price measures (tariffs), many aspects of the regime seem to be at best irrelevant for development and often clearly injurious in ways that are barely touched on by the theoretical literature Professor Bhagwati reviews. As in Professor Krueger's volume, there is strong evidence here not only of the effects of domestic political considerations but also of that appears to have been sheer inadvertence. Quantitative controls became so complex that governments did not realize their impact, as in the case cited for India in which ". . . the import control regime seems to have provided the private sector with incentives to add to capacity in the face of excess capacity."

The gains from an export-promotion strategy are thus largely in the removal of such unintended consequences of import substitution as excess capacity, excess inventories, and bottlenecks. These effects are reinforced by the apparent success of export promotion in inducing greater capital inflows, despite the high profits for local production offered by import-substitution policies. Professor Bhagwati's explanation is, first, that foreign capital inflow is encouraged by the prospect of higher exports, which can finance the servicing and repatriation of the debt. His second point is that the type of "tariff-jumping" direct investment induced by import substitution may lower real income in the receiving country, while under an export-promotion strategy the investment is more likely to take advantage of the country's abundant resources, particularly labor, and thus raise the country's (and the world's) real income.

Professor Bhagwati points out that both tariffs and quantitative restrictions give rise to opportunities for illegal transactions, favoritism, and corruption. However, quantitative restrictions, by producing larger deviations from free market prices than do tariffs, offer larger temptations to illegal behavior. The awarding of import licenses has produced the most flagrant examples, but quantitative restrictions also offer greater incentives to smuggling and false invoicing than tariffs because the implicit tariffs resulting from quantitative restrictions are so high. Explicit tariffs of over 100 percent are rare, but implicit tariffs over 100 percent resulting from quantitative controls are numerous.

Even where the quantitative restrictions do not give rise to illegal transactions or corruption, the effort to avoid favoritism in awarding licenses often leads to mechanical methods of allocation on the basis of "fairness," or "equality of treatment." The result of such efforts is to ignore efficiency in favor of rules of thumb that seem "fair" such as allocation by past shares, capacity, employment, and so on, all of which shelter and thus preserve the least efficient firms.

Professor Bhagwati examines each aspect of the anatomy of exchange controls theoretically and points out the often severe limitations that the required assumptions place on the applicability of the theory. He then combs the country studies and related literature for examples, counter-examples, and statistical tests of the nature and consequences of exchange control regimes. He carefully points out the difficulties in tracing clear effects of exchange controls and calls attention to the exceptions and ambiguous cases.

In a sense, by examining the anatomy of exchange control regimes, Professor Bhagwati opens up an area beyond the usual theory of optimum development policy. What is needed is a theory of how policy will actually be made and administered under different trade regimes given the incentives for the policy-makers, the administrators of the policy within the government, and the firms that must live with or evade the policy. It may be irrelevant to any actual problem whether a quantitative restriction program can be imagined that would maximize real income or growth. A policy of import substitution, particularly under quantitative restrictions, may involve so many opportunities to secure private profits in ways that defeat the ostensible purpose of the restrictions that it is bound to be manipulated to that end. Even if an export promotion policy were not theoretically superior, it might be superior in fact because it offered fewer opportunities for exploitation.

The success of Professors Bhagwati and Krueger in drawing substantial conclusions about trade policy from such intractible materials testifies to the value of this type of large-scale comparative study that could draw on the experience of many countries and expert contributors. In a study of any single country the complexities and national peculiarities would obscure the lessons. A series of studies, in a well-designed common framework, can bring out the major common themes of each country's experience and provide conclusions for scholars and policy-makers.

Robert E. Lipsey
Director, International Studies

Preface

This volume is designed to be a partial synthesis of the major findings of the National Bureau of Economic Research Project directed by me and Professor Anne Krueger. It is meant to be a complement to the more substantial synthesis written by Professor Krueger and therefore is deliberately kept extremely brief in regard to both the description of the country studies and its overall size, the former so as to avoid undue repetition and the latter so as not to strain the patience of the reader who seeks to gain a total view of the Project's findings.

Two caveats must be entered. First, the two synthesis volumes complement each other in focusing on different aspects of the Project. This volume is addressed to the static efficiency and dynamic effects of exchange control regimes whereas the Krueger volume is addressed principally to the causes and consequences of liberalization attempts. Nevertheless, inevitably, several overlaps of topics do exist. In these instances, no attempt has been made to impose uniformity of views. This is, in fact, in the spirit of the Project, and we hope that it also encourages the readers of the synthesis volumes to refer to the original country studies and attempt their own syntheses! Nonetheless, the reader of both volumes should find a substantial conformity in the overall conclusions reached by Professor Krueger and myself, especially in regard to the major questions addressed by the Project.

Second, the syntheses cannot expect to, and in fact do not, capture the full complexities and subtleties that the reader will find in many of the country studies. At least this volume should therefore be treated as a guide to certain key contributions in the country studies rather than as a perfect substitute to reading them for their many insights.

In the course of reflecting over the questions posed in the Project and interacting with the many distinguished collaborators in the Project, I have chalked up a number of intellectual debts. I should particularly like to thank Hal Lary of the National Bureau of Economic Research who oversaw the Project over its long life. Although he is an economist with distinguished contributions of his own, he selflessly gave an immense amount of time, energy, and intellectual ability to the Project. While therefore no volume bears his name, the stamp of his meticulousness, carefulness with data and interpretation, and insightfulness is evident in all the volumes published under the Project, and none of them has failed to improve from his generous input. I should also like to add that I have profited much from the collaboration with Anne Krueger in co-directing the Project. Over the several years that we have worked on the Project, we have discussed many things, and it is now impossible to take the partial derivatives and assign marginal product to either of us. But it is evident to me that, without her many contributions, the Project would have been much the poorer. Next, all the country authors have freely placed at our disposal their ideas, in penciled comments on early drafts, through their excellent studies, and at the on-the-way conferences that were held to discuss the progress of the Project. The penultimate draft in particular has profited immensely from the detailed and careful comments of Bent Hansen, Clark Leith, Larry Westphal, Jere Behrman, Anne Krueger, Hal Lary, T.N. Srinivasan, Padma Desai, and Gideon Fishelson.

Finally, the reader should be warned that, except for minor revisions, the writing of this volume was substantially finished by June 1977.

Cambridge
March 1978

Jagdish N. Bhagwati

Other Books by the Author

The Economics of Underdeveloped Countries
Trade, Tariffs and Growth
The Theory and Practice of Commercial Policy
The Amount and Sharing of Aid
India: Planning for Industrialization (with Padma Desai)
India in the International Economy
Contributions to Indian Economic Analysis (with S. Chakravarty)
Foreign Trade Regimes and Economic Development: India (with T.N. Srinivasan)

International Trade (editor)
Foreign Aid (co-editor with R.S. Eckaus)
Economics and World Order (editor)
Development and Planning (co-editor with R.S. Eckaus)
Trade, Balance of Payments, and Growth (co-editor with R. Jones, *et al.*)
Illegal Transactions in International Trade (editor)
Taxing the Brain Drain: A Proposal (co-editor with M. Partington)
The Brain Drain and Taxation (editor)
The New International Economic Order: The North-South Debate (editor)

PART I
Introduction

Chapter 1

Scope of the Study

This volume and the companion volume by Anne Krueger are the outcome of a Project that was addressed to three principal sets of issues in the area of foreign trade and economic development of developing countries:

1. Given the widespread postwar reliance in LDCs (less developed countries) on exchange controls to manage the balance of payments and cross-sectional differences and changes over time in the nature and degree of such reliance, it seemed necessary to systematize the "anatomy" of exchange control regimes prior to examining their economic consequences in much greater depth than was the current practice. Thus, for example, the consequences of QRs (quantitative restrictions), which were levied so as to confer automatic protection to domestic production, would be clearly different, indeed more adverse, than when QRs were adjusted so as to confer no more than a certain degree of protection. The characterization of the anatomy of exchange control regimes, including the interaction between quantitative and price measures, was thus an important object of inquiry in the Project.

2. The relationship between different types of exchange control regimes and economic efficiency was then the next area of inquiry in the Project. In this matter, we needed to distinguish two broad sets of questions:

a. Were different types of exchange control regimes likely to have systematic differences in regard to their consequences for economic efficiency?

b. Would the conclusions in this regard differ according to whether the consequences were investigated in a static sense (i.e., allocation of given resources) or in a dynamic fashion (i.e., saving, investment, innovation, entrepreneurship, etc.)?

3. Finally, it was clear from even a casual examination of the developing

countries' experience that their exchange control regimes changed from one type to another, with some countries transiting gradually to more liberalized regimes (e.g., South Korea and Israel) and others sticking to roughly the same restrictive patterns for much longer periods (e.g., India). Could we then learn something systematic about the forces that governed the likelihood of success in moving from a restrictive exchange control regime to a liberalized regime?

To investigate these questions, the Project was addressed to an intensive, functional analysis of ten developing countries with diversity of growth, exchange control regimes, size (in terms of population, area, and income), geographical location, and historical experience.[1]

The present volume (as also the companion Krueger volume) draws extensively on the results of these studies[2] to systematize the answers to the questions posed above. At the same time, extensive reference is made, where appropriate, to evidence on specific issues from other empirical studies in the currently available literature.

The present volume focuses essentially on the first two sets of questions distinguished above, the third set of issues (essentially the analysis of the conditions that could contribute to a successful transition to less restrictive regimes) being the principal subject of the Krueger volume. The plan of the volume is to divide its substantive analysis into two parts. Part II deals with the first set of issues delineated earlier, namely, the anatomy of exchange control; Part III deals with the second set of issues, namely, the consequences of exchange control regimes. To avoid undue repetition, the present volume does not review the major economic characteristics of the countries in the Project: these are reviewed in Krueger's companion volume (Chapter 2).

In the analysis of the anatomy of exchange control regimes that follows in Part II, we begin in Chapter 2 with a taxonomic examination of the alternative, direct control dimensions of exchange control regimes. The focus in this chapter is on distinguishing among alternative control methods with which such regimes function: for example, regulating imports by source, by end use, by claimants (e.g., large-scale versus small-scale, foreign versus domestic applicants). Extensive use is made of the country studies in the Project to illustrate specific types of such regulation. There is no attempt made, however, to indicate the precise combination or cluster of such regulatory methods, as distinguished and delineated, that obtained at any period in any of the countries studied in the Project; this task is left until Chapter 3.[3] Chapter 2 concludes with a discussion of the uses of the price mechanism as distinct from controls. Exchange control regimes are rarely "pure," and invariably use is made of price instruments such as tariffs, advance deposits on imports, export subsidies and taxes, and a host of similar instruments. When the phrase "exchange control regime" is used in this volume, it is intended to apply not merely to the control methods and instruments (such as those discussed in depth in

Chapter 2) but also to the associated set of price instruments in use in that regime.[4]

Chapter 3 then shifts attention to a more integrated and functional view of the different control and price instruments, seeking to define specific clusters, types, or combinations of instruments as revealed by the country analyses, distinguishing among these in a manner designed to facilitate analysis of the exchange control regimes. This leads to a delineation of five *Phases* in exchange control regimes, the evolution of the exchange control regimes through these Phases then being also set out in the chapter.[5] In essence, the Phases isolate and denote alternative mixes of resort to price *versus* control measures, the complexity of the control measures, and the degree of discrimination against exports implied by differential, effective exchange rates on imports and exports. In addition to the Phase delineation, Chapter 3 develops explicitly certain general propositions regarding the differential impact of different exchange control regimes and of identical exchange control regimes with different domestic policies.

The delineation of Phases, and the sorting out of individual country experiences with exchange control during the postwar period into these Phases, then permits a systematic analysis of the economic consequences, static and dynamic, of exchange control regimes in Part III. Chapter 4 contains an analysis of the illegal economic transactions as they interact with exchange control regimes. Frustrations of the objectives, alteration of the restrictiveness, and changed economic costs of exchange control regimes that follow from evasions and the growth of illicit phenomena in such regimes need to be noted prior to the more traditional analysis of the economic consequences of these regimes.

Chapter 5 examines the static, allocative efficiency impact of exchange control regimes, extending the analysis also to issues such as excess capacity, competitiveness and cost-consciousness, choice of techniques, and so on. While the focus is mainly on the consequences of tightly restrictive regimes—Phase II type regimes in our Phase delineation—an attempt is also made to see if any evidence exists on the issue whether a shift to more liberalized regime—Phases IV and V—is associated with transition to greater efficiency.[6]

Chapter 6 extends the analysis to the interaction between exchange control regimes and saving, both domestic and foreign. Chapter 7 examines the question whether (1) restrictive regimes, via a differentially low effective exchange rate on exports and other causes, adversely affect *export* performance and whether (2) such an adverse impact on export performance also implies an adverse impact on *economic* performance. Again, the analysis is extended to consider explicitly the question whether a successful shift to a more liberalized regime has been associated with improved export performance and thence with enhanced economic performance. Other, miscellaneous arguments are also reviewed.

Chapter 8 then draws together the major conclusions that emerge from the analysis in the present volume, focusing in a stylized fashion on the lessons to be drawn regarding the optimal foreign trade regime to be adopted by developing countries.

Finally, the reader should be forewarned that the present volume does not generally arrive at strong, prescriptive conclusions in regard to many of the detailed questions that are examined. For example, in Chapter 6, the relationship between exchange control regimes and saving is examined at considerable length, both analytically and in terms of the empirical evidence in the country studies in the Project and elsewhere. But the conclusion is, broadly speaking, that there are several possible linkages here, as also conflicting evidence in some cases. It is thus not possible to argue propositions such as: "restrictive exchange control regimes may be inefficient statically but they lead to more rapid capital formation by generating more saving" or that, conversely, "liberalized exchange control regimes will promote more rapid growth by augmenting savings." While such *general* propositions are not sustainable, *individual* country experiences may, and often do, indicate the dominance of only a subset of the possible linkages and effects, thus sustaining stronger propositions in regard to their own experience. This also suggests that, to a large extent, the reader should approach the present volume as a manual.[7] Anyone who wishes to examine a specific country's foreign trade regime and its consequences can read the present volume and readily have access to possible hypotheses and techniques of analysis (as also evidence, mainly from the Project) that may be used for the reader's own analysis. Many chapters in the present volume are therefore deliberately ambitious in their taxonomy; this should make the manual aspect of the volume's analysis more valuable to the reader.

Nonetheless, both the present volume and the companion volume of Anne Krueger do suggest that, in regard to the famous issue raised by Ragnar Nurkse and others in the early 1950s about the appropriate foreign trade strategy to be pursued by the developing countries, the results of the present Project strongly indicate that the export-promoting strategy has turned out to be superior. This "prescriptive" conclusion, discussed at some length in Chapter 8 here, is important. It warrants a careful scrutiny by the reader of the meticulous and systematic synthesis by Anne Krueger of the findings of the Project on the problems attending on the attempts at liberalizing the foreign trade regime and thus on the lessons to be borne in mind in successfully transiting from a restrictive, import-substituting strategy to a liberalized, export-promoting strategy.[8]

NOTES

1. The studies were conducted with reference to a common plan of research worked out in the form of an analytical framework authored by Bhagwati and Krueger and finalized in light of discussions with the country authors.

2. The ten countries for which studies were undertaken are: (1) *Turkey*, by Anne Krueger, (2) *Ghana*, by J. Clark Leith, (3) *Israel*, by Michael Michaely, (4) *Egypt*, by Bent Hansen and Karim Nashashibi, (5) *The Philippines*, by Robert Baldwin, (6) *India*, by Jagdish Bhagwati and T.N. Srinivasan, (7) *South Korea*, by Charles Frank, Jr., Kwang Suk Kim, and Larry Westphal, (8) *Chile*, by Jere Behrman, (9) *Colombia*, by Carlos Díaz-Alejandro, and (10) *Brazil*, by Albert Fishlow. A study of Pakistan, by Nurul Islam, was commissioned and exists in first draft; it was interrupted by the events that resulted in the creation of Bangladesh. Reference to the Pakistan draft is however repeatedly made in the present volume. The present volume also has had to be written despite the failure to complete the Brazil volume, so that references to that work are to an early and incomplete draft thereof.

3. Chapter 2 is thus written to aid the economist or civil servant who intends to examine the exchange control system in a specific country in an economically meaningful way.

4. On the other hand, the phrase "foreign trade regime" is used generally synonymously with the phrase "exchange control regime" but obviously would also apply to the case where exchange controls have disappeared and only price instruments are deployed.

5. A summary description of the five Phases, as set out initially in plans for the country studies, will be found in the appendix at the end of this book.

6. See also the Krueger synthesis for a more direct focus on the effects of liberalized regimes on economic efficiency.

7. The reference here is to the celebrated *OECD Manual* of I.M.D. Little and James Mirrlees (Paris: OECD Development Center, 1970), which relates to social cost-benefit analysis of projects. While, however, the *OECD Manual* was addressed primarily to civil servants and planners, the present volume is written for professional economists, whether academic or bureaucrats.

8. In fact, the present project differs primarily from the earlier OECD project on trade and industrialization, directed by Messrs. Little, Scitovsky, and Scott, in analyzing in far greater depth the growth effects as well as the conditions determining a successful transition from restrictive to liberalized regimes. Cf. I.M.D. Little, T. Scitovsky, and M. Scott, *Trade and Industry in Some Developing Countries*, OECD Development Center, Oxford University Press, 1970.

PART II

Anatomy of Exchange Control Regimes: Patterns and Sequences

Chapter 2

Anatomy of Exchange Control Regimes

In this chapter, we propose to delineate the alternative forms that direct controls can, and often do, take under exchange control regimes.[1] These possibilities are illustrated extensively from the country studies. They are also taxonomically organized in a functional fashion: thus many so-called administrative details, which are often considered to be economically uninteresting, are shown to be of economic importance, having distinct effects on economic efficiency and on income distribution. The chapter concludes with a brief delineation of the *price* measures that often co-exist with the direct controls under the exchange control regimes.

I. CONVENTIONAL THEORY

The analysis of quantitative restrictions in the trade-theoretic literature has generally relied on the so-called equivalence proposition. This Marshallian proposition asserts that tariffs and quotas are basically equivalent in their real effects, the only difference being in their revenue (and, to that extent, in their income-distributional) effects, as noted in Figure 2-1 and the legend thereto. Thus, if a quota were to be replaced by a tariff set at a rate that *equals* the ratio of the import premium to the c.i.f. import price, the "real" effects on domestic and international equilibrium values of production, consumption, and prices would be identical. The only difference would be that the government would now pick up the import premium as tariff revenue.

Related to this basic equivalence proposition, of course, is the standard Marshallian depiction of the QR regime in terms of the supply and demand

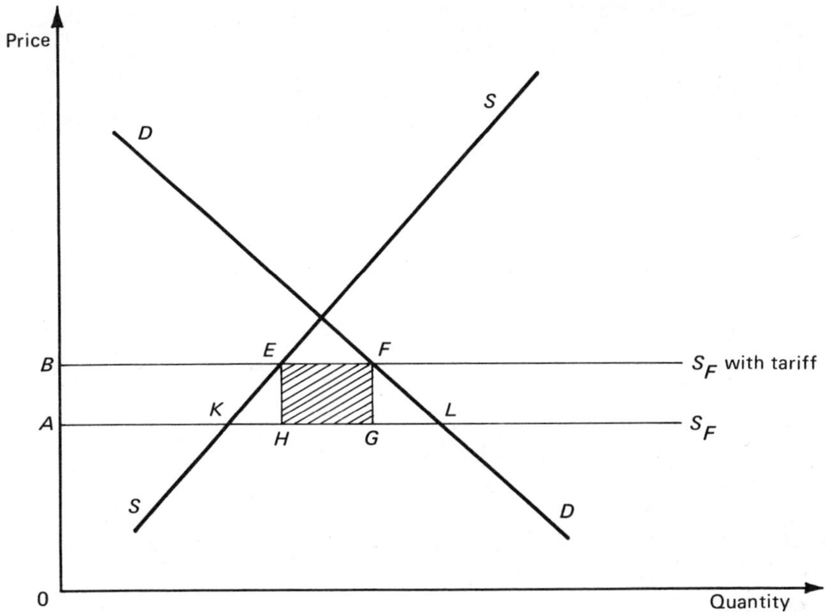

Figure 2-1. The Equivalence of Tariffs and Quotas Under Perfect Competition.

(*DD* and *SS* are the domestic demand and supply curves for a product. S_F is the foreign supply curve. A tariff at rate *BA/0A* shifts S_F upward and reduces imports from *KL* to *EF*. *EFGH* is then the import tax revenue. Alternatively, an "equivalent" import quota of *EF* units could be imposed, leading to the same equilibrium except that *AB/0A* would now be the import premium rate on c.i.f. import price and the revenue *EFGH* would now accrue to the holders of the import licenses.)

schedules of foreign exchange. The QR-equilibrium price of foreign exchange would then be lower than the "true" equilibrium price, the lower quantities would be cleared at an import-premium-inclusive price, and it would generally be argued that the same QR equilibrium could be equally achieved by an equivalent tariff on imports (which would make the effective exchange rate on imports equivalently higher than the effective exchange rate for exports), as noted in Figure 2-2 and the legend thereto.

Such "equivalence" notions have typically provided the underlying conceptual basis for many quantitative and descriptive studies of the trade and payments policies of LDCs. An excellent example is the World Bank study of the structure of LDC protection, which does not extend to discussion of many of the caveats that must surround the resort to the equivalence assumption.[2] At the same time, however, it has increasingly been appreciated in the theoretical

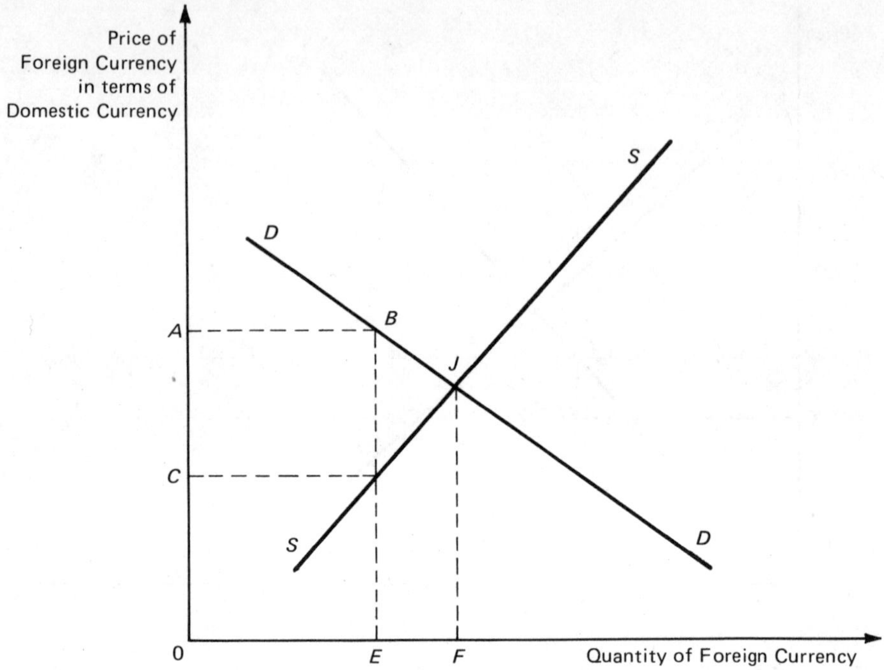

Figure 2-2. The Foreign Exchange Market and Overvaluation.

(*DD* and *SS* are the supply and demand curves for foreign exchange. The equilibrium price should be *JF*. However, *QR*s peg the exchange rate at *0C*, resulting in quantity *0E* of foreign currency being supplied. This amount clears the market at *domestic* price *0A*, the difference *AC* then representing the premium on foreign exchange and the premium rate being *AC/0C*.)

literature that the Marshallian equivalence assumption will hold only under singular circumstances. Yet, as will be evident below, even this theoretical literature is concerned only with a narrow set of non-equivalence circumstances and leaves out many aspects of exchange control allocation mechanisms in practice that, as the country studies in the Project illustrate, have definite efficiency and distributional effects that are asymmetrical to those that would obtain if the same quotas were replaced by *ad valorem* tariffs (levied at rates identical to the observed ratio of import premium to c.i.f. import prices under the quota regime).

Thus, the conventional equivalence proposition has been shown in the theoretical literature to depend on special restrictions. Within the Marshallian framework, Bhagwati has shown that equivalence can break down when the assumption of perfect competition is replaced by, say, monopoly in domestic production, export supply, or quota holding, that is, institutional assumptions that are not exactly foreign to the economic scene of many LDCs.[3] Moreover, within the same partial-equilibrium framework, Fishelson and Flatters, as well as Pelcovits, have discussed the relative merits of quotas and tariffs under conditions of uncertain supply and/or demand using a two-period analytical approach to rank, with respect to welfare, the two instruments for optimal restriction of trade and to achieve target level of domestic production respectively.[4] Their analysis implies that, if the policy instrument cannot be flexibly adjusted to the situation materializing when uncertainty is resolved, the equivalence of tariffs and quotas, as defined, will not hold. Next, McCulloch and Johnson have shown that proportionally distributed quotas (i.e., as when import licenses are assigned *pro rata* to importable production, as with U.S. oil imports) will produce differential welfare levels from tariffs (or "normal" quotas), while achieving the same "non-economic" objectives such as targeted levels of imports or import-to-production ratios.[5] Although they do not consider the equivalence question in the sense defined here (i.e., if the observed premium under the quota equilibrium is replaced by a tariff set at the rate defined by the premium-to-landed-price-of-import, the equilibrium values of prices, production, and consumption, domestically and abroad, will not change), it is readily shown that, if the premium observed under a proportionally distributed quota regime is turned instead into an explicit tariff, the resulting equilibrium will *not* be equivalent.

Finally, using general equilibrium analysis, Rodriguez and Tower have recently demonstrated that, in a retaliation analysis of the Cournot-Johnson variety, the retaliation process, using optimum tariffs, may lead to welfare improvement of either country and to tariff cycles, whereas the same process, using instead optimum quotas, would lead inexorably to an erosion of world trade.[6]

A little reflection will show that what is essentially at the bottom of these demonstrations of non-equivalence is the breakdown of the implicit Marshallian assumption that the supply and demand schedules are given. If they can change *exogenously* (to the use of quotas or tariffs), then non-equivalence will arise purely because the policy instruments being compared are not flexible and cannot be adjusted parametrically to suit the new supply and/or demand schedules. This is clearly the case in the analysis of uncertainty by Fishelson-Flatters and Pelcovits. If the supply and/or demand schedules will change *endogenously* (to the use of the trade policy instrument), then the equivalence will generally break down regardless of flexibility in the use of the tariffs/quotas. This latter is clearly the case in Bhagwati's demonstration where the introduction of monopoly in his analysis of quota holding and of domestic production involves differential, policy-related shifts in the supply and demand schedules; in the McCulloch-Johnson case where proportionally distributed quotas affect supply incentives; and in the Rodriguez-Tower analysis where the duopolistic responses of the retaliating countries generate quite different offer curves during the retaliation process so that optimal policy response is also correspondingly different at each step.[7]

While therefore these recent theoretical developments have underlined the strictly limited, almost negligible, scope of the equivalence proposition, the sources of non-equivalence that they formalize are themselves only a small subset of the many different possibilities that are to be encountered in reality and, in fact, are to be found in the countries studied under the present Project. Thus, take only three examples. (1) Under some exchange control regimes, quotas of imported raw materials are assigned to approved industrial users *pro rata* to their capacity (somehow defined). As argued later, this obviously creates (*ceteris paribus*) an incentive to add to capacity in the presence of excess capacity since capacity attracts premium-carrying import allocations. (2) Alternatively, consider the case of inefficiency following rather from the specification of strict non-transferability of imported raw materials. In the absence of illegal markets, or coincidental balancing of demands and supplies in specific markets, serious bottlenecks could arise with magnified income losses. (3) Or, consider the case where all capital goods imports are controlled to restrict domestic entry; all raw material imports are allocated, *pro rata* to installed capacity, to the existing producers; and competing imports are also strictly regulated in the interest of domestic producers. In this case, there is virtually no real competition with possible efficiency consequences on cost-minimization, and so on.[8]

Clearly, therefore, efficiency, and related distributional, consequences will follow from the methods of allocating quotas (as is, in fact, evident also from the existing theoretical analysis of the proportionally distributed quotas already alluded to). We proceed therefore to a taxonomy of the various ways in which imports are, in fact, regulated under exchange control regimes developing our classification in, we hope, a manner that should lend itself to systematic analysis of the consequences of different types of exchange control regimes. We also take the opportunity to illustrate our taxonomic possibilities by reference to the country studies. In fact, it is these studies that have suggested the different possibilities. We shall also account, insofar as is possible, for the "reasons" that may explain the presence of these different features in our countries' exchange control systems at different times.

II. REGULATING IMPORTS

We begin first by distinguishing among alternative characteristics of import control systems. We can analyze import control regimes by their features on five different dimensions (each of which has implications for economic efficiency and income distribution):

1. The regulation of imports by source
2. The regulation of imports by commodity composition
3. The regulation of imports by end use (in the broadest sense)
4. The regulation of imports by payments conditions
5. The regulation of imports by the degree and kind of restrictions on the disposal of the licenses (or the imports thereunder) once one or more of the preceding forms of regulation have been attempted[9]

While we focus initially on methods of regulating imports, we proceed then to discuss briefly alternative forms of regulating exports. The methods of operating exchange restrictions on capital account also can vary but less so and are well understood; hence we forego discussing them here. Besides, few countries are characterized by or aim at achieving restriction-free capital accounts. The debate among the proponents and opponents of exchange control regimes thus is focused on the control of current account, as distinct from capital account, transactions.

A. Regulation of Imports by Source

A number of our country studies show that the exchange control regime was characterized by restrictions on imports by source. But the reasons for such a phenomenon were diverse. Three were particularly relevant during the 1960s.[10]

1. Aid-tying.

One of the reasons for specification of source on import licenses was aid-tying. Through the 1960s, aid came to be increasingly tied by source (and by commodity specification). The donor countries, when in deficit, thought it necessary to avoid any leakage of their funds into purchases from the surplus countries. And the surplus countries followed suit by giving in to their exporting interests. The Germans found it difficult to counter their exporters who complained that their American rivals could compete for German-aid-financed contracts whereas they could not tender for the U.S.-aid-financed purchases.[11] Thus, the bulk of aid flows came to be tied by source by the second half of the 1960s.[12]

The source specification of import licenses from the United States, the United Kingdom, Japan, and other aid donors was thus evident in Colombia, Pakistan, Israel, India, Phillippines, South Korea, Ghana, and Turkey, among our countries.[13] One example should illustrate. Thus, in Colombia, Carlos Díaz-Alejandro has shown that the use of import controls to enforce aid-tying to U.S. sources was definitely prevalent and his amused comment thereon is worth quoting:[14]

> INCOMEX and related institutions took strong measures to divert purchases toward U.S. products. . . . Those were the days of bitter wrangling over "positive" and "negative" lists, "additionality." U.S. officials were in the awkward position of simultaneously urging Colombians to liberalize import controls, to use controls to enforce tying, and to stop using controls to divert imports toward bilateral partners, such as Spain and the socialist countries.

2. Bilateral Trade Agreements.

An equally important cause of source-tying of imports, for several of the countries in the Project, was the bilateral trade agreements. These agreements were often signed by LDCs with one another and were of special importance in their trade with the Soviet-bloc countries. In what is probably the most important instance of the latter relation, the share of Egypt's trade with Eastern Europe rose fivefold from 1950 to 33.5 percent of imports and 60.7 percent of exports in 1970.[15]

The standard practice in such agreements was to stipulate that the rubles, or any non-convertible currency, so earned must be spent on imports from the country whose currency had been earned from exports under that bilateral agreement. A typical consequence was, of course, that such source-tied import licenses were often sold in the (legal or illegal) market at significantly lower premiums than import licenses without such source restriction, as in India.

The relatively short-lived geographical restriction of Israeli import licensing was clearly due to bilateral agreements. As Michaely notes:[16]

> Paradoxically, significant geographic discrimination started only in 1953, when the general restrictiveness of the system was already rapidly diminishing. This discrimination clearly originated on the export side. In those years, as some capacity for industrial exports developed, it was assumed that such exports would flow provided there was access to protected foreign markets, the instrument for protection being bilateral trade and payments agreements. Consequently, Israel entered into a number of such agreements, in which the partner country was to purchase from Israel mainly industrial products while Israel would buy in exchange mainly foodstuffs and raw materials. The most important partner country to such an agreement was Turkey, with Yugoslavia coming next. Stated in terms of convertible currencies, Israel's imports from these countries were clearly more expensive than similar goods in the free world market. Obviously, each of the partners to such an agreement, tried to sell to the other its most expensive goods and to exclude exports which could compete freely in convertible-currency markets. Although Israel used a specific price mechanism designed to compensate importers for these price differences . . . , this mechanism in itself was quite often inadequate; so that the government resorted to the QR system as a means of directing Israel's import trade toward bilateral agreement countries.

For Ghana as well, Clark Leith has noted the determining influence of bilateral trade pacts on the sourcewise specification of import licenses during the Nkrumah regime in the 1960s:[17]

> The licensing system during 1962 and part of 1963 was not well designed to induce importers to purchase from bilateral-pact countries. Licenses were valid for importation of the specified items from any country. While official entities were redirecting their purchases, for private importers the only apparent advantage that might be achieved by purchasing from trade-pact countries revolved around payment in local currency to the bilateral account in the Bank of Ghana and the consequent reduction in problems associated with arranging payment to suppliers. This was seldom enough to offset the traditional ties with West European and U.S. suppliers. The result of this situation was a substantial undersubscribing of the bilateral accounts in 1962, yielding a positive net balance in bilateral clearing accounts of nearly NC6 million. This phenomenon and its meaning were not unnoticed, and in 1963 specific licenses distinguished between trade-pact sources and other areas. In addition imports of certain goods (8 commodities) could be obtained only from those countries, and 20 percent of other specified imports (28 commodities) were to come from trade-pact countries. For 1964 the redirection of licenses to bilateral trade-pact countries was strengthened. A special exchange allocation was provided, and a list of 35 commodities developed which permitted purchases only in bilateral-pact countries. Further, in order to discriminate among the various bilateral partners, the system of simply distinguishing between bilateral partners as a group and all others was abandoned in favor of specifying the bilateral country from which the licensed commodity had to be imported.

3. Preferential Trade Arrangements.

A related reason for source-tying of import licenses, noted by Carlos Díaz-Alejandro for Colombia, is the existence of preferential trading arrangements (e.g., the Andean Common Market), which, in practice, imply not merely preferential tariffs but also occasionally source-tied import licenses.

Likewise, Chile also had some source-tying of import licenses because of preferential trade arrangements. Thus, in the 1960s, Chile signed two such agreements: the Treaty of Montevideo, which initiated LAFTA, and the Bogota Agreement, which initiated the Andean subregional group.[18]

4. Non-convertibility of Currencies.

A fourth reason for source specification of import licenses was the general non-convertibility of currencies in Western Europe. The source specification of licenses merely reflected then the fact that the foreign currencies earned, or "released" (in case of sterling balances accumulated during World War II by countries such as Egypt and India), were not convertible and had therefore to be spent, if at all, in the countries that issued them or accepted them (as with sterling in the sterling area). This reason for source specification of import licenses, of course, became inoperative as the Western European currencies became convertible in the 1950s.[19]

B. Regulation of Imports by Commodity Composition

Specification of the items authorized for importation was, of course, an almost standard feature of the licenses issued under the exchange control regimes of the countries studied in the Project. Occasionally it was combined with source specification—as in the case of India—so that there was a double restriction with rather serious consequences that we shall consider presently. The reasons for itemwise or compositional specification of import licenses were diverse.

1. Aid-Tying.

Aid-tying was again a reason for such itemwise specification. The source-tying of aid, by itself, was soon discovered to be subject to substitution possibilities, especially when non-project aid was given. To make source-tying more effective, commodity specification in the import licenses was increasingly sought by donor countries. Thus, typically Japanese yen credits (aid) were available for specific commodities, U.S. aid funds for importing U.S. steel, and so on.[20]

The donor countries often argued (with much truth) that they tried to foresee what the recipient-country importers would buy and only then to agree on the list of permissible imports. Insofar as this was a correct description of the process, the cost of such tying would be less than when the tying looked rather to the donor-country's export interests.[21] We must also note here aid-in-kind, for example, PL480 surplus disposal of wheat, cotton, and other commodities, chiefly from the United States, into countries such as India, Pakistan, Israel, and Chile.

2. Protection.

Quite aside from aid-tying by commodity specification, our countries showed quite endogenous reasons for administering import licenses subject to such specification. The most obvious and persistent reason was, of course, the protective one. An important aspect of the QR regimes in all the countries studied was the eventual utilization of the QRs to confer varying degrees of "automatic" protection to domestic activity. "Saving foreign exchange" often became an adequate excuse for protecting domestic industry against import competition. "Prohibited" lists of importable items were also typically used at times to ensure such protection.

The extreme examples of such protective use of the QR regime are the Indian rule of indigenous availability and the (early) Brazilian law of similars, which virtually ruled out imports when local substitutes were available. In the Indian case, the authorities maintained (inadequate) lists of locally producing firms in different products and the burden of proof was on the import-license applicants to show that they could not physically (as distinct from economically) utilize their output.[22] The situation was so odd that, like the East European jokes, it found its way into humor as in the story of the minister inaugurating a hospital. Having been taken to witness a surgery prior to cutting the ribbon, the minister announced in his speech that it was a matter of pride for the country that the hospital was using indigenously manufactured equipment and that, at the surgery he had seen, the anesthetic used had also been "local"!

The less extreme versions of the protective nature of itemwise specification of import licenses (as also of prohibited lists) are well illustrated by the Colombian case. Carlos Díaz-Alejandro brings this out gently but firmly:[23]

> If the application is satisfactory in form, the INCOMEX staff next examines whether products similar to those requested are produced locally. Extensive files on domestic production have been built up during the last few years. There is at this point a frank and clear protectionist bias; in case of doubt, the presumption is that local goods are indeed fully satisfactory candidates for import replacement, at least in their physical attributes. Prospective importers whose requests have been turned down on these grounds bear the burden of demonstrating to INCOMEX that the local product is in fact different from the proposed imports because of quality, product specification, or other reasons. Price differences, unless extreme, are not considered valid grounds for importing. INCOMEX occasionally brings together the potential importer and the local import-competing producer, to iron out serious disagreements regarding prices, quality, and specifications. INCOMEX officials occasionally visit plants of import-competing firms to verify their capacity, output quality, and other characteristics, a time-consuming, subjective, and ad-hoc practice.

The INCOMEX's arguments about occasionally verifying or raising quality issues with indigenous suppliers are, of course, paralleled by the Indian DGTD's arguments to the same effect; they surely carry little weight, given the protective thrust of the regime.[24]

For Israel, Michaely has documented an equally firm use of the quotas to confer domestic protection, although the regime was to be adapted fairly early in the game to restrict the degree of protection that could be so obtained. Thus, in Israel, there existed a general directive to prohibit any imports of goods that were produced domestically. A declaration by a manufacturer to the Ministry of Commerce and Industry that the manufacturer was producing a given good was usually sufficient for the prohibition of imports of the good. During the 1950s a public commission "for the protection of local industries," associated with the ministry, operated with the announced purpose of deciding on requests for protection. However, as Michaely notes, with protection by total import prohibition afforded almost automatically, the commission handled applications of importers who argued that, in their case, imports should be allowed despite the fact that they competed with existing local production. The working of the commission was subject to rules regarding such things as how much excess cost would be permitted to domestic production. In practice, however, Michaely notes that decisions were made *ad hoc* and "occasions on which imports were allowed because local prices were found to be excessive were rare indeed."[25]

The use of "prohibited" import lists to protect domestic production is also noted by Clark Leith for Ghana. Thus, in the instance of the import liberalization beginning with the July 1967 devaluation, Ghana simultaneously expanded the list of restricted or prohibited imports amounting to some eighty or more items primarily as a response to pressure by domestic manufacturers already engaged in production.[26]

Anne Krueger has also noted for Turkey the definite tendency to shift importable items, once they became domestically produced, from the "liberalized" (*L*) list to the "quota" (*Q*) and the "prohibited" (*P*) lists.[27] In an interesting time-series examination of three 100-commodity samples of items on the import lists, she mapped out the transition matrices for these items, tracing their classification under the three (*L, Q,* and *P*) categories in successive programs spread from August 1959 to January 1971. These transition matrices are reproduced here in Table 2-1. They show rather vividly the greater fluctuations in the import-classification treatment of commodities in the early days of planning (during the period from the 3rd to the 16th Import List)—as reflected in the increased importance of the diagonal elements (in the latter period from the 16th to the 24th Import List).[28]

3. Priority Notions.

Leaving aside the protective rationale for regulating the imports of specific goods, some of the countries studied also aimed to regulate the other (non-competitive) imports on "priority" notions of one kind or another. The most extreme example was India where the AU (actual user) licenses issued to producers for imports of intermediates were item specified in considerable detail to ensure that only the (priority) approved production would be made feasible. This also required that value and/or quantity limits were specified for the listed importables, in addition to the list of permissible imports, on each license.

Perhaps the main reason why itemwise specification of import licenses

Table 2-1. Transition Matrices, 100-Commodity Samples: Turkey

1. *3rd to 16th Import List*

	Sample 1				*Sample 2*				*Sample 3*			
From:	*L*	*Q*	*P*	*T*	*L*	*Q*	*P*	*T*	*L*	*Q*	*P*	*T*
To: *L*	16	12	0	28	14	13	7	34	15	7	12	34
Q	4	46	0	50	4	32	15	51	3	24	9	36
P	2	20	0	22	1	5	9	15	0	6	24	30
T	22	78	0	100	19	50	31	100	18	37	45	100

2. *16th to 24th Import List*

	Sample 1				*Sample 2*				*Sample 3*			
From:	*L*	*Q*	*P*	*T*	*L*	*Q*	*P*	*T*	*L*	*Q*	*P*	*T*
To: *L*	22	7	1	30	28	5	1	34	30	0	8	38
Q	4	39	3	46	3	36	4	43	4	34	12	50
P	2	4	18	24	3	10	10	23	0	2	10	12
T	28	50	22	100	34	51	15	100	34	36	30	100

Notes:
L = Liberalized List
Q = Quota List
P = Prohibited List
T = Total

Source: Krueger, *Turkey*, op. cit., Chapter VI, page 32, Table VI-4.

frequently arose was the desire to ensure the domestic availability of "essential," imported goods. Thus, in the Philippines, quotas were determined generously for priority items and restrictively for "non-essentials," the different items of interest having been initially classified into four groups.[29] Moreover, the list of import classes was later increased in the 1950s from four to nine groups, and as in India and Turkey in particular, a definite tendency existed to shift consumer goods not regarded as highly essential into very restrictive import groups. For example, 52 out of the 190 consumer items shifted in the Philippines between 1953 and 1959 were placed in the unclassified group, a move resulting in the virtual banning of imports of these items.[30]

The degree and nature of specification by items therefore varied among the countries and within countries over time, depending on the balance of payments position and prospects, the degree and nature of aid dependence and aid-tying, the pressure of protective interests, and the susceptibility of the governments to notions of "priority" in resource-allocation decisions.

Note also the general point that the *de jure* specification of itemwise, source, and other restrictions is, to some extent, an inverse function of the degree to which such purposes can be *de facto* achieved by *indirect* inducements cum penalties on deviant behavior. Thus, on source discrimination, it is occasionally the case that importers can be and are nudged into importing from specific areas even when area restrictions are not explicitly specified. The penalty for not abiding by the implicit restrictions is usually the elimination of access to future licenses and, given the profits from the premiums thereon, that indeed can be a deterrent. In fact, according to some aid-recipient officials, aid-tying by source has at times been "enforced" in this way—*via* the prospect of aid reduction if "additionality" criteria were not met in importing from the donor source.[31] Nonetheless, having made the point that the restrictions on import licenses may be *de facto*, rather than *de jure*, we must note that none of our countries has shown much hesitation in specifying the bulk of its intended restrictions on a *de jure* basis.

4. Goods vs. Bads.

Next, while there is no new wrinkle here, we should also list the prohibition of "bads" that all trade regimes are addressed to: for example, the prohibition of heroin imports except for prescribed uses.

5. Probability of Illegal Capital Flows.

Finally, we may note the resort to regulation, including occasional prohibition, of imports of goods likely to be instruments for effecting illegal capital transfers. As discussed at greater length in Chapter 4 on *Illegal Transactions and Exchange Control*, this was the case with used-goods imports in Turkey and Colombia. It also led to closer scrutiny and regulation of imports of capital goods under direct foreign investment in India.

In conclusion, we should also note in regard to itemwise control of imports that the different countries in the Project used a variety of administrative means to implement such control. Moreover, the labels used for similar methods were quite diverse; for example, "automatic approval" items in South Korea were essentially the same as "open general license" items in Pakistan and India. However, one general substantive distinction between alternative means used is perhaps worth stressing and comes from the South Korean reform of 1967. Korea then shifted from a "positive list" to a "negative list" system of import control. Under the positive list system, only those items listed in the trade program could be imported or exported, as specified in that program. Under the negative list regime, however, the trade program listed only items whose imports (or exports) were prohibited or restricted.[32] Thus, all other (unlisted) items were routinely importable under the automatic approval (AA) umbrella. This shift clearly increased flexibility considerably; but this, in turn, basically reflected a desire to have fewer imports tied by specification. In the absence of such an objective, the relative weight of the negative list to the AA imports would surely have increased, nullifying the flexibility attributed to the negative-list regime.

C. Regulation of Imports by End Use

Quite aside from the specification of importable items and permissible source in import licenses, all QR regimes can be characterized by what end uses they seek to allow. Essentially, these regimes have to settle the question: "How much should be given to whom for what use?" The corresponding regulations thus have two component aspects: (1) Allocation by functional end use (e.g., production vs. consumption, production for export vs. domestic sales, investment vs. consumption) and (2) allocation among rival claimants once the functional end use was determined (e.g., division of licenses among different regions, between large and small applicants, among different industries, among different firms within an industry, between the private and the public sectors)

1. FUNCTIONAL END USE.

The division of available foreign exchange among alternative functional end uses was common to all our countries though the extent and pattern differed. The most recurrent patterns here related to (1) imports of capital goods, consumer goods, and intermediates, (2) imports of intermediates for domestic as against export production, (3) import licenses given to reward exporters, and (4) import licenses given to attract remittances, capital inflows, and so on. We will consider each in turn.

a. Capital Goods, Consumer Goods, and Intermediates. The desire to control the amount of foreign exchange going to the importation of *consumer* goods has been evident in a number of LDCs, and not just the countries in this Project, since the last world war. The impulse toward this policy in many LDCs has been clearly the view that the imports of "inessential" consumer goods should be considered a "non-priority" utilization of scarce foreign exchange, a theme that recurs throughout the studies in our Project as well. This philosophy, which may be aptly described as "priority illusion in foreign exchange utilization" because it rarely prevented the countries in question from the allocation of resources for producing the same consumer goods, is to be contrasted with the economic philosophy under which countries, such as India and Ghana, professed actual plans and targets for import substituting in these consumer goods industries and utilized the import-control system to provide the necessary, automatic protection. In this latter case, the targets were buttressed by industrial licensing (in India and Pakistan) and corresponding control over the expansion of capacity in these, as in other, industries. The targets were progressively worked out by reference to overall macro-planning techniques such as consistency models of different types ranging from crude material balances to optimizing, intertemporal, and multisectoral models (as in India's case).

Note further that the preceding analysis applies to "inessential" consumer goods and that "essential" consumer goods such as food have remained relatively large proportions of total imports in many LDCs. Furthermore, as in Chile, whenever foreign exchange "shortage" became more acute, governments have often tended to postpone the importation of capital goods rather than of essential consumer goods for obvious reasons.[33]

At the empirical level, the data in a recent analysis by Bhagwati and Wibulswasdi of the shift in import structure of twenty-eight LDCs during 1954-1956 to 1965-1967 may be cited here for they broadly confirm the relative decline in the imports of consumer goods as a group and of "inessential" consumer goods in particular.[34] Moreover, on comparing with the shift in import structure of twelve DCs (developed countries), these authors find that the major contrast is in the category of non-food consumer goods, where the DCs actually experienced an *increase* in the relative share of this category in overall imports whereas, as seen from Table 2-2, the LDCs experienced a decline. While the Bhagwati-Wibulswasdi LDCs overlap with only about half of the countries in the present Project, it is clear that the generally low and declining share of non-food consumer goods category in overall imports has characterized many of the countries in the Project, especially India, Israel, Philippines, Turkey, and Egypt.[35] In particular, the import structure for most of the countries in the Project has shifted heavily in favor of intermediates and capital goods.

In keeping with this shift, it is interesting that the distinction between producers/users/industrialists on the one hand, and traders/sellers/importers on the other, had become administratively built into the import-licensing procedures, with economic consequences that will be spelled out later. Thus, in India, the major categories of licenses were AU (actual user) and CG (capital

Table 2-2. Comparison of the Shifts in the Import Structures in LDCs and DCs

	Total of 28 LDCs Percentage Shares in Total Imports			*Total of 12 DCs Percentage Shares in Total Imports*		
	1954-1956	*1965-1967*	*Changes*	*1954-1956*	*1965-1967*	*Changes*
I. Food and Beverage	16.6	14.6	−2.0	26.6	19.0	−7.6
II. Non-Food Consumer Goods:	10.6	9.4	−1.2	4.9	10.1	+5.2
Durables	4.5	4.5	No change	2.3	5.0	+2.7
Nondurables	6.1	4.9	−1.2	2.7	5.1	+2.4
III. Total Consumer Goods	27.2	24.0	−3.2	31.6	29.1	−2.5

Source: Bhagwati and Wibulswasdi, op. cit., Table 5, p. 235.

goods), which were given *directly* to the producers and investors (who, in consequence, enjoyed the benefit of the import premium themselves) and permitted the imports of raw materials and capital equipment for use in production, whereas an increasingly small category was the EI (established importer) import licenses, assigned to traders, and predominantly consisting of consumer goods. The same division of licenses, and with the same tendency to give intermediate and capital goods licenses directly to producers rather than traders, was to be found in Colombia and Turkey.

In the Turkish case, in particular, these producer allocations were affected not directly from the licensing authorities to the producers but *via* the chambers of commerce and of industry, which examined individual import claims by their members and negotiated presumably for the resulting total import bills with one another at the union of chambers and, in turn, with the official authorities dispensing imports. In consequence of the competing claims by traders and producers, as elsewhere, the Turkish situation was also marked by a bifurcation of the traditional chamber of commerce and industry into two chambers. As Anne Krueger remarks:[36]

> The importers are of course interested in increasing the flow of resaleable goods into the country, in receiving foreign-exchange allocations themselves and in keeping finished goods on the list of eligible imports. Industrialists are by contrast interested in their own quotas of intermediate goods and raw materials and in reducing the importers' quotas to limit competition with their products.

Furthermore, as elsewhere, the (value) proportion of import licenses going to importers steadily went down in Turkey, from 48 percent in 1962 to 23 percent in 1970.[37]

We may now turn to the division of foreign exchange among capital goods and intermediates, materials, and so on, for current production. Nearly all the regimes studied in the Project divided up the "available" foreign exchange into allocations of raw materials and intermediates and of capital goods. No criteria for this division can be discerned in the countries in the Project except that, in countries that sought to maintain overall plans (as in India, Pakistan, and Turkey), there was some attempt at providing for sufficient capital goods imports to support the planned industrial investment.[38] In practice, however, even in this regard, the fluctuating availability of foreign private and official capital made for inevitable *ad hocery*, and few of the stated targets in regard to provision of targeted capital goods imports were achieved in the countries that practiced such targeting.[39]

b. Export-Import Links: Intermediates. The QR regimes in many of the countries in the Project were also to be distinguished at some stage of their evolution by schemes for linking the allocation of a fraction of their raw materials and intermediates licenses to exporting producers. This phenomenon occurred generally when the effects of the overvaluation on export performance were becoming visible and attempts had to be mounted *within* the QR framework to increase the export incentive.[40]

These links were either *de jure* or *de facto*. Thus, the *de jure* links typically took the form of some kind of import entitlement such as the early Indian import entitlement schemes and the later import replenishment schemes. Under these schemes, the producer-exporter was given allocations of licenses to import *raw materials* in quantities that either replenished those used up in the exportation or were provided in greater quantitites as an added incentive. The *de facto* links consisted, on the other hand, in stressing to the producers that, unless their export performance improved or was sustained, the "normal" allocations of AU (actual user) licenses to import raw materials could get cut or that a better export performance would make the import authorities look more kindly on future applications for spares, expansion, and so on.[41]

Similar links were found in other countries as well: South Korea, Colombia, the Philippines, and Chile, in particular. Thus, in the Colombian case, Carlos Díaz-Alejandro argues that:[42]

> [The import licensing] mechanism has been increasingly used to ensure that new projects, particularly those granted tax or other advantages, commit part of their expected output for exports; for several projects specific export targets have been laid down at the time of their approval by INCOMEX in the form of formal contracts. It is not in the INCOMEX style to insist rigidly on exact compliance with such targets, but the companies know that systematic departures from these promises can lead to a displeased and colder INCOMEX in the future.

A sample survey of Colombia's 1970 registered imports and statistical analysis did indicate that, for the industrial importers, there was a very weak, negative relationship between 1970 "minor exports" per 1970 imports and the chances of getting import applications approved.[43] But this has to be put against both the INCOMEX claims that industrial exporters were treated better in the award of import licenses and another analysis based on the same sample survey that shows, for example, that for industrial importers, the average characteristics of firms with rejected applications showed a substantially lower level of minor exports during 1970 than the firms with approved applications.[44]

For the Philippines, Baldwin notes the No-Dollar Import Law of 1955 as having been designed to encourage exports by permitting exporters to barter a certain amount of their exports for imports, with the permitted imports mainly restricted to producer goods and essential raw materials.[45]

In Chile, *de facto* links existed for large-scale mining and for other exports.[46]

c. Export-Import Links: Unrelated Goods. The export-import links occasionally went *beyond* rewarding the producer-exporter with the intermediates used in production. The import entitlements were made expendable on imports of "unrelated" goods as a pure incentive. Thus, the Pakistan bonus voucher scheme deliberately permitted the import of a number of high-premium consumer goods items against the import entitlements earned by exporters eligible for the scheme.[47] Similarly, the Indian authorities had an unpublicized scheme for importing, on an *ad hoc* basis, scarce dry fruit by exporters who needed the "extra" incentive to complete export deals remuneratively.[48] Frank and others have also noted such a scheme for Korea where, in the latter part of 1966, an export-import link system was reintroduced. Export performance was linked with the import rights for popular consumer items and not merely to imports of inputs for exported commodities. Thus, the exporters of radios and electronic products were given import rights to television accessories, exporters of domestically assembled watches and exporters to Switzerland the import rights to Swiss watches, and so on.[49]

d. Links to Remittances et al. Finally, note that the functional end use of import licenses, defined broadly to include their use to promote a specific economic function (e.g., encouraging exports or investment), was not restricted merely to export-import links. It turned up in the form of links designed to promote remittances, for example. Thus the national defense remittance scheme, introduced in India in mid-1966, entitled the (inward-) remitter to import licenses that fetched a sizeable premium in the market.[50] In Israel, they had the so-called "imports-without-payment" market with supply fed from three sources: foreign capital transfers, immigrants' capital, and gifts from abroad. Michaely notes that, by the end of 1948, the government allowed foreign investors to transfer their capital in the form of goods from a specified list on condition that foreign exchange amounting to 30 percent of the import license be sold to the treasury at the official rate. Import licenses thus issued were more or less marketable, although not in a sanctioned market.[51]

2. Allocations Among Claimants Within Category of End Use.

The functional end use having been decided, the most recurrent problems for the authorities in our countries related to the allocation of the quotas within each end-use category among competing claimants.

a. Large vs. Small Applicants. It appears as if the majority of the QR-regime authorities like to think of themselves as biasing access to imports in favor of the smaller applicants. Indeed, in countries such as India and Pakistan, this was considered to be one of the benefits of the import control system vis-à-vis the market allocations.

In point of fact, little of the evidence produced in our country studies would seem to support such a thesis: *ex post* outcomes appear to have been disturbingly concentrated on the large-scale applicants, though one cannot meaningfully assert that such concentration would have been higher or lower under a non-QR market system.

Thus, in the Indian case, Bhagwati and Srinivasan argue that, while the import control authorities claimed that the small-scale sector would benefit from the control regime,

> it is extremely difficult to take this . . . seriously. In point of fact, there is reason to conclude that the control system discriminated against the small-scale sector: as when import cuts in face of sudden accentuation of the foreign exchange shortage fell relatively more acutely on the small-scale sector and much less on the (well-connected) larger firms.[52]

Similarly for South Korea, Frank and others note that under the Trade Transaction Law of 1957 there were minimum export volumes, steadily rising, before an exporter-importer could be registered by the authorities.[53]

For Ghana, however, Clark Leith indicates a deliberate bias in favor of the larger importers:[54]

> [For traders' imports] a system involving grades for importers was introduced, with grades ranging from A (large trading firms) through D, based on historical shares of turnover, taxes paid, and employment . . . [In the post-Nkrumah period] the system of grading commercial importers established in the early days of import licensing was retained. . . Grades were assigned according to past volume. Importers with N¢ 2 million annual volume over the period 1961 to 1965 were assigned the top grade. . . Within each grade [alone] commercial importers were assigned approximately equal foreign-exchange allocations. The objective in this approach was to "obtain goods on competitive terms and at reasonable prices to the consumers," hence the reliance on larger firms with proven trade and financial contacts and facilities to ensure that the country had adequate supplies of essential commodities.

The advantage of the larger claimants in the QR regime thus stemmed from the desire of the authorities to have "reliable" firms with "proven experience," in the Ghanaian case. It was paralleled by the Colombian case where the INCOMEX appears to have been happy with the simplicity and "ease of administration" that dealing primarily with the larger claimants seemed to confer on the authorities. Thus, during 1970, Carlos Diaz-Alejandro has estimated that only 119 companies and public institutions accounted for nearly 48 percent of the total import bill. Moreover, some 500 private companies were not only major actors in the import field but also acted as major exporters and tax collectors (i.e., generators) for the government. He also found, on examining the reimbursable imports category, that the largest industrial companies had the highest percentages of approved requests for imports, and that the advantage of the very largest companies in percentage of approvals went up when both the reimbursable and non-reimbursable requests were considered together.[55] His further comments on this issue are worth quoting:[56]

> Given the burden of work, and the speed with which applications must be handled, there is an inevitable tendency to accept without much analysis most "reasonable" requests from established, well-known (i.e., large) companies, and to examine more closely and reject, in case of doubt or stringency, those of less well-known, smaller newcomers, many of which may not even bother to apply. . . [The junta] argues that at times of exchange stringency, proportional cuts in import requests are larger for bigger than for smaller firms, and that it tends more readily to overlook faulty request forms from small than from large importers.
>
> But, on balance, the larger and better-known importers find it easier than others to communicate with the junta. Given the Colombian milieu, potential small importers may actually exaggerate in their own minds the complications of dealing with INCOMEX. . . Some junta officials candidly admit that this may be so, but . . . argue that there are no other practical ways of handling the enormous mass of actual and potential applications. What is wrong, they ask, with tilting in favor of applications from long-established corporations, with honorable records, and of being skeptical of new and unknown applicants, who may turn out to be no better than phony industrialists, disguised smugglers, and black-market operators?

Aside from the ease of administration and the readier access to INCOMEX by the "well-connected" larger companies, Carlos Díaz-Alejandro's analysis also points to additional factors that helped to bias the concentration of imports toward the largest firms. These included the fact that the larger industrial companies could get more non-reimbursable licenses against foreign credits and investment (to which they had greater access because of their size in the first place).

The bias of the import-licensing mechanism against the small-scale sector was noticeable in Pakistan as well. Nurul Islam observes that this bias arose principally from the fact that the firms in large-scale industry had access to their own allocations of (premium-exclusive) raw materials, whereas the small-scale entrepreneurs were expected to rely on commercial importers whose allocations in any case were steadily diminished (as in India). This situation continued right up to 1968, until which time the small-scale and cottage industries had to rely on commercial importers for the supply of both imported raw materials and capital goods because the system of industrial licensing for the distribution of import licenses based on the recommendation of the provincial departments of industry was restricted to large-scale industry. The survey conducted by the provincial governments for the assessment of the raw material requirements covered only the registered firms in the large-scale industry. Thus, the units in large-scale industry had access to (at least a fraction of their) raw material and capital goods imports at premium-exclusive, landed prices. On the other hand, the units in the small-scale industries had no such access and were also faced with possibly lower (*pro rata* to capacity) allocations of imports via commercial-importer licenses than their counterparts in the large-scale industries.

In addition to this subtle implication of the licensing mechanism against small-scale firms, the Pakistani import licensing system had the typical bias against smaller firms that arose from making *pro rata* to capacity allocations to producers or making historic-share allocations to commercial importers. Thus, Nurul Islam has noted that, under the system of commercial licensing, the controller in Pakistan distributed import licenses to traders or importers who imported to resell in the market. The selection of "eligible importers" from a large number of potential importers was made by the adoption of "a rule of thumb," which defined eligible importers as those who had an import performance to their credit during the period July 1950 to November 1952, when there was essentially free importing under the open general license (OGL) system. Each importer of the OGL period was then given a monetary "category" for each type of good that the particular importer imported. The monetary value of each category was determined by the average imports during the five OGL shipping periods between July 1950 and December 1952. A category was not a definite commitment by the government to issue to the importer a license of equivalent value, but rather the actual value of each license was expressed as a certain percentage of the monetary value of each category. The variation in this percentage was the main instrument by which the controller enforced a liberal or stringent import policy.[57] A similar phenomenon obtained in the allocation of industrial imports directly to producers. We will, however, return to this theme later when we discuss the criteria for allocation among firms within the same industry.

Altogether therefore the import allocations in many of the countries in our Project would seem to have been biased in varying degrees in favor of the larger applicants. The reasons included: (1) ease of administration in dealing with smaller numbers of successful applicants; (2) a feeling that larger firms were more "reliable"; (3) a sense that larger firms would get better c.i.f. terms from foreign suppliers;[58] (4) the greater access (and contacts) of the larger firms to the bureaucracy and politicians, in general, and to the licensing authorities, in particular; and (5) the important edge obtained by the larger firms, whether traders or producers, quite simply because nearly all the licensing authorities tended to allocate quotas *pro rata* to "past shares" or "capacity installed" or such size-related variables. The operative "fair-shares" rules of thumb were therefore loaded in favor of larger quotas for the larger firms. The reward of the rich was, much as in the market system, here and now, but that of the poor was often in a later millenium!

b. Regional Allocations. The import control authorities have often had to grapple with the problem of allocations among claimants from different regions within the country. This is a distributional issue, much like the problem of large *versus* small applicants, but more explosive since interregional politics are often important and, as Pakistan's experience demonstrates, can be even critical.

The import control regime can be found to be justified on the ground that it permits a "fair" or "balanced" regional distribution of import licenses. It is argued that the market will not work in this way. But control regimes have not often worked better either.

Thus, while INCOMEX in Colombia claimed, as do most licensing authorities elsewhere, that regional considerations were important, they resolutely refused to comply with persistent requests to open up regional offices, citing possible corruption at regional level, and the complaints of inattention and neglect continued from firms outside the Bogota and Medellin region. Carlos Díaz-Alejandro's sample survey also seems to confirm the possible validity of these complaints. The industrial companies in the Bogota/Medellin region did better than those in the rest of the country in terms of percentage of total import requests approved; and even if attention were confined to the reimbursable requests, the percentage of approvals was higher for Bogota and Medellin for both industrial and commercial categories.[59]

For Pakistan, the neglect of the East Pakistan region by the licensing authorities would appear to have been even more drastic. Yet, given the economically less developed nature of the region compared to West Pakistan and the lack of entrepreneurial activity and tradition on the same scale, it would appear that the neglect was probably as much a consequence of the fact that large importers were favored (for reasons discussed in the preceding subsection) as it was politically motivated.

In India, the regional allocations of import licenses for investment and for materials and intermediates were generally perceived to be satisfactorily resolved. The state administrations were actively involved in the ultimate allocations of most scarce items, including foreign exchange, and few regional grievances in this regard were allowed to simmer on without some form of conciliatory response. In short, thanks to the conciliatory and responsive nature of the political regime, the precise regional allocations of import (as other) licenses rarely became a matter of public debate and concern. The apparent absence of this issue from divisive debate was a reflection, in fact, of the importance attached to it *prior* to the allocational decisions.

Special attention to regional distribution of import licenses has been noted also in Chile by Jere Behrman. In fact, the "special regimes" according discriminatory treatment generally by region accounted for 30 percent of total imports in 1961 and for as much as 74 percent of imports in 1970. The objective was to subsidize the integration of remote areas into the national economy.[60] However, it should be noted that the overwhelming bulk of the discriminatory benefits for these remote areas took the form of *price* measures (e.g., higher protective tariffs for industry) rather than biased, beneficial allocations of imports through the *control* mechanism.

c. Public Sector vs. Private Sector Allocations. Yet another basic problem of allocation in many of our countries related to the division of available foreign exchange between the public and the private sectors. This was a decision that was rarely settled by letting public sector concerns get their "fair share" (in any functional category) in the same fashion as the private sector concerns.

For one thing, many public sector concerns, including those undertaking industrial activities, are in monopolistic positions in some of the countries in our Project. This is true of Egypt and, in some instances, of Chile, Ghana, and India as well. The allocations to these concerns then raise issues identical to those underlying interindustrial allocations, as distinct from interfirm, intraindustrial allocations.

Next, the public sector monopolies have sprung largely from ideological reservations of certain industries (as in India) or overall sectors (as in Egypt) on the ground that they are "key" or "basic" activities, represent "commanding heights of the economy," and so on. A "priority" allocation of scarce imports to these public sector enterprises has thus frequently been a consequence of these notions that led these activities into the public sector domain in the first place.

Finally, when it comes to the allocation of materials and capital-goods licenses to concerns in the public and private sectors belonging to the same industry (e.g., steel in India), the import authorities often seemed keen to claim that no favors were shown to the public sector while the private sector asserted the opposite. This was the case in India; and, for Colombia, a bias in favor of official import needs was reported by Alejandro Díaz.[61] For the Philippines, as well, Baldwin reports that supplies and equipment for the government were not subject to import quotas, implying a general view about the priority of all governmental demands for imports. Similarly, in Chile, Behrman notes several ways in which governmental importers managed to have better access to scarce imports.[62] Finally, we may note also that items such as weapons purchases are always treated separately and that "embodied" aid such as PL480 surplus food has always been channeled through public agencies. Hence the relative division of these imports between the private and the public sectors is only an academic question.

d. Interindustrial Allocations. The allocation of imported capital goods, and of raw materials and intermediates, among alternative industries/activities was naturally a primary function of all the control regimes in our Project.

i. Capital Goods. In regard to capital goods, the interindustrial allocations tended to be aligned with the planned, targeted expansion of capacity in the different industries in the countries where the method of targeting and often concommitant industrial licensing was practiced. Thus, the criteria for allocation of capital goods imports have to be sought, in turn, in the more fundamental criteria that determined the basic choice of relative expansions of different industries during a planning period. In turn, these targets tended to reflect varying degrees of planning sophistication at a macro level, as stated earlier. On the other hand, in countries such as Colombia and the Philippines where no such targeting and industrial licensing were in vogue, the allocation of foreign exchange among rival claimants in different industries appears to have been more market-oriented. There was little attempt at regulating the interindustrial allocation of capital goods (except insofar as the applying industry could use indigenously produced capital goods, in which case the protective rules could take over and the import applications denied). In such "non-planned" regimes presumably the allocations of capital goods were made to applicants on a first-come first-served basis until the foreign exchange provided for this purpose ran out. A few exceptions were made for industries producing "essential" items, the chief exception in most countries being defense.[63]

A natural question, of some interest, is whether the import-licensing authorities under either type of regime, with or without industrial capacity targets and industrial licensing, attempted to refuse the allocation of capital goods to industries that already had some excess capacity (thus implicitly trying to use some type of "productivity" criterion to allocate imports). It appears that the different import-licensing authorities reached their decision on this issue in light of three considerations: if there was excess capacity, the creation of additional capacity was wasteful; if additional capacity was not licensed, the degree of competition in the industry would be reduced; and if aid or foreign private capital were available specifically for expanding capacity in an industry, despite excess capacity therein, this opportunity should not be allowed to lapse. Thus Leith notes for Ghana under the National Liberation Council (NLC) that the import license system came to be used as an industrial licensing system as well. The Ghanaian Ministry of Industries saw a conflict between the need for competition among domestic producers and the wasteful expenditure involved in duplicating underutilized domestic facilities. But during the NLC period this was generally resolved in favor of "rationalization" of industries and against new entrants.[64]

For the Philippines as well, Baldwin argues that since 1970 the Central Bank attempted to prevent foreign borrowing to expand investment in industries listed as "overcrowded."

In India, on the other hand, the balance of forces seems to have gone more toward capacity creation in face of excess capacity. The targeting of capacities under the plans implied that the corresponding allocations of foreign exchange for supporting imports of capital goods would be more or less sanctified. Moreover the import control authorities predominantly seem to have confined themselves then to allocating the "available" foreign exchange for intermediates among all the capacity holders according to "fair shares" (as we shall presently note).

The main thrust in all the "planned" regimes appears to have been toward capacity creation in light of explicit or implicit targets of industrial expansion. As Bhagwati and Srinivasan have noted, however, the working of the import control regime seems to have also provided the private sector with incentives to add to capacity in the face of excess capacity. Unless this were so, it would be difficult to see why entrepreneurs would choose to add to capacity just because the import authorities were willing to give capital goods licenses for such capacity creation. Thus, in India, the allocation of raw materials *pro rata* to capacity installed implied that the installation of new capacity would enable access to imported materials and hence to associated profits. We quote Bhagwati and Srinivasan on the subtleties of the interaction between the licensing rules and the creation of incentives to add to underutilized capacity in India:[65]

> The tendency to relate equity in allocations of AU licenses to installed capacity led to an incentive to create capacity by linking the availability of premia-fetching imports with creation of more capacity. Thus, as Bhagwati and Desai have argued, an entrepreneur, with a given capacity that was underutilized for lack of imported inputs, could not (under the Indian QR-regime) expand output through additional utilization of capacity. The only way he could increase production was by getting capacity installed and having some import quota allotted to him on basis of it. But even if the entrepreneur were allowed access to more imports at market prices[66] so that he could expand utilization of existing

capacity, he would have to purchase inputs at import-premia-inclusive market prices, whereas expansion of capacity would enable him to expand output by access to premia-exclusive import allocations. This would then certainly bias, *ceteris paribus*, his choice between these two courses of action toward creating more capacity. . . .

Even more important in practice . . . is the fact that (for most industries, until 1966 at least) licensing constrained the creation of capacity and QR policy guaranteed domestic sales at high enough prices to let licensed firms make large profits even at low levels of capacity utilization. Thus, even when there was excess capacity, it would pay a new firm to enter the industry, provided it could get the license to do so, then get its pro-rata-to-capacity share of scarce AU imports, and still earn a large profit. On the other hand, with free entry and competition for imported materials in the market, such a venture would have been untenable.

ii. Intermediates and Raw Materials. Few criteria can be distinguished among the countries studied in the Project as far as the allocations of foreign exchange among different industries for their requirements of raw materials and intermediates are concerned. "Essential" industries were favored, no doubt, but the definition of essentials varied from capital goods industries to consumer goods industries. Besides, in the regimes that claimed to plan their growing industrialization, there was a real problem raised by the fact that nearly all activities had been implicitly sanctioned or explicitly licensed, so that nearly everything was "essential" or "priority." Undoubtedly, the end result for the bureaucratic decision-making turned out in nearly all cases to be the allocation of foreign exchange according to (1) some historic shares among industries, (2) targeted shares in total production during the planning period,[67] (3) *ad hoc* bargaining and reflection of pressure groups, (4) "priority" notions of varying operational importance[68] and/or (5) outright corruption (as in Ghana during part of President Nkrumah's regime, involving two of his ministers).[69]

It is of some interest to note, however, that consumer durables industries appear to have been regarded as generally "luxury" or "inessential." Thus, in India and Pakistan there is some evidence that the cut in allocation of their actual user (AU) licenses during acute foreign exchange crises was disproportionately higher than for the other industries.[70] In Egypt as well, Hansen and Nashashibi note that in 1965, when the foreign exchange crisis became acute, automobile assembly imports were slashed. Since these industries were usually set up at a very low scale, again in view of their "luxury" nature and the consequent desire to contain the availability of such goods, the investment in their capacity appears to have been doubly wasteful. Low scale meant that average costs of production were excessive, and the deprivation of raw materials and intermediates resulted in underutilization of even that low capacity. Both factors made it highly probable that an alternative strategy of merely importing relatively cheaply the small number of such luxury items (e.g., air conditioners, cars, refrigerators) and shutting off their imports whenever foreign exchange availability got worse would have been more economical.

e. Interfirm Allocations. We need again to distinguish between the allocations of capital goods and of raw materials and intermediates.

i. Capital Goods. For capital goods, to add to capacity or to invest afresh in an industry, the firms that had access to the bureaucracy and to foreign technology and credits appear invariably to have been favored with successful applications to invest in nearly all the regions we have examined. This, in turn, often meant, as we noted for Colombia earlier, that the larger firms were relatively better off than the smaller firms under the import control mechanism. In India, this happened again to be the case. The authorities were to become conscious of the phenomenon after a decade of operation and tried to bend the system in the direction of favoring smaller scale applicants by setting up new guidelines for import and investment licensing, with possibly harmful impact on the overall amount of investment in the economy.[71]

ii. Intermediates and Raw Materials. In regard to intermediates and raw materials for current production there appears to have been a common tendency to adopt "fair shares" as a working rule for interfirm allocations. The precise rules, however, varied from *pro rata* to installed capacity to *pro rata* to production in base year allocations. It is interesting that no import control authority among the countries studied ever attempted to lay down explicitly the rules in this regard, and varying elements of executive discretion always remained, defying the analyst's ability to decipher what exactly were the criteria utilized in the end.

For Ghana, Leith has noted how the Ministry of Industry utilized various categories such as "essential consumer goods," "exporting industries," and "import-substituting industries," and made initial allocations among them. Then, for the interfirm allocations, Leith records a rather complex decision process (as perceived by the authorities):[72]

> . . . The Ministry of Industries . . . attempted to make *pro rata* allocations among firms within a category based approximately on previous market shares but taking into account their assessment of the firms' "performance" in such things as employment, taxes paid, and what was called general efficiency of operation.

The method of allocations used by the import control authorities in Pakistan illustrates rather better the "fair-shares" doctrine and the *modus operandi* of its execution. A "quota system" was designed there to routinize the issue of licenses to industrial importers for the import of raw materials and spare parts. Each eligible industrial importer, called a "quota-holder," was assigned a quota, specifying the importer's "requirements" for industrial raw materials and spare parts for one shipping period. This enabled the provincial directorates to determine simultaneously the commodities (i.e., spare parts and raw materials) that should be imported and the industrial importers who were eligible to import them in each shipping period. These quotas were revised every three years. The provincial directorates then determined the *percentage of the quota* that each quota-holder would be allowed in each shipping period, the percentage allowance reflecting the foreign exchange availability relative to total quota needs.

Two points finally need to be noted here. First, the tendency to go by "fair-shares" rules was probably motivated as much by notions of fairness as by the bureaucrat's desire to *appear* impartial and just. Any attempt at biasing allocations in relation to "efficiency" or "performance," evaluated subjectively by the bureaucrats, would have landed them into situations where charges of corruption could have been freely laid at their doorstep. Second, the effect of such "fair-shares" rules was to create economic incentives for inefficiency. Thus, for India, we have already noted in the preceding subsection that the result was to encourage the expansion of capacity despite excess capacity when the allocations tended to reflect shares in installed capacity in the industry. Yet another effect was that the more efficient firms could not readily drive out the inefficient ones by competing freely for more scarce raw materials and intermediates. The effect of competition was thus blunted by the import control regime that gave these imports at artificially low rates to both the efficient and the inefficient firms in the first round.

f. Domestic vs. Foreign Applicants. Finally, although instances of this practice are infrequent, there is some evidence that the import allocations were used to "indigenize" trade. The most striking example is furnished by the Philippines where, under the 1950 Import Control Act, marked preference was given to Filipino citizens and the Import Control Board was instructed to reserve 30 percent of the total import quota for any article in the fiscal year 1950-1951, 40 percent in 1951-1952, and 50 percent in 1952-1953 to new Filipino importers. Furthermore, at least 60 percent of a company's stock had to be owned by Filipinos for a firm to qualify under this provision of the law. Existing import businesses, which had long been dominated by Westerners and Chinese, received only nominal quota allocations. As a probable result of this policy, Baldwin notes an increased Filipinization of the import trade. Thus, between 1948 and 1958, the value of imports by Filipinos rose from 23 percent to 54 percent, and the share of Chinese traders fell from 39 percent to 14 percent.[73] A similar "Ghanaization" of business, using the import-licensing system, has also been noted by Leith.[74]

D. Regulation of Imports by Payments Conditions

We could also classify the regulation of imports, as is evident from the analysis and examples in the foregoing discussion, by the payments conditions associated with the financing of the imports. Four types of such regulation may be distinguished:

1. REMITTANCE-TYING.

As illustrated by the Israeli, Indian, and Pakistani cases noted above, imports from remittances were regulated with more laxity than imports financed from other foreign exchange funds.

2. BARTER.

Similar laxity was evident in imports financed from accumulated foreign balances under barter and/or bilateral trade agreements in countries such as Egypt, Ghana, and India.

3. FOREIGN CREDITS.

Again, capital goods imports in general were often easier in most countries when accompanied by foreign credits. This practice was, in fact, a motivating factor in getting the Japanese foreign-aid program, with its primary emphasis on yen credits for imports of Japanese machinery, off the ground in the late 1960s.

E. Degree and Types of Restrictions on Transferability

The final dimension on which the import control regimes need to be distinguished from one another is the degree and nature of restrictions on the transferability of either the import licenses or the imports brought into the country under these licenses once the other dimensions, which we have already distinguished above, were defined.

While it may be thought that these restrictions would be fairly similar across countries, our studies threw up remarkable contrasts. Thus, for example, the Indian regime was characterized by extremely stringent restrictions on the transferability of licenses and imports thereunder. The Colombian system permitted the transfer of imports rather freely while frowning on those producers who earned import allocations only to transfer them to other producers. The Turkish regime seemed to have no stigma of any kind attached to transferring licenses or imports thereunder even though this was illegal. Finally the Pakistani system had elements of both rigidity and transferability.

The restrictions on transferability were of different kinds. They related to (1) whether the license could be sold to other parties, (2) whether the imports, once effected, could themselves be resold to other parties, and (3) whether these other parties had to meet certain eligibility criteria.[75] Depending on how many of these restrictions were in effect, the degree of non-transferability could be the cause of great or little inflexibility in the system.

In India, the actual user (AU) import licenses for direct imports by producers were generally non-transferable by individual firms, even for use by other plants in the same firm. Combined with the equally rigid pattern of permissible imports—specified in itemized detail on the AU licenses in most cases—it was inevitable that the result would be inflexibility leading to economic inefficiency. Bhagwati and Srinivasan have speculated on the motivations underlying this remarkably rigid regime and argued that the theoretical premise that AU allocations were being made on the basis of well-defined priorities at the detailed-industry level led the authorities to rule out legal transferability of the licenses among the different industries. Bureaucratic logic took the inevitable next step and eliminated transferability even among units within the same industry, thus making AU licenses (legally) *altogether* non-transferable by the licensee units.[76]

In Colombia, the situation was *de facto* more flexible. Carlos Díaz-Alejandro argues that:[77]

> It is INCOMEX's expectation that goods imported in the industrial category will be used only by the company to which the license has been issued. When INCOMEX was questioned about the legality of resales of merchandise imported for industrial companies, its answers were surprisingly fuzzy. The license itself is clearly non-negotiable, as it is issued only to a specific company or person. The reselling of the imported items by industrial users is apparently not strictly illegal, but it is frowned upon by INCOMEX. . . . Companies shown to be systematically selling part of their imported industrial inputs to others are punished by INCOMEX with total or partial rejections of future requests. Similar punishment is dealt to individuals or companies discovered trying to import under several social or private names. . . . INCOMEX, however, does not punish temporary swapping or lending of imported items among industrial firms. Indeed, it finds such practice quite reasonable, particularly if done during periods of stringency and in a "non-speculative" manner. Apparently, during 1971 very little reselling or swapping of non-commercial imports took place, although some INCOMEX officials indicated that that practice was widespread during difficult years, e.g., 1967.

It is interesting and important to note that the import control regimes, even when characterized by the extreme rigidities of the kind just described, had three different types of "safety valves" that helped ease the resulting bottlenecks and waste.

First, the establishment of links between imports and exports *via* import entitlement schemes (South Korea, India), "bonus voucher" schemes (Pakistan), "special unnumbered license" category (Ghana),[78] and the like often created a new channel for imports of scarce materials. These schemes worked by making the import premiums the inducement for exports. Hence the worst bottlenecks, leading to the highest premiums, tended to be relieved through the presence of such schemes.

Second, there were always the illegal transfers of non-transferable licenses and imports.

Third, in nearly all countries, the presence of some commercial (or trader, established importer) licensing, as also the occasional shift of items to open general licensing or the introduction of "automatic" licensing (Pakistan) and "repeat" licensing (India) for producers who had used up their allocations of imports, managed to blunt somewhat, and from time to time, the worst effects that a rigid set of non-transferability rules would have created for those who otherwise would not have had access to the imported items that created the bottleneck.

III. REGULATING EXPORTS

The anatomy of direct exchange controls, when we turn to exports, is drastically simplified for the reason that, asymmetrically with import controls, the basic control relates mainly to the surrender of receipts to the exchange authorities within a specified period.[79] However, in several of the countries in the Project, there were occasional instances of regulation of exports (1) by destination, and (2) by (itemwise) composition though, naturally, there was no counterpart to the regulation of imports by end use or by the degree of restrictions on transferability of licenses.

The regulation of exports *via* licensing, by destination, and by items can occur simultaneously when exports of specific items need to be "diverted" under bilateral trade agreements to fulfill prior official commitments to deliver. On the other hand, there were few explicit instances of this nature to be found in the countries in the Project since this task was undertaken *via* the use of state trading agencies with attendant monopolization of export trade in such items. This resulted in *implicit* licensing of the exports of such items by destination (as in Egypt).

More frequent, though still uncommon, instances of (only) itemwise regulation of exports were to be found, however, in the countries studied. These arose from the simple need to maintain adequate domestic availabilities of specific "sensitive" items. This was the case with vegetable (cooking) oils in India. Similarly, in the Philippines, in 1948 the government restricted the export of vital foodstuffs and industrial goods (but this action was held in violation of the Philippine Trade Act of 1946). Again in 1951, as an anti-inflation measure, the reexport of "vital materials" was banned. At the same time, restriction of exports to make the domestic price to producer-users cheaper also was not uncommon. Thus, in Israel, the cotton Marketing Board is not permitted, in the interest of domestic spinning establishments, to export as much cotton as it wishes or finds profitable to sell abroad.

Itemwise regulation of exports in the interest of *quality control*, aimed at maintaining long-term competitiveness for the country's exports, was also evident in some cases. Thus, in the case of Israel, the producers of citrus and groundnuts have been obligated to sell their yield to the corresponding marketing board, which then exports the high-quality produce and sells the low-quality produce domestically. The marketing-board arrangement therefore acts in lieu of export licensing, to restrict and regulate the export of the items in question.

Perhaps the more noteworthy practice relating to the itemwise regulation of exports, however, was *via* the fixing of export targets, much as the import quotas were fixed for specific items. We may quote Frank and others on this:[80]

> Another facet of the military government's export strategy was the institution of full-scale export *targets* in 1962. Before the beginning of each year, the Ministry of Commerce and Industry was to set the new year's targets on the basis of past export performance and new export forecasts for separate commodities. Annual export targets were usually classified by commodity, region, and country of destination. Commodity targets were assigned to industrial associations and firms, and the regional and country targets to South Korean trade and diplomatic missions abroad. The Ministry maintained an "export situation room" to check actual performance during the year against the annual targets. In addition, an Expanded Export Conference, which was chaired by the President and attended by ministers, government officials, bankers, and exporters, usually met several times during the year to deliberate on the annual targets.

Targeting of exports to the same degree as in South Korea does not appear to have been present in the other countries in the Project. However, the practice of tying in export obligations before new capacity was licensed seems to have been common during the late 1960s in India and Pakistan. Carlos Díaz-Alejandro describes the activities of the INCOMEX in Colombia in similar terms.[81]

In short, the countries in the Project *either* had sporadic export regulations of a quantitative nature to handle critical shortages in small sectors of the economy, *or* in a few instances (e.g., Egypt, Ghana, and India) were having to divert exports geographically to fulfill barter-trade agreements, *or* in yet fewer instances (e.g., South Korea) were using effective export targeting as an export-augmenting device on a broad front. In none of these cases, however, did the scope of export regulation (by quantitative, control methods) match the scope of the control mechanism regulating imports.

IV. REGULATING SERVICES

The direct regulation of services is symmetric with the control mechanism for imports and can be so analyzed, as we noted earlier, in terms of identical dimensions. Thus, obvious parallel examples can be cited. For example, aid-tying can lead, and has led, to (partial) tying of imports of shipping services to U.S. shipping for PL480 exports in a number of countries in the Project that were the beneficiaries of such aid. Similarly, expenditure on travel abroad has been controlled in nearly all countries, and this control mechanism has distinguished among classes of users, functional end use (e.g., for business, for students, for pleasure, for visiting relatives, for medical treatment, and so on) in much the way that imports of goods have been regulated in these regimes,[82] while they have also been subject (in Chile and India, e.g.) to severe cuts at times of exceptional foreign exchange shortage.

V. REGULATING CAPITAL FLOWS

As with the regulation of services, no particularly significant, differential aspect of the regulation of capital flows in the countries in the Project can be distinguished for spelling out here. However, one significant interaction effect between capital account controls and controls on trade on current account does need to be highlighted as it is not always appreciated. In many of the countries in the Project there is some evidence that the need to enforce capital account controls more effectively led to specific controls on current account. Thus, as we note in Chapter 6 on illegal transactions under exchange control regimes, used machinery imports were occasionally ruled out because they facilitated capital outflows through overinvoicing. Similarly, in Turkey the purchase of airline tickets with domestic currency had to be controlled as it became a loophole through which Turkish liras could be converted into foreign exchange (*via* resale abroad of these tickets). In Ghana refunds on air tickets abroad were prohibited. It is indeed a moot question whether foreign exchange controls can be made reasonably effective on capital account in the absence of general controls on current account. This is an issue that has not been tested for the countries in the Project as practically none of them has managed to reach this degree of liberalization.[83]

VI. OVERALL SETTING

We may next note that the *control* mechanisms and methods described and analyzed above were combined with varying degrees of resort to a variety of *price* measures in each of the countries in the Project. Thus, on the import side, there were "prior deposit" requirements, tariffs, multiple exchange rates, and exchange auctions, to take the most important examples. On the export side, there was resort to duties, cash subsidies, export-import links yielding access to lucrative imports, preferential access to profitable investments, tax rebates on imported inputs, and so on.

The exchange control regimes varied, not merely in respect to the control mechanisms discussed so far but also in regard to their varying and variegated resort to price measures in regulating imports and exports. In the next chapter, we will define phases in the evolution of exchange control regimes in the countries in the Project, drawing on the blend between control and price instruments in the trade and payments regime as a distinguishing feature. Immediately, however, we proceed to describe some of these price instruments in depth and illustrate them from the countries in the Project.

VII. PRICE INSTRUMENTS: IMPORTS

The use of the price mechanism to influence imports was widespread among the countries in the Project. But it took diverse forms and had varying objectives. Thus, the forms extended to tariffs, "prior" or advance deposits, sales taxes on commodities primarily imported, multiple exchange rates, exchange auctions, and forthright parity changes. And the objectives varied from the imposition of tariffs to mop up the premiums on the import licenses to their use as protective devices and their deployment as an instrument to improve the balance of payments deficit.

Since the most complex interaction of intended objectives, requiring careful attention and analysis, arises in the case of tariffs, and since the other price instruments raise few new issues, we focus here exclusively on the use of tariffs, drawing on the country studies again to illustrate the alternative objectives to which they were addressed. In regard to the other price instruments, note merely two things: (1) the use of exchange auctions, while proposed in other countries at the time,[84] has been attempted in a significant manner only for Brazil for a brief period; and (2) interestingly, the use of "prior" or advance deposits as an instrument for taxing imports has been used predominantly in Latin American countries, to varying extent in Turkey and Ghana, but almost never in India and Pakistan.

Turning then to the use of tariffs, we should note their major distinguishing characteristic, namely, that they are used not merely for (direct) balance of payments objectives, as are instruments such as prior deposits, but also traditionally for revenue collection and for protection.

1. QRs vs. Tariffs.

What is interesting, however, is that, in terms of their *protective* effects, tariffs were typically "swamped" by QRs in many of the countries in the Project for quite substantial periods. This was the case in Pakistan, Turkey, and India for the bulk of the period studied; it was so for the Philippines and Israel for long periods except when liberalization really took root; and it has been the case for Chile, Colombia, and Brazil occasionally, except when multiple exchange rates, exchange auctions, or sliding parities served to dampen the premium on imports. For South Korea, the only year for which evidence was collected is 1968 when QRs were unimportant, as indeed they continued to be later. One has indirect evidence however that, during the pre-1960 period, QRs swamped tariffs.[85]

Thus, for Turkey, Anne Krueger was able to report on Ahmet Aker's data on c.i.f. landed (inclusive of tariffs) and wholesale (inclusive of import premium) prices for 1968, for seventy-four commodities covering 8.6 percent of Turkey's imports.[86] It turned out that, for thirty-one commodities in this sample, the premium exceeded the landed cost, with twenty-seven of these showing a difference in excess of 100 percent of the landed cost. The importance of the premiums is also evident from the following analysis:[87]

> . . .the 1967 value of imports of each commodity in the sample was obtained. The value of the premia as given by Aker was then computed under several assumptions as to what mark-up would yield a normal rate of return. Three mark-up rates were used: 20, 50 and 100 per cent. The results of the computations were:

	(millions of TL)
Value of imports in the sample, c.i.f.	547
Landed cost of imports	1,443
Wholesale value of imports	3,568
Premia:	
20 per cent markup	1,836
50 per cent markup	1,404
100 per cent markup	682

> The average EER for the sample, thus, was TL 23.76 = $1 contrasted with the official rate of TL 9 = $1. This EER is slightly above the rate calculated in Appendix A. The premium however, equalled TL 30.21, TL 23.1, or TL 11.22, depending upon the assumption made about the normal mark-up. That would

> vary from one product to another, but in this author's judgment, a 50 per cent mark-up is probably the best estimate. On that basis, a dollar's worth of imports cost the importer TL 23.76, and his return from it was TL 58.75, giving him an average windfall gain, or premium, of TL 23.11 per TL 9 of licenses received.
>
> Thus by 1968 the premium on import licenses was considerably in excess of the duties and surcharges imposed upon imports. Industrialists receiving import licenses for intermediate goods imports were, in effect, subsidized by the amount of the premium they received, and protected by the amount of the EER plus the premium on imports competing with their own production. The premia associated with final outputs were at least as high as those on intermediate goods . . . therefore, the protection afforded through quantitative restrictions considerably exceeded that through tariffs and surcharges. Quantitative restrictions were thus of much greater importance than price interventions in providing incentives for import-substituting production.

Anne Krueger also notes that the structure of import premiums bore no relationship to the structure of landed costs. The premiums on import licenses varied considerably from commodity to commodity, and the tariffs and surcharges absorbed different proportions of the final prices on these commodities.[88]

For the Philippines, Baldwin records for the period before 1962 a similar situation. He utilizes three alternative methods to demonstrate the importance of implicit tariffs.[89] First, he estimates the implicit tariffs from surveys of prices during 1950 and 1951, indicating that the range of implicit protection was very large, going from nearly 400 percent to almost 700 percent on such luxury items as oranges, cigarettes, and salt to quite moderate levels on evaporated and condensed milk. On the other hand, the protection afforded a given bundle of non-essential consumer goods by explicit fiscal and monetary measures (i.e., tariffs, prior deposits, etc.) in 1951 was only 69 percent. The comparable figure for essential consumer goods was 21 percent. Assuming that the sample was representative, implicit rates of 200 percent or more in 1951 were not unusual for non-essential consumer goods. Since prices of this group of items rose about 80 percent between 1951 and 1959, levels of implicit protection of 400 percent or more at this time apparently existed for some items. Since the protection from explicit fiscal measures on this category of goods was 149 percent, this implied that windfall gains of over 200 percent were being made on these commodities. Second, Baldwin argues backward from the behavior of import prices and domestic wholesale prices for the same category of goods between 1959 and 1962 when import controls were completely dismantled. He shows that their peso cost, inclusive of tariffs, and so on, rose by 90 percent during the period whereas the wholesale price index for this group of non-essential consumer goods rose by only 10 percent, indicating large premiums before the dismantling of the import controls. Third, Baldwin utilizes comparisons between U.S. and Philippines prices of comparable goods for selected items, estimating what the Philippines prices should be (based on U.S. prices plus transportation, tariff, and other charges) and what they actually were. Baldwin concludes from these statistical analyses that:[90]

> It is clear from these three estimates that exchange controls added greatly to the degree of protection provided by explicit fiscal and monetary measures. In 1959, for example, implicit protective rates of 400 percent were not uncommon for nonessential consumer goods, whereas the average explicit degree of protection in 1959 for this category was around 150 percent. For the essential-consumer-goods group, average implicit and explicit protective rates in the same years were roughly 30 and 5 percent, respectively.

Clark Leith records for Ghana in 1968 a situation where QRs were important for a fair number of industries. While he could not obtain premium data for twenty out of the forty-seven industries for which he estimated protection, thirteen out of the remaining twenty-seven had implicit tariffs in excess of the explicit tariffs.[91] By 1970, with the imposition of an import surcharge on several items and the shift of these items to open general licensing, the role of import premiums had declined but still persisted in a few industries.[92]

For India, the evidence of the importance of implicit tariffs is quite overwhelming. Indeed, except for a period of three years after the June 1966 devaluation, the dominance of implicit over explicit tariffs seems to have been quite general. Thus, as with Leith in Ghana, the analysis of protection in India would have been totally misleading if Bhagwati and Srinivasan had not analyzed it on the basis of implicit protection.[93]

For Israel also, Michaely notes that, as of 1956, moderate to strong restrictions affected over half of the total value of imported goods, with only raw materials bearing a small brunt of this regime (Table 2-3). Indeed, until the liberalization of the 1960s, the protection of industries producing final consumer goods by import prohibition was "comprehensive and almost total."[94]

Table 2-3. Effectiveness of Import Restrictions in Israel, 1956

(proportions of imports in each class, by value of imports, in percent)

Import Category	*Formal or Effective Liberalization (1)*	*Moderate Restrictions (2)*	*Strong Restrictions (3)*	*Total (4)*
Foodstuffs and fodder	40	4	56	100
Raw materials	60	32	8	100
Finished goods	35	33	32	100
Total import of goods	45	31	24	100

Source: *Israel,* op. cit., Chapter 2, Table 2-3.

In none of the countries in the Project, however, were explicit tariffs altogether dominated by implicit tariffs. Nearly all countries had open general licensing or, as with South Korea since the mid-1960s, items not on any import lists were available for free importation.[95] Nor did any countries in the Project forego the use of explicit tariffs for any length of time for, as already stated, the use of explicit tariffs could be addressed to several objectives, including that of reducing the magnitude of the implicit tariff by cutting into the import premium resulting from QRs. Indeed, we turn now to a discussion of the tariffs as addressed, *ex ante*, to these diverse objectives, treating tariffs to mop up premiums and tariffs to provide protection, in turn.

2. Tariffs to Mop up Premiums.

Tariffs with the explicit objective of depriving import licenses of their windfall premiums were adopted in some of the countries in the Project. Such tariffs naturally bear close affinity to tariffs customarily adopted for revenue purposes insofar as the premiums are turned thereby into governmental revenue.

The Ghanaian surcharges of August 1970 and the Indian tariffs of 1964 and 1965 clearly fall into this category. However, the most striking example comes from South Korea where Frank and others note:[96]

> With the adoption of a unitary fixed exchange rate in June 1961, the differential between the import price and the domestic price became greater for some items restricted by import quota. Thus in July 1961, a Temporary Special Customs Law was enacted to capture the windfall profits that would otherwise accrue to importers receiving import licenses for restricted items. Under the law, about 700 items subject to import quotas were classified into four categories, I to IV, in order based on the ratio between the domestic price and the c.i.f. import price and the estimated degree of nonessentiality. A temporary special tariff was imposed on these classified import items in addition to regular tariffs. The special rates were 100 percent of import value on category I, 50 percent on category II, 30 percent on category III, and 10 percent on category IV. Adjustments were made periodically in the classification of items. . . .
>
> Also after the May 1964 devaluation, a new Temporary Special Tariff Law was enacted to soak up margins between c.i.f. import prices and domestic prices of restricted import items. About 2,200 import commodities, for which the "foreign exchange ratio" exceeded 30 percent, were classified in categories I and II. The special tariff was imposed on the difference between the domestic wholesale price of an imported good and the landed price of that import plus regular tariff, commodity tax, incidental expenses, and normal profit. A tariff rate of 90 percent was applied to category I and 70 percent to category II.
>
> To administer the special tariff, the Bank of Korea and the Ministry of Finance made a monthly survey of domestic wholesale prices of import commodi-

ties. On the basis of this price survey, the list of items for the special tariff was expanded from about 2,200 in 1964 to about 2,700 after 1965. Those items to which a regular tariff did not apply were, however, exempted from the special tariff. [Foreign exchange ratio = (domestic wholesale price of imported goods) minus (regular tariff + commodity tax + normal expenses) divided by (normal foreign exchange price of the import on c.i.f. basis). This formula was basically an estimate of the premium which could be obtained by an importer licensed to import a restricted item.]

3. Protective Tariffs.

We next consider the relative importance of protective tariffs, as recommended by regulatory agencies such as tariff commissions and boards, as distinct from tariffs levied during the budgetary process explicitly for purposes other than the protection of domestic import-competing industries.[97] It is interesting to note, here, that even the *ex ante* role of tariffs as protective devices had shrunk in many of the countries in the Project. Thus, in India and Pakistan, detailed analysis shows that the tariff commissions had often been reduced to a relatively minor role, with few industries appearing before them for the purpose of claiming tariff protection.[98] Clearly, most industries were sufficiently protected by the QR system and did not therefore feel it necessary to argue the traditional protective case before a regulatory body!

A question of some interest is then why a few industries did ask for tariff protection. Here, the answer seems to lie in the possible desire of these industries to provide for a rock-bottom rate of protection just in case the QR regime was changed and the protective incidence of quotas was eroded. After all, payments positions could ease, criteria of allocation of imports could shift, and there was therefore not the same level of assurance perhaps about the continuity of QR protection.

VIII. PRICE INSTRUMENTS: EXPORTS

In conclusion of our taxonomy, we now may address briefly the range of price instruments utilized to affect exports. Aside from parity changes, these price instruments divide into direct (cash) subsidies and taxes and indirect subsidy and tax schemes. The latter, in turn, take numerous forms as is evident from the country studies in the Project, and quite clearly have differential economic effects.

Examples of direct taxes and subsidies can be found in South Korea, Pakistan, India, and other countries. Typically, because of the "large-country" (i.e., monopoly power in trade) problem associated with exports of primary products in markets where the country may have an imperfectly competitive position, some of the countries in the Project used export *taxes* while using export subsidies on manufactured exports instead mainly to counter the export-reducing effects of overvaluation of the exchange rate.

The role of direct cash subsidies, however, appears to have been minimal, with substantial emphasis being placed in most countries on the *indirect* schemes. Leaving aside the routine schemes offering rebates and drawbacks, and also marketing and credit advantages, the major indirect instruments for export subsidization were essentially those that exploited the exchange controls on imports to channel the premiums associated with the restricted imports to those who successfully exported. Examples of these "link" schemes can be found in South Korea, Pakistan, and India where they were formally instituted (as already noted in our taxonomy of the direct controls of imports), whereas they were informally used in other countries such as Colombia (where, as Carlos Díaz-Alejandro has noted, the INCOMEX gently but effectively also managed to prod the import licensees into export performance by implicit threats of not so favorable treatment of import requests if the exports did not materialize).[99] In turn, these links set up numerous efficiency implications. These have been systematically analyzed in the India study in the Project, which the reader may wish to consult,[100] and are addressed more generally here in the concluding Chapter 8 on the optimal foreign trade strategy suggested by the results of the Project.

NOTES

1. The detailed comments of Bent Hansen, Ana Martinera-Mantel, Barry McCormick, Clark Leith, Gideon Fishelson, Larry Westphal, Padma Desai, Rodney Falvey, Jere Behrman, and Anne Krueger on an earlier draft of this chapter have been very helpful.

2. Cf. Bela Balassa et al., *The Structure of Protection in Developing Countries* (Baltimore: Johns Hopkins University Press, 1971).

3. J. Bhagwati, "On the Equivalence of Tariffs and Quotas," in R.E. Baldwin et al., *Trade, Growth and the Balance of Payments: Essays in Honor of G. Haberler* (Chicago: Rand McNally, 1965). Later contributions, including a further discussion of the different dimensions of equivalence (i.e., domestic price, production, consumption, foreign price, and imports), include: J. Bhagwati, "More on Equivalence of Tariffs and Quotas," *American Economic Review* 58 (1968):142-146; H. Shibata, "A Note on the Equivalence of Tariffs and Quotas," *American Economic Review* 58 (1968):134-142; G. Yadav, "A Note on the Equivalence of Tariffs and Quotas," *Canadian Journal of Economics* 1 (1968):105-110; and Tsvi Ophir, "The Interaction of Tariffs and Quotas," *American Economic Review* 59 (1969), drawing upon 1956 dissertation at Hebrew University.

4. Cf. G. Fishelson and F. Flatters, "The (Non-) Equivalence of Optimal Tariffs and Quotas under Uncertainty," *Journal of International Economics* 5 (1975):385-393; and M. Pelcovits, "Quotas *versus* Tariffs," *Journal of International Economics* 6 (1976):363-370.

5. Cf. R. McCulloch and H.G. Johnson, "A Note on Proportionally Distributed Quotas," *American Economic Review* 63 (1973):726-732.

6. Cf. C. Rodriguez, "The Non-equivalence of Tariffs and Quotas under Retaliation," *Journal of International Economics* 4 (1974):295-298; and E. Tower, "The Optimum Quota and Retaliation," *Review of Economic Studies* 52 (1975):623-630. Two points may be noted: (1) the Metzler paradox requires that the tariff *increase* imports: this implies that an import quota (which can only restrict, *not* expand, imports) cannot be equivalent to the Metzler tariff (cf. R.Falvey, "A Note on the Distinction Between Tariffs and Quotas," *Economica* 35 (1975): 319-326); and (2) furthermore, as noted by both Rodriguez and Tower, for similar reasons, an optimum quota response may not be feasible with an import quota but, as in the Metzler case, would require the use of an export quota.

7. In fact, once endogenous changes in supply and demand schedules are seen to invalidate equivalence, it is easy to imagine numerous such applications. Thus, for example, the Bhagwati-Hansen theorems on the welfare effects of smuggling ("A Theoretical Analysis of Smuggling," *Quarterly Journal of Economics* 87 (1973):172-187; reprinted in J. Bhagwati, ed., *Illegal Transactions in International Trade*, Series in International Economics, vol. I (Amsterdam: North-Holland, 1974), are based on assuming tariff-induced smuggling; if the tariff is replaced by a quota, R. Falvey, "A Note on Preferential and Illegal Trade Under Quantitative Restrictions," *Quarterly Journal of Economics* 92 (February 1978):175-178, has shown that the results are not identical.

8. Evidently, in all these cases, analyzing these exchange controls merely by turning the observed import premiums into *ad valorem*, "equivalent" tariffs would be, at best deficient and misleading, and at worst quite seriously wrong.

9. Where we use the word "imports" here the reader should infer that we also include the utilization of foreign exchange for purposes other than the import of goods alone.

10. The reader should *not* infer anything about the relative importance of these reasons from either the order in which they are discussed or the relative space devoted to them.

11. For details, see J. Bhagwati, "On the Tying of Aid," UNCTAD Secretariat, 1968; printed in UNCTAD II Papers and Proceedings; reprinted in J. Bhagwati and R. Eckaus, eds., *Foreign Aid* (Harmondsworth: Penguin Books, 1970).

12. Since the 1960s, however, the policies and practices of most aid donors have shifted significantly away from tied procurement. There now exist agreements among the major aid donors (1) with respect to untying of contribution to multilateral development institutions and (2) with respect to the untying of their bilateral assistance programs for procurement within the developing countries. In addition, many donors have as a result of a shift in the nature and emphasis of their programs increased the level of their local cost financing activities and reduced the level of their direct commodity procurement, all of which has reduced both the incidence of tying arrangements and the possible influence of tying arrangements on LDCs' exchange control regimes.

13. An interesting example of a country that reportedly refused, on exchange control considerations, to benefit from aid-financed contracts is Thailand. The United States, under PD31, permitted a small set of LDCs to tender for U.S.-aid-financed contracts *provided* that, in turn, they spent the dollars so earned on U.S. exports. This would have required opening "restricted" accounts. Thailand did not wish to do this and opted out of the PD31 benefit.

14. Carlos Díaz-Alejandro, op.cit., Chapter 5, pp. 147-148. INCOMEX is the import licensing authority. On the other hand, USAID has argued that "one reason for the U.S. practice [was that] Colombia was using its licensing procedures to give preference to its European bilateral trading agreement partners at the expense of traditional U.S. suppliers" (private communication dated September 13, 1974).

15. Cf. *Egypt*, op.cit., Table 1-6, p. 22. For Chile, *before* the period of our study, Behrman notes that there were bilateral trade agreements with DCs as well and that the share of bilateral to total trade was as high as 60 percent for imports and 25 percent for exports in 1936. Cf. *Chile*, op.cit., pp. 99-100.

16. Michaely, *Israel*, op.cit., Chapter 2, pp. 53-54.

17. Leith, *Ghana*, op.cit., pp. 26-27.

18. *Chile*, op.cit., pp. 102-103.

19. Finally, although there do not appear to be any significant examples of this in the country studies in the Project, Bent Hansen has suggested that an additional factor leading to source specification in licenses may be included, to complete the set of possibilities. Thus there may be politically motivated discrimination (as in the case of trade embargoes imposed, for example, on Cuba by Brazil, Chile, and Colombia or Ghana's prohibition on use of licenses to purchase imports from South Africa, Rhodesia, and Portuguese territories).

20. An additional reason for such commodity-tying, at least with U.S. aid, was concern over the types of items that may be procured with the aid funds: the familiar champagne glasses and pink bidets issue.

21. Although source-tying would have been made most effective only by specification of commodities in which the donor was *least* competitive, and such an idea was discussed in certain donor-country aid agencies, there is no evidence that it was systematically applied. Cf. Bhagwati, ibid. In fact, after June 1969, USAID claims to have relaxed commodity specification on U.S.-aid-financed imports substantially, allowing a "very long list of 'development-type' goods" (private communication, September 13, 1974).

22. See Bhagwati and Srinivasan, *India*, op.cit., Chapter 2.

23. Ibid., Chapter 5, pp. 135-136.

24. DGTD stands for the Directorate General of Technical Development; see Bhagwati and Srinivasan, ibid., Chapter 2, for further discussion.

25. *Israel*, op.cit., Chapter 2, pp. 51-52.

26. *Ghana*, op.cit., Chapter 2.

27. *Turkey*, op.cit., Chapter VI. Refer to this for details on the transition matrices reported in the text above.

28. Krueger also notes that: "The transition matrices fail fully to reflect the extent of the increasing use of the 'Prohibited List': (1) since all three samples were drawn from import lists, any item continuously prohibited could not be drawn. . .; and (2) for many of the items which continued on the lists, only a subcategory of the original classification was eligible for importation in later Programs" (Chapter VI, p. 162).

29. *Philippines*, op.cit., pp. 31-33.

30. See *Philippines*, ibid., Table 2-5, p. 34.

31. For further discussion, see Bhagwati, "The Tying of Aid," op.cit. This prospect was apparently pointed out at times by sympathetic aid agencies to recipient countries as arising from the possibility of effective slashing of aid programs on balance of payments grounds by the foes of these programs.

32. *South Korea*, op.cit., Chapter 5.

33. See, for example, *Chile*, op.cit., Chapter 5 and Chapter 6, especially pp. 157-161.

34. This is demonstrated in J. Bhagwati and C. Wibulswasdi, "A Statistical Analysis of Shifts in the Import Structure in LDC's" *Bulletin of Oxford University Institute of Statistics* 34, 2 (1974):229-239. For further analysis, especially of the distinction between essential and non-essential consumer goods, refer to this paper.

35. Cf. *Israel*, op.cit., Table 2-10, p. 49; *Egypt*, op.cit., Table 1-5, p. 21; *Turkey*, op.cit., p. 127; and *Philippines*, op.cit., Table 2-6, p. 36.

36. *Turkey*, op.cit., Chapter VI, p. 151.

37. Ibid., Table VI-1, p. 151.

38. For Egypt, Hansen and Nashashibi suggest that raw material imports were generally considered more important than capital goods imports.

39. This can be inferred by comparing the planned "requirements" of capital goods imports in the official documents with the actuals year by year over the plan periods. This type of comparison for India and Pakistan supports the statement in the text.

40. Such a situation is characterized as Phase II in the evolution of exchange control regimes in Chapter 3.

41. For details, see Bhagwati and Srinivasan, op.cit., Chapter 7.

42. *Colombia*, op.cit., Chapter 5, p. 144.

43. Ibid., Chapter 6, pp. 160-168, especially Table 6-7.

44. Ibid., Table 6-6, p. 163.

45. *Philippines*, op.cit., Chapter 2.

46. *Chile*, op.cit., Chapter 4, pp. 103-114.

47. Cf. the work of H. Bruton and S.R. Bose, Pakistan Institute of Development Economics, Karachi; cited by Nurul Islam, *Pakistan*, op.cit.

48. Cf. J. Bhagwati and Padma Desai, *India: Planning for Industrialization*, (Oxford University Press, 1970), Chapter 18.

49. *South Korea*, op.cit., Chapter 4, p. 51.

50. *India*, op.cit., Chapter 4.

51. See *Israel*, op.cit., Chapter 2, pp. 36-39, for further details.

52. *India*, op.cit., pp. 39-40. Additional evidence on this bias against the small-scale sector is presented in Bhagwati and Desai, op.cit., Chapter 5.

53. Thus, they note that:

> . . . all exporters and importers were required to register at the Ministry of Commerce and Industry. A prerequisite for registration was a minimum export of $3,000 for exporters and a minimum export of $10,000 for importers in 1958. This form of trading system is unusual in that the importer's registration was granted according to his export performance. Minimum exports for registration were raised in 1959 to $5,000 for exporters and $20,000 for importers. To *maintain* the status of exporters and importers, traders had to sustain an annual export performance exceeding a certain standard. Minimum exports were $10,000 for export business and $50,000 for import business in 1958. A year later minimum requirements for registration were raised by 100 percent. Cf. *South Korea*, op.cit., pp. 39-41.

54. *Ghana*, op.cit., pp. 24, 31-32.

55. "Reimbursable imports" are those requiring payment in foreign exchange supplied by the central bank, while non-reimbursable imports (typically capital goods) are those financed by external sources. Cf. *Colombia*, pp. 126-127.

56. *Colombia*, op.cit., Chapter 5, p. 139.

57. Ibid., Part III, Chapter 1, p. 8-9; unpublished manuscript for the NBER Project.

58. In fact, for Ghana, points (1) to (3) together are cited by Leith as resulting in the "assured" supplies of essential consumer goods at "reasonable prices."

59. *Colombia*, op.cit., Chapter 5, pp. 168-172.

60. *Chile*, op.cit., Chapter 4, pp. 95-98.

61. Op.cit., Chapter 5, p. 143. "On balance, however, there is a presumption that official requests should be given priority, and they are said to fare better than private requests, particularly at times of exchange stringency."

62. *Chile*, op.cit., pp. 4-28 and 4-30.

63. Cf. Hansen and Nashashibi, *Egypt*, op.cit., Chapter 2. They emphasize that construction of new plants financed through special arrangements with foreign donors and purchases of weapons fell outside the foreign exchange allocation system described by them.

64. *Ghana*, op.cit., p. 32.

65. *India*, op.cit., Chapter 13, pp. 188-190.

66. This could happen through illegal purchases in the black market. It also became possible when the import entitlements under the export promotion schemes were made legally transferable since 1965.

67. Cf. Bhagwati and Desai, op.cit., p. 291; and *Pakistan*, op.cit., Part II, Chapter 1.

68. See, for example, the statement of "essentials" and "non-essentials" in *Philippines*, op.cit., Chapter 2, pp. 33-34.

69. Cf. *Ghana*, op.cit., pp. 25-26.

70. Cf. Bhagwati and Desai, op.cit., p. 291.

71. Cf. *India*, op.cit., Chapter 8.

72. *Ghana*, op.cit., p. 32.

73. *Philippines*, op.cit., p. 35.

74. *Ghana*, op.cit., pp. 35-36.

75. The distinction between transferring licenses and imports is substantive because the former may imply greater flexibility since licenses may not be too rigidly defined itemwise, for example. Again, there may also be greater flexibility to choose the time of purchase in the former case.

76. *India*, op.cit., Chapter 2.

77. *Colombia*, op.cit., Chapter 5, p. 146.

78. Cf. *Ghana*, op.cit., p. 21, footnote 37.

79. The anatomy of exchange control regimes as applied to exports becomes much more complex, moreover, when price-related instruments are considered, as in Section VIII.

80. *South Korea*, op.cit., Chapter 4, pp. 46-47; italics inserted.

81. *Colombia*, op.cit., Chapter 5, p. 144.

82. For details in one instance, see for example Jere Behrman, *Chile*, op.cit., Chapter 4, pp. 49-54.

83. Later, in Chapter 3, we describe this stage as Phase V.

84. Cf. J. Bhagwati, "Indian Balance of Payments Policy and Exchange Auctions," *Oxford Economic Papers*, 14 N.S. (February 1962).

85. Cf. *South Korea*, op.cit., page 194; and private communication from L. Westphal.

86. *Turkey*, op.cit., Chapter VI, Table VI-11.

87. Ibid., Chapter VI, pp. 177-178. Krueger also notes that, after the devaluation in 1958 until 1962, the resale market for import licenses was sluggish and premiums had become negligible, whereas in 1955-1958, the premiums had run as high as eight times the parity rate.

88. Ibid., Chapter VI.

89. *Philippines*, op.cit., pp. 98-103.

90. Ibid., p. 101.

91. *Ghana*, op.cit., Chapter III. Note that Leith estimated the explicit tariffs from average duty collections in view of several exemptions, and that the import premium data were based on unit value comparisons.

92. Ibid., Chapter III. Note that such a use of tariffs to reduce the pressure on QRs often precedes or accompanies what are described in Chapter 3 as Phase III attempts at liberalizing the QR regime. A use of tariff surcharges before the June 1966 devaluation in India is another instance of this phenomenon.

93. However, note that (as discussed in depth in Chapter 5 below) the measurement and analysis of protection becomes extremely complex in the presence of QR regimes and the mere use of implicit tariffs, based on premium data, can be seriously misleading in understanding the nature and degree of protection and its effects.

94. *Israel*, op.cit., Chapter 2, pp. 32-36.

95. Indeed, for South Korea, the role of implicit tariffs had declined to negligible proportions by late 1960s; cf. *South Korea*, op.cit., Chapter 10.

96. *South Korea*, op.cit., Chapter 4, pp. 44 and 49. One footnote in the quote has been eliminated.

97. Note again that this distinction applies only *ex ante*.

98. This is evident from Nurul Islam, *Pakistan*, op.cit., as also from Padma Desai, *Tariff Protection and Industrialization: A Study of the Indian Tariff Commission at Work* (Delhi: Hindustan Publishing Corporation, 1970).

99. In fact, such moral suasion, with the stick held firmly in hand, was evident in the Indian regime as well, whereas the INCOMEX used formal links of imports to exports in certain cases as well. Thus, a blend of both formal and informal links appears to have been used, rather than total reliance on one or the other method.

100. *India*, op.cit., Chapter 3, pp. 59-74; this analysis, in turn, borrows heavily from Bhagwati and Desai, op.cit., Chapter 19.

Chapter 3

Sequential Phases and Contrasting Structures in Exchange Control Regimes

The preceding chapter analyzed taxonomically, with several illustrations from the country studies in the Project, the numerous dimensions on which exchange control regimes can, and do, differ from one another in their use of both QRs and price instruments. In the present chapter, we now shift the focus of our analysis to two sets of questions about exchange control regimes or, more broadly, foreign trade regimes, regarded as integrated structures or "clusters":

(1) Can we state any general propositions about the economic consequences of different exchange control regimes?

(2) Can we delineate certain basic "types" or stages of exchange control regimes in a manner that is economically meaningful for analyzing the time sequencing of the regimes within a country and across countries?

I. GENERAL PROPOSITIONS

The analysis of exchange control regimes and their consequences in the different country studies reflects and underscores three basic propositions that may now be stated and briefly discussed.

Proposition (1): Identical component features of exchange control regimes have, generally speaking, differential economic consequences if the exchange control regime is dissimilar on other dimensions.

Proposition (2): The economic consequences of an identical exchange control regime will, generally speaking, vary with differences in the structure of domestic objectives and attendant policies.

Proposition (3): Alternative exchange control regimes have, generally speaking, different economic consequences.

A. Proposition (1)

The differential effects of identical component features of exchange control regimes, arising from differences in the regimes on other dimensions, may be briefly spelled out here by reference to specific examples.

1. Non-Transferability of Licenses.

The effects of non-transferability of import licenses clearly depend on the exact structure of the exchange control regime. Thus, in India, where the non-transferability rules had been carried to the utmost extreme such that firms could not legally sell import licenses or imports, the adverse effects *via* the creation of bottlenecks were progressively blunted as the regime was amended—as part of moves in the direction of export subsidization—to allow for growing numbers of import entitlement schemes under which eligible exporters retained varying fractions of their export earnings for their own use. This was also the effect of the introduction of the export bonus voucher scheme in Pakistan. Under both schemes, the regime enabled the importation of items fetching high premiums and hence reflecting critical bottlenecks and shortages.

2. Itemwise Specification of Licenses.

Yet another illustration of Proposition (1) is afforded by the itemwise specification of import licenses. If such specification is *combined* with the sourcewise specification of licenses, then the effect is equivalent to that of effective "double-tying" of aid. The results, in terms of the additional expense of importing the specified items *via* exercise of monopolistic power by suppliers, are correspondingly more probable. By contrast, mere itemwise specification of importable items, with the sources of origin left open, need not cause monopolistic pricing by suppliers because it would always be possible to switch sources and thereby introduce competition among suppliers.

B. Proposition (2)

We now turn to the proposition that identical exchange control regimes will, in general, lead to different consequences depending on the structure of domestic policies with which they operate. This is ideally illustrated by the following example.

INTERACTION WITH INDUSTRIAL LICENSING.

The allocation of imported intermediates, on a *pro rata* basis related to capacity installed in an industry, is an occasional feature of the import-licensing regimes, as noted in Chapter 2. However, it is clear that its deleterious effects on competition, for example, are seriously aggravated if it is combined with domestic industrial licensing (in pursuit of economic objectives such as the regulation of the pattern of investment or of non-economic objectives such as the control of concentration of economic power).

Thus, in India and to some extent in Pakistan, the *pro rata* to capacity allocations of imported materials would have blunted competition in any event by giving existing firms "equal, guaranteed access" to the imported inputs regardless of their efficiency. In the marketplace, however, without this regime these firms would have had to compete for this access, and the inefficient firms would have been at a disadvantage.[1] But given the strict industrial licensing of both expansion by existing firms and investment by new firms, within overall targets, the effect was to reduce "potential" competition by entry to negligible levels. Not merely could the more efficient existing firms not drive out the less efficient ones but free entry was not possible by new firms either. In addition, foreign competition was ruled out by a policy of automatic protection. Hence the total effect was virtually to eliminate effective competition except in industries that had happened to overexpand by miscalculation of the planners and the investors.

C. Proposition (3)

Having noted briefly the interaction effects between (1) the different components of an exchange control regime and (2) the exchange control regime and domestic policies, we may finally address a few remarks to the simpler fact that differences in exchange control regimes will generally result in differential consequences. It should suffice to draw attention to one pointed illustration.

PRO RATA ALLOCATIONS OF MATERIALS.

Thus, a regime that makes allocations of imported materials to firms *pro rata* to installed capacity, as was the case in Pakistan and India, will have consequences such as the creation of a bias toward expanding capacity in the face of underutilized capacity.[2] It will also affect the structure of incentives *among* different industries for expansion, thus implying differential resource allocational effects, depending for example on the rate at which such *pro rata* allocations are made in the different industries.[3] If, however, the allocations were to be made *via* the use of tariffs that mopped up most of the premium[4] or the use of exchange auctions (as in Brazil after 1953) or the use of traders/importers who then earn the import premium rather than the producers, these effects would be eliminated and different consequences would follow.[5]

II. SEQUENTIAL PATTERNS AND PHASES

The foregoing general propositions can be supplemented by more specific delineation of exchange control regimes into certain basic types or, what we term, Phases that have a broadly differentiated impact on economic efficiency and performance.[6]

This notion of Phases, shortly to be defined but essentially based on the restrictionist content and associated blend of control and price instruments, reflected initial familiarity with the evolving exchange control regimes in specific countries[7] and the strongly suggested hypothesis that these regimes went through a sequencing. In the analytical framework that defined the broad contours of the country studies in the Project, this notion of sequencing was sharpened and spelled out in the shape of alternative Phases in the exchange control regime. These Phases in the exchange control regimes were designed essentially as a classificatory and descriptive device to capture meaningfully the evolution of the exchange control system in terms of its restrictionist content and the dimensions and pattern of its use of control and price instruments.

The analytical framework distinguished among five Phases. The exchange control regimes in the countries in the Project were to be traced through, placing them in one of these Phases at a point in time.[8] It was expected that the resulting patterns would also be highly suggestive of hypotheses concerning the success or failure of attempts at liberalization, hypotheses that are considered explicitly in the companion volume by Krueger.

A. Phase I

This Phase is characterized by the systematic and significant imposition of quantitative controls. It might start in response to an unsustainable payments deficit resulting from intense or sustained prior inflationary pressure (due, for example, to the initiation of a large-scale development plan and consequent extraordinary increases in government expenditures) or from a sharp drop in world prices for some major exports (as in 1953). These reasons for instituting controls are of interest in ascertaining the logic of the evolution of exchange control regimes but are not critical to the definition of Phase 1.

Throughout Phase I (which, of course, can be of varying duration), controls are generally maintained and often intensified. This continuation or increased severity might result from any of several interrelated factors: (1) the continuation of initial controls might be necessary to contain an *ex ante*, unsustainable payments deficit; (2) the initial set of controls might result in evasions of the system through illegal transactions that negate any possible impact on the balance of payments; (3) once controls are instituted, policy-makers may perceive the new instruments as handy for a variety of purposes in addition to controlling the payments situation and begin employing them for such purposes; and (4) policy-makers may perceive their actions as freed from a balance of payments constraint and adopt policies that in fact require restrictiveness afresh to offset further adverse effects on the balance of payments.

B. Phase II

This Phase is characterized by continued reliance upon quantitative restrictions and, indeed, generally increased restrictiveness of the entire control system. However, Phase II is distinguished by two additional and related aspects of the QR system, both relatively unimportant during Phase I: (1) for a variety of reasons, indicated below, the detailed workings of the control system become increasingly complex; and (2) price measures are adopted to buttress the functioning of the control system. Both of these characteristics of Phase II stem from dissatisfaction with the results of an undifferentiated system and are often the result of many small decisions rather than an overall policy design.

(1) Although neither term is quite appropriate, Phase I decision-making and policies may be characterized as "crude" and "unsophisticated." Quantitative restrictions are applied with relatively few rules, and treatment of competing claims to import licenses tends to be relatively undifferentiated in the sense that rules for allocation tend to be of an "across the board" nature, such as allocating to everyone a certain percentage of this person's imports over a specified number of earlier years or allotting licenses *pro rata* with applications. The major motivation for changes in the control system during Phase I is a concern with evasions, both legal and illegal, of the system. Thus, export licensing may be adopted to ensure that exporters do not succeed in their attempts at capital flight; controls over tourist and other invisible transactions are aimed at preventing the emergence of a black market, and so on.

In Phase II, however, the rules of the regime have become more complex and differentiated. The growth of the bureaucracy to administer the allocations and the inevitable tendency to differentiate increasingly among alternative end uses and claimants as the control regime is perceived to be a continuing state of affairs interact to produce a complex system (whose possible dimensions ought to be generally evident to the reader from Chapter 2).

(2) The other major feature of Phase II is an increasing resort to price

measures to supplement the QR regime. This generally occurs with respect to both exports and imports. The continuation or intensification of foreign exchange shortage leads to recognition that additional export earnings would be desirable. Rebate schemes, import replenishment schemes, special credits for exporters, and a variety of other devices may be instituted that offset part or all of the discrimination against exports implicit in an overvalued exchange rate. Like the quantitative restrictions discussed above, however, export incentives tend to be adopted in a piecemeal and fragmented fashion. As for imports, price measures are also adopted to absorb part of the excess demand for imports. Tariffs may be increased or surcharges added to the cost of importing. Guarantee deposits are generally required on various categories of imports. These and other measures tend to reduce (but hardly eliminate) the windfall gain or premium accruing to the recipients of import licenses.

The following aspects of the price situation in Phase II are then evident: (1) the exchange parity is "overlaid" by tariffs and subsidies, levied in lieu of formal parity change; (2) the effective exchange rate for exports, on the average, is rarely as high as the effective exchange rate on imports, implying a bias against the (relative) incentive to export; (3) the domestic currency is overvalued at the current parity plus trade tariffs and subsidies, implying a premium (on the average) on imports; and (4) this import premium varies across different activities, implying differential incentives to produce and invest in these different activities.[9]

C. Phase III

Phase III is entered against the backdrop just defined, and it can take various forms. It may consist of a mere "tidying-up" operation directed at replacing the diverse import premiums by reasonably uniform tariffs such that the differential incentive effects caused by diverse premiums on different imports are greatly reduced or virtually eliminated. Alternatively, the tidying-up operation may replace the existing tariffs and export subsidies with a formal parity change, the result being that the (average) effective exchange rates on exports and imports do not change much but the dispersion of tariffs is replaced by the uniform devaluation—an action again of rationalization in this instance. On the other hand, Phase III may be substantially ambitious and take the form of what might be described as a devaluation cum liberalization package. Such a package may have a gross devaluation large enough to leave a net devaluation despite the removal of the trade tariffs and subsidies, with accompanying grants by donors of additional credits to facilitate early expansion of imports, debt rescheduling, and similar measures aimed at quick and easy liberalization of imports.

D. Phase IV

Phase IV is entered when Phase III has resulted in *continued* liberalization. This means that the average import premium has fallen, the bias against exports has substantially diminished (the effective exchange rate for exports having come closer to the effective exchange rate for imports), and the degree of dispersion in the incentives to expand different activities has diminished through greater uniformity in these incentives *via* the foreign trade sector.

Needless to say, this outcome can only be anticipated from a Phase III episode when the latter takes the ambitious form of a concerted effort of the kind presupposed in a devaluation cum liberalization package. Even then, as is documented in the companion Krueger volume, the outcome has often been a reversion to Phase II. But the transition to Phase IV, which can be regarded as the successful culmination of Phase III efforts, cannot be expected when Phase III takes the form of a simple tidying-up operation, consisting of rationalization measures of the type already described above.

E. Phase V

The transition from Phase IV to Phase V occurs when the exchange regime is virtually liberalized in the sense that there is full convertibility on current account and quantitative restrictions are not employed as a means of regulating the balance of payments. Thus, an economy in Phase V is not an exchange control regime in the usual sense of the term, and Phase V represents a total alternative to the QR regimes of Phases I and II. The pegged exchange rate is at its equilibrium level, a flexible exchange rate policy is in operation, or monetary and fiscal policies are employed as the instruments to achieve payments balance in contrast to a reliance on the exchange control mechanism.

It will be evident shortly that Phase I has characterized the early experience with exchange control in nearly all the countries in the Project. Indeed, it is no more than the period of entry into exchange control regimes of a sustained variety. At the same time, Phase V turns out to have been more an ideal than a reality even for the few countries (with the possible exception of Israel) in the Project that have managed to transit from Phase II into seriously sustained Phase III episodes and Phase IV.

III. PHASE EVOLUTION AND PATTERNS IN COUNTRIES IN THE PROJECT

For each country in the Project, the delineation of Phases was undertaken. For details the reader should consult the country volumes. Here, it should suffice to put these countries onto a common chart, Figure 3-1, which helps underline possible patterns among the countries. In drawing conclusions, we need to keep in mind that the delineation of Phases cannot be exact. Phase II, III, and IV in particular are difficult to differentiate sharply. Hence it is wise to forego the temptation to discuss questions such as the length of the periods under each Phase in the different countries. Instead, the following points of interest need to be made.

A. Patterns

Although the detailed Phase evolution is different for each country in the Project, certain suggestive groupings are indicated. One group seems to have more or less progressed through the Phases from I to IV. This group contains Brazil, Israel, and South Korea. Another group appears to have made repeated attempts at Phase III episodes, which have not endured but rather been followed by relapse into Phase II. The behavior of these countries is best described as cycling back and forth mainly between Phases II, III, and IV and, rather rarely, Phase I as well. The countries that clearly fall into this group are Chile and Colombia. In a similar vein, Ghana and the Philippines seem to have gone through one major such cycle and Turkey through two. Finally, there are the countries that have generally been in Phase II over *long-sustained* periods with rare (if any) jabs at Phase III episodes that were unsuccessful. The classic case here is India, with Egypt falling neatly into the group before the nationalizations of the early 1960s (and after, if one construes the nationalization of foreign trade as Phase II).

B. Discernible Trends

We may look at the Phase experiences from yet another angle by examining trend differences during the period 1950-1972. A few observations are in order.

One notices that Phase I is really an early form of exchange control regime as a liberal regime is initially abandoned. It rarely seems to be a Phase to which a regime at a *later* stage *reverts,* so that cycling through the Phases, for example, generally bypasses Phase I altogether and is confined to Phases II, III, and IV. Moreover, Phase V appears to have eluded most countries. The success stories in the transition to a liberalized regime are mostly ones of transition to Phase IV, as with South Korea and Brazil. Israel is the only exception to this observation.

As for trends, the following propositions may be advanced.

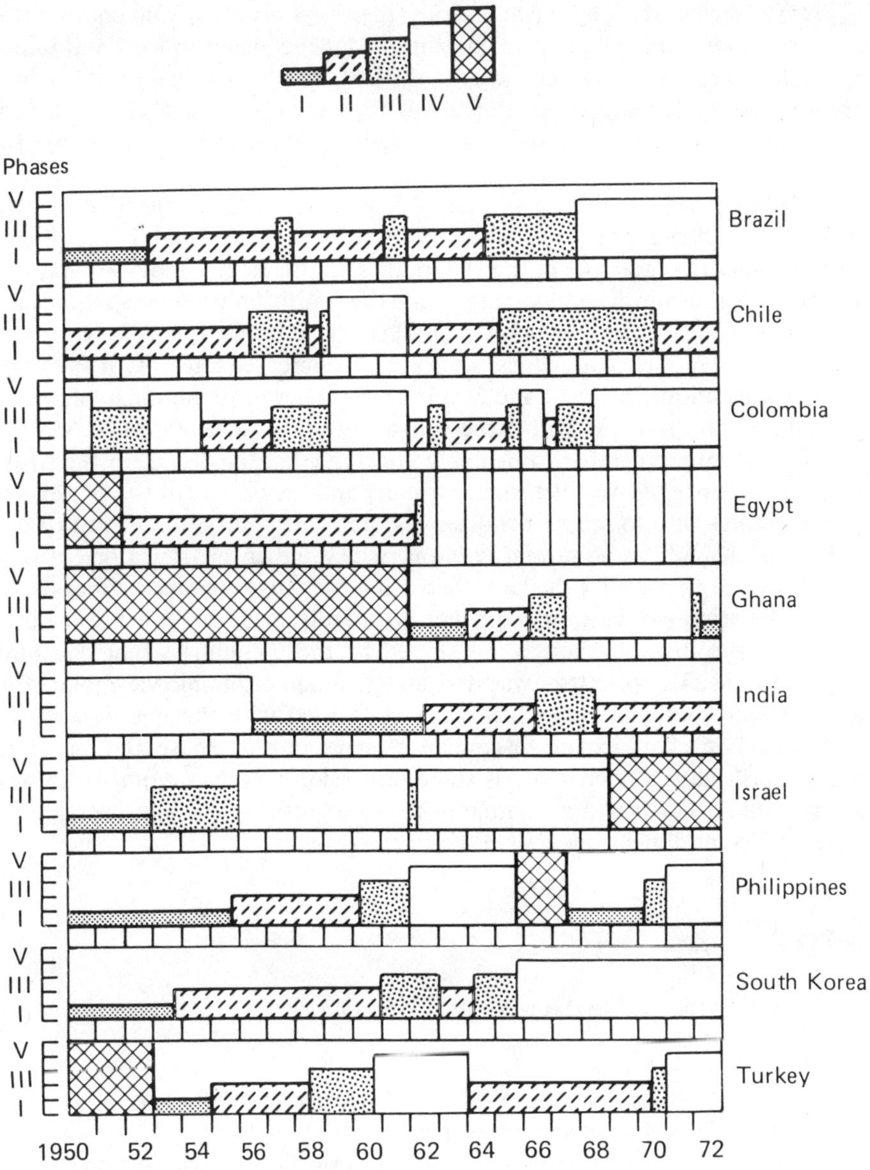

Figure 3-1. Phases of Exchange Control Regimes.

Source: Based on the country volumes, op.cit., in the NBER Project and compiled by Krueger, *Liberalization Attempts*, op.cit., from these country regimes (except for Colombia) with the assistance of the country authors and Hal Lary.

(1) It is clear that, by the mid-1950s, there was practically no country (the only exception being Ghana, which achieved independence in 1957 and joined the ranks of restrictive regimes only in the early 1960s) that had not gone over from a Phase V situation into Phase I or further into Phase II. Liberal trade and payments regimes had thus virtually become non-existent by the mid-1950s.[10]

(2) Furthermore, during the latter half of the 1950s, fully half of the countries studied appear to have remained in Phase II or Phase I type restrictive regimes. This was true of the Philippines, South Korea, India, Egypt, and Brazil. Israel, however, had already made the transition to Phases III and IV, and Chile, Colombia, and Turkey had taken steps in this direction.

(3) The 1960s were to witness substantially increased attempts at Phase III type liberalization. In Brazil and South Korea this was to culminate in a successful shift to Phase IV, with Israel managing to shift even to Phase V.[11]

By and large, therefore, one might conclude that the decade of the fifties was one of restrictive regimes in major part, and the decade of the sixties was one of greater shift to more liberalized regimes. The analysis in the rest of this volume is then addressed primarily to the issue whether the transition between the 1950s and (especially) the late 1960s from exchange control regimes of the Phase II variety—a phenomenon that is broadly evident from the country studies in the Project, though not shared by those countries that had only abortive Phase III episodes—was desirable from an economic viewpoint. Put another way, our analysis will now be concerned with the question of the economic impact of exchange control regimes of the Phase II type. This analysis will naturally encompass some discussion of the *alternative* regimes such as Phase IV. It will also attempt to distinguish, where appropriate, between different dimensions *within* the Phase II regimes.

NOTES

1. Similar blunting of competition would have occurred even under allocations based, for example, on historical shares.

2. See the analysis in Chapter 5 below.

3. Cf. Bhagwati and Desai, op. cit., Chapter 17; also see Chapter 7 below.

4. For examples of this from the country studies, see Chapter 2.

5. Note also that the distributional and political implications of these alternative regimes would also be different: for example, the former would lead to more opposition by producers to devaluations than the latter for the premium on imports would already have been lost to the producers under the latter. These issues have been discussed in *India,* op. cit., and *Turkey,* op. cit.

6. Within each of the Phases to be defined, we must note that economically significant differences may exist among some of the dimensions distinguished in Chapter 2: for example, in Phase II, the QRs may be used to confer automatic protection or protection only within prespecified limits of excess cost over c.i.f. values.

7. Thus, writing in 1968 with the Indian experience in mind, the present author had argued:

> The typical stages in the transition of a less developed country, from one parity to another, may be described as follows:
>
> (1) Balance-of-payments difficulties, under a fixed parity, lead to the establishment and frequently to the more or less permanent continuation of a regime of quantitative restrictions. The result is the establishment of several *ad hoc, de facto* effective tariffs on different activities—a set of multiple import rates. There also comes about a net export rate (equal to parity) that falls below the effective import rates. (They exceed parity by the premium on imports, which may vary between different imports if the exchange markets are effectively segmented.) This export rate not only discriminates against exports but also compounds the distortions that would arise from a multiplicity of rates on imports.
>
> (2) Gradual shift towards a system of effective export subsidies occurs as the tight balance-of-payments situation and the quantitative restrictions continue, in order to increase export earnings. The effect is to reduce the differential between the export and the import rates, while often leading to multiple rates on exports as well, since official subsidies on exports almost always are discriminatory in practice.
>
> (3) As the import premium continues, while lessened (*ceteris paribus*) by the export subsidization, governments turn gradually (under public criticism) to using tariffs more actively so as to cut into this premium and earn the scarcity profits themselves. The result is that, with both export subsidies and import tariffs being used in this fashion, there comes about a *de facto* devaluation on current visible transactions (extended gradually again to invisibles, such as remittances from settlers abroad and tourist earnings, but practically never to transactions on capital account).The *de facto* devaluation, however, is characterized by numerous rates on imports and exports, and conceals effective export rates on specific commodities that may exceed or fall below their effective import rates, so that numerous distortions remain embedded in the system.
>
> (4) As the realization grows that a *de facto* devaluation has occurred, in an inefficient manner, the way is seen to rationalize the situation by devaluing the rate formally and thereby managing to reduce, if not eliminate, the reliance on export subsidies and import tariffs, though even this is done with considerable reluctance.
>
> (5) Then the process can, and frequently does, start all over again, with the system of quantitative restrictions again taking the brunt of initial adjustment and then gradually being eased by export subsidies and import tariffs.
>
> There are several variations on this general sequence, of course. In place of a freer use of import duties, for example, exchange auctions (as in Brazil) or multiplicity of exchange rates, fixed directly by exchange-control authorities (in many Latin American countries), have been used. Similarly, there are wide variations in the forms of export subsidy and the manner in which selectivity is exercised in granting them.

See J. Bhagwati, *The Theory and Practice of Commercial Policy*, Frank Graham Memorial Lecture (1967), Special Studies in International Economics, International Finance Section (New Jersey: Princeton University Press, 1968), pp.48-49.

8. Clearly, as will be evident below, identification of Phases must rest partly on judgments. On the whole, however, the identification process has been both relatively uncomplicated and fruitful.

9. See the appendix for the definition of effective exchange rate and other concepts (as well as a summary description of Phases) at the end of the book.

10. In Chile, this had been so since the early 1930s! Cf. *Chile*, op. cit., pp. 21-27.

11. None of these countries, however, had dismantled the QR mechanism.

PART III
The Consequences of Exchange Control Regimes

Chapter 4

Illegal Transactions and Exchange Control

Among the significant economic effects attendant upon the working of exchange control regimes are those that relate to illegal transactions. Since we have defined exchange control regimes comprehensively to include those foreign trade regimes that have a large complement of price instruments as well as quantitative restrictions, we need to distinguish between the price and quantitative instruments in discussing the emergence of illegal transactions.

The use of QRs is not, of course, a necessary condition for such illegal transactions since tariffs can equally create an incentive for smuggling and faked invoicing. In the analysis that follows we therefore plan to note also the *distinctive* aspects of QRs in regard to the growth of illegal transactions.

These illegal phenomena can be divided into three broad classes: (1) those that relate to abuses in awarding, claiming, and disposing of licenses; (2) those pertaining to illegal trade transactions such as smuggling and faked invoicing; and (3) those relating to capital flows, including both capital flight abroad and inward flows seeking better exchange rates in the black market. We consider these now in turn. Finally, we turn to examining reverse links between illegal transactions and exchange control rules and methods.

I. ILLEGALITY IN AWARDING, CLAIMING, AND DISPOSING OF LICENSES

The most notable instances of illegality in awarding licenses have naturally appeared in regard to import control.

1. We have noted in Chapter 2 how, in several import regimes, the bu-

reaucrats generally sought to follow fair-share rules in their choice of criteria for awarding licenses among competing claimants and that this phenomenon was partly attributable to their desire to protect themselves against allegations of corruption and favoritism. However, breakdowns in the actual honesty and integrity of the bureaucracy dealing with the award of licenses were not uncommon.[1] Perhaps the most notable and extreme example of illegal manipulation of allocational criteria in import licensing is provided by Ghanaian experience. Leith notes that the extensive, personalized routing of import licenses by Mr. Djin, Minister of Trade in the Nkrumah cabinet from late 1963, resulted in "fraudulent exploitation, corruption and malpractices" according to the investigative commission after the overthrow of the Nkrumah regime. The displacement of Mr. Djin by President Nkrumah was to be ironic. As Leith writes.[2]

> In the first half of 1965 a number of steps were taken in an attempt to reverse the situation created by Mr. Djin. President Nkrumah replaced Mr. Djin by Mr. Kwesi Armah as Minister of Foreign Trade. . . . In addition, a foreign-exchange budget was published for the first time. The only significant result of these moves was a more systematic form of corruption. Mr. Armah, rather than restricting himself to profiting on some licenses, proceeded to develop a system that would permit him to share in the profit on all licenses. As the post-Nkrumah commission reported: "He [Mr. Armah] introduced the system whereby all applications for import licenses had to be addressed to him personally under registered cover and he alone was responsible for processing the said applications. . .[T]here was open corruption and malpractices in the matter of grant of import licenses during this period. Import licenses were issued on the basis of a commission corruptly demanded and payable by importers on the face value of the import licenses issued. The commission was fixed at 10%, but was in special cases reduced to 7½ or 5%."

Political scientists have observed that the Ghanaian political system had been characterized by subordination to the goal of economic profit to its participants as distinct from any general ideology. Hence, even when we have allowed for the customary postcoup exaggerations, it remains basically plausible that the import control regime was subject to serious abuse during the ministries of Messrs. Djin and Armah.

2. There was illegality also in the claiming of import licenses, *given* the criteria. Thus, in India, the Estimates Committee of the Indian Parliament cited as an abuse of the import control system the following (among several) practices:

> (i) applying for licenses on the basis of forged essentiality certificates of the Director of Industries or certificates obtained by misrepresentation;

(ii) applying for licenses on the basis of forged quota certificates or such certificates obtained by false or forged documents of past imports;

(iii) applying for licenses on the basis of false turnover by producing certificates from a Chartered Accountant obtained by misrepresentation or in collusion with the Chartered Accountant; and

(iv) applying for licenses on the basis of imports or exports which do not qualify for establishment of quota.[3]

In Turkey, Anne Krueger records that since new firms in an industry were to be given a quota initially on criteria rather different from established producers, there were reported to be many instances of entrepreneurs 'going into business' for the purpose of obtaining imports and reselling to larger firms.[4]

3. Finally, there was the illegality involved in the resale of the licenses or the imports themselves in the regimes that prohibited such transferability. For Turkey Anne Krueger has noted that, while industrialists could not legally resell their imports, resale occurred in many ways. As some of the smaller firms found it more profitable to sell their imports to larger firms than to produce themselves, a legal means of resale (resulting, however, in *de facto* illegal transfer of imported goods) was for a small producer to ask a large producer to place his order with the larger establishment's. The ostensible purpose of permitting this practice was to enable the small producer to get a better price on his import order than was thought possible with a very small allocation. When the consignment arrived, however, the small firm could claim that the larger house had violated their understanding. The consignment in quality, technical specifications, or other regards was not what the small firm required or could use. The larger firm would then settle the matter by paying off the smaller firm for its goods and keeping the imports for its own use, all this at the appropriate premium-inclusive price. Several other means of resale were also devised, including even reported instances where the local chambers organized resale markets.[5]

II. FAKED INVOICING AND SMUGGLING

Both QRs and tariffs set up incentives to smuggle goods through illegal channels and to fake invoices on trade through legal channels. In either case, the illegal transaction yields profit. With QRs, for example, the premium on c.i.f. value of imports may be high enough to cover both the risk on smuggling or underinvoicing of imports[6] *and* the premium on the foreign exchange with which to pay the exporter. With tariffs, the same argument applies, except that the tariff rate must be considered in place of the import premium.[7] The argument applies equally, *mutatis mutandis*, to export smuggling and to faking of invoices pertaining to exports.

Note that, while the argument is equally applicable to QRs and tariffs, a QR system is more *likely* to generate the phenomenon of illegal trade, either smuggled or *via* faking of invoices, simply because QRs tend to give rise to rather more extreme levels of "implicit" tariffs. For example, it is relatively rare to find explicit tariffs that exceed 100 percent *ad valorem* in our countries. However, it is more readily possible to find (even numerous) instances of implicit tariffs in the 100 percent range or over.

A. Faked Invoicing

There seems to be fairly impressive evidence of underinvoiced imports in the case of two countries, Turkey and the Philippines, that relates to tariffs. Evidence for underinvoiced imports in response to tariffs *and* import premiums under QRs is available for Turkey and Pakistan.

For Turkey, the tariff-related underinvoicing of imports was recorded by Bhagwati, for 1960 and 1961, using the classic partner-country trade data comparison technique.[8] Utilizing such comparisons for Turkey's trade with Italy, Germany, the United States, France, and the Netherlands, and allowing for possible *statistical* reasons for such discrepancies as were evident, he concluded that significant discrepancies were left, for which the only explanation appeared to be underinvoicing of imports.[9] The categories of goods that showed perverse discrepancies also generally had tariff rates ranging up to 30 percent and rarely below 10 percent, whereas the black market premium for foreign exchange had rarely exceeded 15 percent according to official observations, so that it seemed reasonable to conclude that the discrepancies represented underinvoicing of imports by and large. This conclusion was further reinforced by the fact that understatement of value in the field of manufactures—especially machinery, which is frequently made to order and rarely carries standard prices that the customs can readily check—is readily possible, and it was precisely in these areas that the perverse discrepancies occurred in the Turkish case.

Baldwin also records underinvoicing of Philippines imports, relying however on aggregate data on imports (as distinct from Bhagwati's more disaggregated examination of Turkish trade data to adjust for possible misallocations of specific items among different sources of origin or SITC categories). He cites Philippines' partner-country trade data, compiled by George Hicks, for 1950-1958 and concludes that there was possible underinvoicing of both exports and imports. Citing high tariffs and/or import controls as the cause of underinvoiced imports, Baldwin argues that textiles were possibly the best-known illustration of this phenomenon. Baldwin also conducted a test of the hypothesis that the degree of import undervaluation is positively related to the height of duty levied on an item. The 1967 f.o.b. (free-on-board) import values from the Philippine Central Bank and f.o.b. export values of the same items from the U.S. Department of Commerce for a sample of sixty-two commodities were compared. The regression equation relating to this comparison was as follows:

$$y = 1.65 + 14.70x$$

where $y = \dfrac{\text{U.S. data on U.S. exports to the Philippines}}{\text{Philippine data on Philippine imports from the U.S.}}$

and x = 1969 *ad valorem* tariff rates in the Philippines (in percent)

The t-value on the coefficient of x was 4.27, which is significant at the 1 percent level, and the coefficient of correlation was .48. Thus Baldwin concluded that the hypothesis that the higher the tariff the greater the degree of undervaluation was supported by the statistical analysis. Moreover, the degree of undervaluation increased very sharply as the duty rose.[10]

In regard to the effects of import premiums, as distinct from those of tariffs, there is evidence in the country studies from Turkey and outside the Project studies from Pakistan (as we shall presently discuss). Thus, for Turkey, Anne Krueger cites a study by Cahid Kayra for the period 1963 to 1969, which undertook a detailed reconciliation of Turkish and partner-country trade statistics, including adjustment for transport costs, differences in the timing of imports, and other factors, and turned up substantial evidence of underinvoicing of imports and shifted classifications in categories where sizeable savings in import duties or gains in premiums were possible.[11]

There is little such systematic evidence on faked invoicing in the other country studies in the Project. A notable exception is the Chilean study where some evidence on faked invoicing is available by a comparison of trade statistics for operating partners; but the argument is not carried far enough to make the evidence reasonably compelling.[12] The only other evidence on faked invoicing in the Project is based on interviews. Thus, for India, Bhagwati and Srinivasan record overinvoicing of several non-traditional exports carrying high rates of import entitlements and high premiums thereon in turn, as with art-silk fabrics. They also note that the elimination of these extreme incentives with the June 1966 devaluation may have resulted in a seemingly less satisfactory showing of export performance than was actually the case, merely because the degree of overinvoicing had been seriously reduced.

Going outside the country studies, however, we can mention here the excellent analysis by Munir Sheikh of faked invoicing in Pakistan during 1965-1968.[13] Using the partner-country comparison technique, Sheikh worked with thirty-six different commodities and with partner countries that supplied over 80 percent of Pakistan's imports. He then divided the commodities into two broad groups, "restricted" and "liberal," based on a careful examination of the incidence of import licensing thereon. The results showed a very strong tendency for commodities in the restricted category to have the Pakistani import values fall significantly below the partner-country export values, indicating underinvoicing of imports for each of the four years considered. Sheikh further managed to establish a relationship between underinvoicing and the classification of a commodity in a high-tariff category or a low-tariff category. The former category meant that the goods therein were more prone to underinvoicing.[14]

Finally, for Ghana, we also have a careful analysis by David Scheffman of trade data discrepancies in Ghanaian cocoa trade, suggesting underinvoicing of exports in this instance.[15] Choosing S.I.T.C. classification 072-100 (cocoa beans, raw or roasted), which constitutes the major portion of the Ghanaian cocoa exports, and considering 1964-1969, Scheffman shows that substantial underinvoicing of cocoa exports is apparent with Canada, Norway, and the United Kingdom.

B. Smuggling

The detection of smuggling has also exercized the ingenuity of economists. An obvious approach is to infer the volume of smuggling from the data on confiscations. This is however problematic unless one knows the expected risk of confiscation with which smugglers are working. Much of the evidence on smuggling is therefore impressionistic. Thus, Anne Krueger notes for Turkey that she herself encountered "an incredible variety" of imported goods not eligible for importation on the shelves of local groceries and in the windows of various shops and that smuggling was sufficiently widespread so that its existence was officially acknowledged at the end of the First Five Year Plan.[16]

Similarly, Baldwin, records an estimate of smuggling into Philippines as follows:[17]

> An estimate from the government's Anti-Smuggling Action Center places the annual value of smuggled cigarettes at about $37 million in the 1962-65 period and $9 million from 1966 to 1968. Although estimates of the influx of other smuggled goods are not available, the Anti-Smuggling Action Center does report the value of confiscations of these other goods. If the ratio of the total volume of cigarettes smuggled to the volume of cigarettes confiscated holds for these other goods, the total value of smuggled goods, including cigarettes, comes to about $19 million in both 1966 and 1969, or around 2 percent of total imports.

Finally, it is worth recording here a technique, used independently by Timothy King for Mexico and by Richard Cooper for Indonesia, to detect smuggling. It works for tariffs but not for QRs because it compares the tariff-inclusive price of imported goods in domestic markets with the actual prices at which they sell. Both King and Cooper, using this technique, were able to show that smuggling had managed to drive the actual prices below the tariff-inclusive prices and that this discrepancy tended to increase with the tariff rate.[18]

III. CAPITAL FLIGHT

The faked invoicing that we considered in the preceding section, as also smuggling for that matter, was regarded strictly from the viewpoint of the incentive to undertake such illegal transactions without focusing on whether its effect was to create a supply of or demand for illegal foreign exchange. The latter question becomes relevant, however, when we try to detect capital flight. This phenomenon represents a demand for illegal foreign exchange that is fed by the supply created by phenomena such as "leaked" inward remittances and capital flows and primarily by underinvoicing exports and overinvoicing imports.

Note that the incentives to underinvoicing exports and overinvoicing imports as a vehicle for capital flight are the opposite of those discussed in the preceding section as leading to overinvoicing exports and underinvoicing imports for tax or other benefits. Both sets of phenomena may exist side by side, complicating the task of empirical verification.

A. A Statistical Analysis

One important impact of exchange control in LDCs is indeed that capital flight would occur in illegal fashion.[19] Whether, of course, such flight is still below the level that would occur in the absence of exchange control is an issue that is difficult to settle empirically. We would be inclined to assume that the extra costs of illegal methods of capital outflow tend to reduce its level. However, to the extent that exchange controls may generate expectations of devaluation, this may induce capital outflow as a hedge.

We decided therefore to explore the possibility of making partner-country trade data comparison to see whether the phenomena of overinvoicing imports and underinvoicing exports can be detected to infer such capital flight from the LDCs. Note, of course, that the illegal outflow of foreign exchange, so detected, may not fully represent capital flight in the strict sense and may be financing partly the underinvoicing of imports (as detected for Turkey in the preceding section) and related phenomena that require the illegal use of foreign exchange. Also, the analysis leaves out of consideration possible capital flight *via* smuggling.

We confined our analysis to comparisons of the trade data of LDCs with the Organization for Economic Development and Co-operation (OECD) countries, examining altogether twenty-eight LDCs for 1966. This, of course, means that capital flight that occurs *among* LDCs would not be shown up, even in principle, by our methods. There is "word-of-mouth" evidence of such flight occurring from some of the African countries to India by the Indian settlers, and from Indonesia, Malaysia, and Philippines to Hong Kong and Taiwan by the overseas Chinese communities.

Our method is subject to considerable "noise." There are a number of purely statistical reasons why partner-country data may not match. Nonetheless, it is interesting to see whether, on comparison, OECD imports from each LDC are sufficiently above that LDC's exports to OECD countries to indicate underinvoicing of that LDC's exports and consequent presumption of capital flight. It is also interesting to see whether each LDC's imports from OECD exceed the OECD exports to that LDC by a sufficient amount to indicate overinvoicing of imports and hence capital flight again from the LDC.

B. Analysis of Findings

Table 4-1 summarizes for each of the twenty-eight LDCs the percentage difference between imports and exports as a proportion of exports, the export figures being those recorded by the LDCs and the import figures being those recorded by the OECD countries. It is really quite remarkable that, in the total OECD columns, we find that for all but two countries there is an excess of import figures over the corresponding export figures. However, note that the exports are f.o.b. and imports are generally c.i.f., so that the excess is actually smaller than it looks. But even if we estimate average insurance and freight at a crude 10 percent on f.o.b. value, it would still leave twenty LDCs as export-underinvoicers.

Noting that the United States and Canada record their imports by f.o.b. values, we also calculated separately the trade flow from each LDC to the two countries combined. Column 2 of Table 4-1 shows the discrepancy between the combined imports of the United States and Canada and the corresponding exports by LDCs as a percentage of the import figures. The excess of import figures over the corresponding export figures in this case would be presumptive evidence for export underinvoicing practices in LDCs. Of the twenty countries noted earlier, such positive excess shows up for all but one (Pakistan).

Table 4-1. Exports of LDCs to OECD Countries Compared with Corresponding Imports by OECD Countries from LDCs, and Black Market Premium of U.S. Dollars, for 28 LDCs: 1966

Country (by region)	*Total OECD 100 · (M – X)/X (1)*	*U.S.A. and Canada 100 · (M – X)/M (2)*	*Black Market Premium of US$ (%) (3)*
South America			
Argentina	24.2	17.5	23
Brazil[a]	14.0	4.1	10
Chile	4.5	4.4	49
Colombia[a]	14.2	9.3	n.a.
Mexico	37.0	14.0	0
Central America			
Costa Rica	6.8	6.6	17
El Salvador	0.1	–5.3	13
Guatemala	24.2	16.3	15
Honduras	27.3	3.8	0
Nicaragua	14.7	3.2	19
Africa			
Ethiopia[a]	14.6	15.1	24
Ivory Coast	26.9	19.2	n.a.
Libya	11.1	5.2	20
Nigeria	9.9	1.1	n.a.
Tunisia	47.2	34.7	67
Far East			
Hong Kong	13.7	9.6	1
Korea	–4.6	–16.7	0
Philippines	16.1	16.5	2
Taiwan	7.0	–2.1	3
Thailand[a]	6.4	3.6	0.6
South Asia and Mid East			
Ceylon[b]	20.1	12.9	94
Egypt	30.7	13.9	111
India	23.7	5.3	74
Iran	35.2	21.4	4
Pakistan	14.3	–3.5	75
Europe			
Greece	27.9	16.1	4
Turkey[a]	15.4	9.6	40
Yugoslavia	–1.0	–1.0	17

Notes. 1. OECD countries in Tables 4-1 and 4-2 include only EFTA, EEC, USA, Canada and Japan. 2. *M, X* represent imports and exports, respectively.

[a]1967 data.

[b]1968 data.

Sources: United Nations, Statistical Papers, Series D (Commodity Trade Statistics). OECD, Statistics of Foreign Trade, Series C (Commodity Trade). Pick, Franz, *Pick's Currency Yearbook*, Pick Publ. Co., N.Y. Also printed in J. Bhagwati, ed., *Illegal Transactions . . .* , op. cit.; page 151.

Moreover, the magnitudes of the discrepancies are quite significant. They are larger than 10 percent in eleven cases, and between 5 to 10 percent in five others. These sixteen countries may therefore be classified as "plausible" export-underinvoicers.

We would further argue that, unlike the imports of LDCs that we shortly analyze, a significant part of the export sector is usually free from very large subsidies and taxes and the export duties on traditional exports are usually well balanced by subsidies on non-traditional exports. Hence, no pronounced effect of trade tax and subsidy policies need be expected to affect the trade declarations in the direction of either net overinvoicing or net underinvoicing of exports.

We would thus presume that the above results strongly signify capital flight from LDCs, especially in light of the supplementary evidence concerning the black market premium of U.S. dollars in each LDC, averaging for the year corresponding to the trade figure calculations, presented in the last column of Table 4-1. In view of its "black" nature, the estimates of a premium on foreign exchange presented here may not be very reliable. They nevertheless substantiate our result quite well. Among the nineteen export-underinvoicers, eleven show black market premiums exceeding 10 percent (some as high as 100 percent) and four others smaller but still positive premiums. In the cases of Colombia, Nigeria, and the Ivory Coast, information on black markets is not available.

A breakdown of the nineteen countries by the degree of underinvoicing of exports to the United States and Canada and the height of black market premiums, based on columns 2 and 3, can be shown as follows:

Trade Data Discrepancy (%)	*Black Market Premium (%)*				
	>20	*10-19*	*1-9*	*0*	*No Data*
>10	5	1	3	1	1
5-10	3	—	1	—	1
1-4	—	2	—	1	—

Using the height of black market premium as an indication of the profit from the illegal sales of foreign exchange in the black market,[20] we may then deduce that in more than half of the nineteen countries under consideration, the incentives for export underinvoicing are quite clearly evident.

The data in Table 4-2, on the other hand, relate to LDC imports. We try to see if the same conclusion can be drawn from these statistics, with overinvoicing of imports being the instrument whereby capital flight occurs from LDCs.

Table 4-2. Imports of LDCs from OECD Countries Compared with Corresponding Exports by OECD Countries to LDCs for 28 LDCs: 1966

Country (by region)	100 · (Imports – Exports)/Exports		Percentage share of SITC 5-8 in total LDCs imports
	Total trade	SITC 5-8	
South America			
Argentina	0.6	–0.4	91.8
Brazil[a]	1.3	–4.7	75.5
Chile	16.6	17.1	82.8
Colombia[a]	12.1	–12.1	68.8
Mexico[a]	–7.7	–4.4	85.7
Central America			
Costa Rica	19.0	17.9	86.6
El Salvador	8.1	10.5	87.9
Guatemala	–0.6	2.4	87.6
Honduras	14.5	17.8	89.2
Nicaragua	7.8	8.5	88.4
Africa			
Ethiopia[a]	–1.2	–0.1	84.2
Ivory Coast	13.0	7.0	80.9
Libya	–9.9	–10.9	83.4
Nigeria	14.9	15.2	85.4
Tunisia	0.1	1.4	75.2
Far East			
Hong Kong	–11.6	–11.4	84.1
Korea	–0.4	–10.0	67.4
Philippines	–7.6	–8.3	80.1
Taiwan	–3.3	–3.4	75.4
Thailand[a]	14.0	11.0	88.5
South Asia and Mid East			
Ceylon[b]	–5.7	–11.0	71.2
Egypt	8.3	6.4	60.6
India	–1.0	–15.7	55.0
Iran	–1.3	0.8	90.7
Pakistan	–1.3	–7.6	77.4
Europe			
Greece	–0.2	–0.2	81.7
Turkey[a]	–13.4	–10.2	91.1
Yugoslavia	–1.3	6.2	72.6

Notes and Sources: Same as Table 4-1.

We did not expect to see, on the LDC-import side, a clear demonstration of capital flight for two reasons. First, the customs authorities are more vigilant about faking of transactions on the import side than on the export side because traditionally duties have been levied on a much wider range of imports than of exports in LDCs. Hence the faking of import invoices is likely to be confined to essentially manufactured (Standard International Trade Classification [SITC] 5-8) imports where product differentiation, and so on, make it generally possible to "get past the customs" with faked invoices. Second, since imports are almost never subsidized at the customs point, there is always a net tariff on imports into any country (resulting from the gross tariffs which exist in practice) that acts *ceteris paribus* to reduce overinvoicing of imports (for overinvoicing implies paying more tariff duty). Thus, depending on the relationship of the tariff structure to the import structure (since the same duty on different types of products can create different effects just because different products are differently susceptible to the possibility of faking trade declarations, as we have just argued), one may find the incentive to overinvoice imports, to facilitate capital flight, overcome in various degrees and result, in some cases, even in a net incentive to underinvoice imports.[21]

Our expectation that the import side would show mixed results was borne out in fact, as Table 4-2 shows. Altogether seven LDCs show a percentage excess of imports over exports, on exports, of over 10 percent for total trade, with six more LDCs having a positive (but less than 10 percent) excess and fifteen LDCs having a negative excess figure. This would suggest, once we take into account the fact that imports are c.i.f. and exports are f.o.b. value, that seven LDCs with excess on top of 10 percent in Table 4-2 are clearly overinvoicers whereas all the rest are not, while those having negative figures are probably clearly underinvoicers. The same exercise, repeated for only SITC categories 5-8, shows that these conclusions roughly carry over, except that only five LDCs became clearly overinvoicers: Chile, Costa Rica, Honduras, Nigeria, and Thailand.[22] If we could show that the average tariff level on SITC group 5-8 in these five LDCs is lower than in the remaining LDCs in our sample, we would have a reasonable presumption that these five LDCs are experiencing capital flight through overinvoicing whereas in the other LDCs, the higher tariff level is tending to create a counter-incentive to underinvoice imports. However, neat as this would be, a failure to find a lower average tariff level in the five LDCs would still not rule out the presumption of capital flight for two reasons: (1) as argued above, it is not the usual average tariff level that is really relevant for our analysis but the tariffs weighted in such a way as to reflect the "invoice-fakeability" of the importable commodities, and there is really no feasible way in which this could be done with available information; and (2) what matters in determining whether imports will be overinvoiced or underinvoiced is not just the tariff level but also the premium on black market foreign exchange.[23] This premium is not uniform across the LDCs in our sample, as is evident in Table 4-1, column 3. Hence, we have little choice except to infer from Table 4-2 merely that the phenomenon of overinvoicing of imports, as a vehicle of capital flight, seems to be much more restricted than the phenomenon of underinvoicing of exports. This asymmetry of conduit behavior for capital flight in the exports and imports of LDCs is, on the other hand, a conclusion of some interest to policy-makers in these countries.[24]

IV. REVERSE LINKS BETWEEN QRs AND ILLEGAL TRANSACTIONS

Next, we should note that, while the trade and payments regime affected the incidence of illegal transactions, the reverse link was also evident in some of the countries in the Project. Three instances of interest should suffice to illustrate this phenomenon.

First, some of the QR regimes (e.g., Chile, Colombia, and Turkey) ruled out the importation of used goods because it was difficult to determine their market price and hence any associated faking of invoices. Thus an obvious and apparently advantageous segment of the world market was ruled out merely because it may lend itself to abuse.

Second, since smuggling would be difficult to pin down if legally and illegally imported commodities were simultaneously entering the domestic market, it was occasionally the practice in some of the countries in the Project to shift such items as were "easy" to smuggle into "prohibited lists." If then these items turned up in the market, they would have a very high probability of having been smuggled and hence of being detected as such, thus deterring the smuggling.

Third, the Colombian INCOMEX had an interesting argument on the blend of tariffs and QRs to deter smuggling. Thus, Carlos Díaz-Alejandro writes:[25]

> Apart from the smuggling of spare parts and some consumer goods, such as furs, perfumes, jewelry, and cigarettes, INCOMEX feels that the system is relatively free of leaks and well organized, in the sense that importers know what to expect. Its officials argue, not without reason, that the combination of moderate tariffs plus import controls forms a more powerful barrier to smuggling than a situation with higher tariffs and no import controls. A key element in their reasoning is that, as more items are shifted from the prohibited list to the prior license list, more uncertainty will be planted in the minds of would-be smugglers, whose profit margins could be reduced or wiped out if INCOMEX suddenly permits imports of moderately taxed goods.

This argument is not fully spelled out as given because it is theoretically possible to vary tariffs as one varies QRs. However, it acquires cogency in light of the difficulty in varying tariffs as frequently as QRs did change in nearly all the countries in the Project.

APPPENDIX V: NOTES ON THE WELFARE-THEORETIC ANALYSIS OF ILLEGAL ACTIVITIES INDUCED BY INTERFERENCES WITH THE FOREIGN TRADE REGIME

The text of this chapter has been confined to analyzing the empirical and statistical aspects of illegal transactions induced by interferences with the foreign trade regime. Almost nothing was said, however, about the welfare effects of these phenomena.

As it happens, a great deal of literature has recently grown up on this precise theme. Bhagwati and Hansen initiated the analysis by modifying the traditional 2 × 2 model of trade theory to include a foreign reciprocal demand curve for illegal trade. In this model, the illegal trade transformation possibility was less favorable than for legal trade, this feature being the analytical device (earlier used by Paul Samuelson to deal with transport costs in the 2 × 2 model) to reflect the *incremental* resource costs used up in undertaking the illegal trade.[26] Using essentially the same approach, Johnson as also Bhagwati and Srinivasan later analyzed the relative rankings of optimal and maximal revenue tariffs in the presence of smuggling.[27]

Sheikh made an important modification in the analysis to allow primary factors to be used in producing an intermediate non-traded good that would be used in fixed coefficients for undertaking illegal (but *not* legal) imports.[28] While therefore the Bhagwati-Hansen-Johnson-Srinivasan technique of building incremental social costs of illegal trade was in keeping with the 2 × 2 model's technique of subsuming such costs into the transformation function itself (traditionally for legal and now also for illegal trade), the Sheikh model was a step in the direction of modeling the primary factor costs of trade directly—albeit, however, by the artificial device of the non-traded input into illegal trade. Needless to say, as should be obvious to trade theorists, this difference in the production cum trade structure of the model led to certain differences in the conclusions regarding the conditions under which illegal trade may or may not improve welfare.[29]

Finally, attention has been focused recently on the possible asymmetries between the welfare effects of QRs and tariffs in the presence of illegal transactions. As already noted in Chapter 2 above, Falvey has extended the Bhagwati-Hansen type of analysis to the case where QRs, rather than tariffs are in place. The outcomes can be different because QRs provide an upper limit to legal imports whereas tariffs do not.[30]

Of equal interest and potentially complementary to the theoretical analysis of Bhagwati-Hansen is the forceful argument of Anne Krueger that QRs, even when otherwise equivalent in the Bhagwati-sense to tariffs, have one *additional*, asymmetrical effect, namely, that they lead to competitive rent-seeking that uses up real resources and hence entails a greater loss of welfare than a Bhagwati-equivalent tariff would.[31] Whereas the Bhagwati-Hansen-Johnson-Srinivasan-Sheikh type of illegal trade analysis focuses on the welfare effects of trade restrictions, brought about by attempts of *illegal importers* to profit from the discrepancy between foreign and domestic prices that QRs and tariffs equally imply, Krueger's elegant analysis eschews this and focuses instead on the notion that QRs, which carry premiums, attract the use of resources in order to earn them. While this analysis of what are presumably legal resource costs incurred in securing import premiums—though illegal activity such as bribing, as noted in Section I of this chapter, may attend also on competitive rent-seeking—would appear endemic to QRs, it would appear that a complete comparison of tariffs and QRs should, in this case, include also the "revenue-seeking" that would follow from the tariff revenues earned instead in the case where tariffs are used. Needless to say, the real resource costs of revenue-seeking (by lobbies seeking preferential allocation of tariff revenues for their own benefit) may be less than the real resource costs of rent-seeking in the QR case. But then, the asymmetry arises from the possible differences in the nature of these "quasi-economic" activities in the two cases rather than from the fact that only QRs, and not tariffs, attract such activities.

NOTES

1. Thus, see the discussion in Bhagwati and Desai, op.cit., pp. 308-311, for Indian examples and evidence.

2. Ghana, op.cit., pp. 25-26. Footnotes in the quotation have been eliminated.

3. *Fortyeighth Report* (1963-1964), Lok Sabha Secretariat, Government of India, New Delhi, pp. 104-105; cited in Bhagwati and Desai, ibid., pp. 308-309.

4. *Turkey*, op.cit., Chapter VI, pp. 140-152 and 168-169.

5. Ibid., Chapter VI, pp. 168-169.

6. With import licenses generally specified in value terms, underinvoicing would permit the importation of greater quantities than otherwise.

7. For a more detailed discussion, see J. Bhagwati, "Fiscal Policies, the Faking of Foreign Trade Declarations, and the Balance of Payments," *Bulletin of the Oxford University Institute of Economics and Statistics*, 29, 1 (February 1967). Also see J. Bhagwati, ed., *Illegal Transactions and International Trade: Theory and Measurement*, Studies in International Economics, vol. 1 (Amsterdam: North Holland Publishing Co., 1974).

8. Cf. "On the Undervoicing of Imports," *Bulletin of the Oxford University Institute of Economics and Statistics,* 26 (November 1964): 389-397, reprinted in Bhagwati, ed., ibid., 1974.

9. J. Bhagwati, ed., ibid., 1974, pp. 145-146.

10. *Philippines*, op.cit., pp. 109-110.

11. *Turkey*, op.cit., Chapter VI, pp. 169-170.

12. See *Chile*, op.cit., Table A-1, variable 1.25.1-2, p. 314.

13. Munir Ahmed Sheikh, *Economics of Smuggling: Theory and Application*, Ph.D. dissertation submitted to the University of Western Ontario, Canada, August 1973, Chapter IV; published in *Bulletin of the Oxford University Institute of Statistics*, 36 (November 1974): 287-296.

14. For details of the statistical analysis, refer to Sheikh, ibid., pp. 148-159. Sheikh could *not* establish any relationship between the degree of tariff protection (i.e., the tariff rates themselves) and underinvoicing; only the two-group analysis yielded results.

15. D.T. Scheffman, "An Analysis of Trade Data Discrepancies: The Case of the Ghanaian Cocoa Trade Data," University of Western Ontario, *mimeo*, (no date).

16. *Turkey*, op.cit., Chapter VI, p. 171.

17. *Philippines*, op.cit., p. 109.

18. For detailed discussion, see T. King, *Mexico: Industrialization and Trade Policies Since 1940.* (London: Oxford University Press, for OECD Development Center: Paris, 1970); R. Cooper, "Tariffs and Smuggling in Indonesia," Chapter 13 in Bhagwati, ed., *Illegal Transactions . . .*, op.cit., and J. Bhagwati, "Introduction," in Bhagwati, ed., ibid. The papers by C.G.F. Simkin and Helen Richter in this volume also discuss alternative ways in which the existence of smuggling may be pinned down, essentially involving the construction of "outflow" data based on domestic production *minus* domestic absorption and subtracting the recorded exports therefrom.

19. The following analysis was undertaken with Anne Krueger and Chaiyawat Wibulswasdi and has also been printed as Chapter 10 in Bhagwati, ed., *Illegal Transactions . . .*, op.cit., 1974. The reader should refer to this volume, particularly to Chapters 7, 9, and 12 for many of the purely statistical reasons that can often cause discrepancies in partner-country trade and data comparisons. Thus, to illustrate, in Table 1, the South Korean negative discrepancy is certainly attributable in part, and perhaps entirely, to the extremely rapid growth of Korean exports and the fact that Korean export records would lead the importing countries' import records.

20. The "net" profit is, strictly speaking, relevant here, netting out for any incremental costs that may be incurred in undertaking illegal activity.

21. This, in effect, was observed in Bhagwati's study of Turkish trade data and Baldwin's study of Philippines data where (as we noted in the preceding section) imports carrying high tariff duties were observed to be underinvoiced. In some countries another motive for underinvoicing imports is that import licenses are issued for a dollar value. Thus, by understating price, the importer can buy more.

22. It is interesting to note that Honduras is the only case where the "faking" presumably occurs on both import and export sides. In all four other countries, export underinvoicing may be practiced to only a limited scale as evidence shows up only in the export-trade with United States and Canada but not with total OECD countries. The Honduras case may seem peculiar since its liberal exchange control regime allows capital to be transferred rather freely. There is, however, a requirement (for statistical purpose) that buyers of exchange must file the applications stating how the exchange will be used (IMF, 19th Annual Report on Exchange Restrictions, p. 185); this may provide an incentive to "fake" the invoices so that illegal uses of exchange can be concealed.

23. For, if imports are overinvoiced (underinvoiced), the importer must sell (buy) in the black market an amount of foreign exchange equal to the difference between the correct and the faked price on the invoice. Hence, two critical variables in the importer's decision will clearly be the duty and the black market premium on foreign exchange. See Bhagwati, *Illegal Transactions . . .*, op.cit., Chapter 9.

24. One should stress again, however, the relatively weak efficacy of the partner-country data comparison technique in view of possible "noise" from complicating factors.

25. *Colombia*, op.cit., Chapter 5, p. 148.

26. J. Bhagwati and B. Hansen, "A Theoretical Analysis of Smuggling," *Quarterly Journal of Economics*, 88 (May 1973): 172-187; reprinted in Bhagwati, ed., *Illegal Transactions . . .*, op.cit., 9-22.

27. Harry G. Johnson, "Notes on the Economic Theory of Smuggling," *Malaysian Economic Review* (May 1972); and J. Bhagwati and T.N. Srinivasan, "Smuggling and Trade Policy," *Journal of Public Economics* (August 1973); both reprinted in Bhagwati, ed., *Illegal Transactions . . .*, op.cit., 27-38.

28. M. Sheikh, "Smuggling, Production and Welfare," *Journal of International Economics* 4 (November 1974): 355-386.

29. These differences stem primarily from the fact that, in modeling the incremental real costs of illegal trade *via* explicit use of primary factors so utilized, the analyst is directly affecting the production possibility set for the traded goods in this model (these goods entering the social utility function in the usual manner), whereas in the Bhagwati-Hansen-Johnson-Srinivasan model the production possibility set is unaffected and only the foreign transformation possibilities incorporate the effects of illegal and legal trade. Cf. the extended discussion in Bhagwati, ed., *Illegal Transactions . . .* , op.cit., page 3.

30. Rodney Falvey, 1978, op.cit.

31. Cf. A.O. Krueger, "The Political Economy of a Rent-Seeking Society," *American Economic Review*, 64 (June 1974): 291-303. Her model is Harris-Todaro type and closer to the Sheikh model than the Bhagwati-Hansen-Johnson-Srinivasan model in its treatment of the real costs incurred in smuggling (in their case) and in rent-seeking (in her case).

Chapter 5

Allocative Efficiency

The effects of exchange control regimes on efficiency within a developing country can be analyzed at several levels. In this chapter, we focus essentially on the so-called static efficiency effects—for example, the effects on the allocation of investments among alternative activities,[1] on utilization of capacity, on holdings of inventories, and so on—while deferring to later chapters the consideration of effects on domestic saving and capital formation, export performance, entrepreneurship, and innovation, which are considered to be the "dynamic" aspects of economic efficiency.

This division of efficiency effects, it can hardly be overemphasized, is both artificial and semantically loaded against the set of effects described as static and in favor of the effects termed dynamic. Thus, if the (static) efficiency of investment allocation drops so that the same inputs produce less output than is feasible, surely it will, *ceteris paribus,* reduce the growth of the economy.[2] The static effects of a foreign trade regime may thus impair the economy's growth far more effectively than the sum total of the dynamic effects. In fact, one of the significant conclusions of the Project, which will become evident to the reader in the following analysis, is that the static effects of exchange control regimes of Phase II variety seem to be generally adverse and significant whereas their dynamic effects, when decipherable from the complex evidence as significant, may be adverse and hence reinforcing in character rather than beneficial and offsetting to the static, adverse effects.

In this chapter, we first discuss at a very broad level (in Section 1) some evidence from countries in the Project regarding the productivity of investment during Phase II regimes and outside thereof. We next consider, more directly, for Phase II regimes (1) the possible malallocation of investment among alternative activities using the estimates gathered on this question in the framework of domestic resource costs (DRCs) in most of the country studies (in Section II);[3] (2) the possible accentuation of underutilization of capacity (in Section III); (3) the possible impact on holding of increased inventories (in Section IV); and (4) the diverse effects on choice of techniques, and so on, due to the artificial cheapening of capital goods imports that typically obtains under exchange control regimes (in Section V).

I. SOME OVERALL INDICATORS

The simplest, but least reliable, method of establishing a link between the foreign trade regime and the economic efficiency of an economy is to examine indicators of "productivity" for possible association between levels, and turning points therein, and the state of the trade regime. For Ghana, Israel, and Chile, this has been attempted by the country authors, using different indicators, and drawing pointed attention to the inadequacy of such an approach. They also stress that its results are consistent with the hypothesis, based on *a priori* argumentation, that Phase II regimes, in generally leading to a disregard of opportunity costs in allocational decisions, should cause a decline in efficiency (in the manner discussed at length in the subsequent sections of this chapter).

Clark Leith, for Ghana, cites the fact that both investment and its productivity, as measured by the *marginal output-capital ratio*, declined sharply in the period following the exchange control restrictions since 1960 and 1961, in fact plummeting to very low levels in the late Nkrumah period and during the austerity of the early N.L.C. (National Liberation Council) government,[4] and beginning to recover only thereafter. *In itself*, of course, this broad level form of argument is not compelling. In particular, shifts in the marginal output-capital ratio may result from marked changes in the composition of output and may reflect exogenous factors such as large declines (or increases) in agricultural output around the trend. Nonetheless, Leith argues that it is suggestive of a possible relationship. He then develops arguments to show that the exchange control regime during the 1960s did produce specific inefficiencies.

For Israel, Michael Michaely, who can contrast a Phase IV period with Phase II, argues the many reasons why inefficiency and waste should be widespread when QRs are intensive and observes that a shift to price determination of imports would lead, at the time of the shift, to a particularly large increase in productivity because this waste would be reduced.[5] He then uses Kendrick-type estimates of overall factor productivity, based on Gaathon's earlier work, for the period 1951 to 1965, dividing the period into three subperiods: (1) 1951-1952, peak time of the QR system; (2) 1953-1955, the main years of transition to price regulation; and (3) the following Phase IV years from 1956 to 1965. His conclusions from this evidence are that the data are in conformity with the postulated effect of QRs, namely, the rate of increase of productivity rose markedly from 1951-1952, the peak period of QRs, to 1953-1955, the period of rapid transition to the price mechanism as a means of regulating imports as well as other activities in the economy. For the economy as a whole (excluding housing and the public sector), the rate of increase of productivity was not as fast in the decade from 1956 to 1965 as in the transitional years, 1953-1955—though this is not true for the manufacturing sector, and it was faster than in the period of controls, 1951-1952. Michaely is, however, careful to argue that the causal connection between severe QRs and slow increase in productivity does not follow necessarily from their coexistence. This is especially because the Israeli economy during its earlier years underwent fast and radical changes in size and structure. In particular, the rapid increases in productivity in the first few years following 1951 could have occurred because "immigrants, who made up a large fraction of the population, may have been placed in jobs they were not suited to during the period of mass immigration, and later sought and found more appropriate occupations." For this and other reasons,

> productivity should have been expected to rise rapidly in the years 1953-1955 even without a change in the QR regime. Therefore it cannot be claimed that the whole of the rapid rise that actually took place in those years should be attributed to the change in the exchange system. Unfortunately, there is no feasible way of distinguishing the various factors that contributed to the increased productivity of that time. Thus, it may only be stated that the hypothesis that a shift from QRs to price regulation of the economy leads to faster growth through increased productivity is at least not contradicted by the facts of the Israeli experience.[6]

For Chile, Behrman has a detailed analysis of the relationship between liberalized and restrictive regimes, on the one hand, and the productivity of capital in the shape of the marginal output-capital ratio, on the other hand. He concludes that the degree of restrictionism has been inversely associated with such productivity, pointing *both* to efficiency-type effects of restrictionist trade regimes (e.g., the inability to import economical second-hand goods under restrictionist regimes, the possible increase in inventory holdings, and the shift to inefficient domestic equipment) *and* to compositional effects (e.g., shift of investment to sectors with higher capital intensity during restrictionist regimes).[7] On balance, Behrman's arguments and evidence imply that the (Phase II) restrictionist regimes reduced the marginal output-capital ratio and that this, in turn, did imply efficiency effects rather than purely compositional differences in the pattern of investments under Phase II and more liberalized regimes.

II. INTERACTIVITY ALLOCATION OF RESOURCES: DRCs ET AL.

There are several reasons to conclude that the exchange control regimes studied in the countries in the Project were ill-suited to the task of having the "true" costs and benefits reflected in economic decision-making as, for example, in regard to production, inventory-holding investment levels, and techniques in the economy. This is not to assert that, *in principle*, one cannot combine direct allocations (as in the operation of a QR regime) with an optimal allocation and utilization of resources. Rather the argument relates to the operation of the "visible hand" system, as typically observed in the developing countries examined.

The reader's assessment of the prospects of having a rational allocation and utilization of resources under exchange control regimes, however, is certain to be influenced by the evidence that we will discuss for these countries.

At the outset, it would be useful to keep two points in mind. First, the foreign trade regime in some cases—as in India and Pakistan in particular—was merely supportive, in the main, of the allocation of resources that was already decided upon *via* industrial targeting within the context of overall plans and which was buttressed by an elaborate industrial-licensing machinery. However, even in these countries, one can attribute more of a direct causal role to the foreign trade regime in influencing the pattern of investments. For example, in India, there was a growing small-scale sector that escaped industrial licensing and responded to market incentives, and additionally, there was much actual investment, even in the large-scale sector, that could not be targeted in sufficient detail in advance and which came up for licensing in response to market incentives, of course. Furthermore, while the foreign trade regime may have been supportive in regard to investment allocations, that feature certainly did not preclude the regime from having substantial effects in other areas of resource utilization, for example, on capacity utilization, inventory holdings, and so on.

Second, the evidence that we will present is not fully conclusive in each of its constituent elements. However, taken as a whole, it is very persuasive and supportive of the thesis that exchange control regimes of Phase II variety have adverse effects on the efficiency of the economic system. Thus, when we can show that the methods of allocation used by exchange control authorities systematically ignored economic costs and returns and when it is then shown that the returns on different activities that have emerged under this regime diverge greatly from one another, it would seem to be reasonable to conclude that the former has something to do with the latter. In the analysis that follows, however, we will be careful to spell out the caveats that must not be forgotten in reaching our conclusions as we work through each argument bearing on the matter at hand.

A. Evidence on Allocation Criteria

The task of securing information on the criteria used for the allocation of imports among alternative sectors and uses is not merely tedious but difficult and, at times, impossible because such information is often withheld from public scrutiny. The only countries in the Project for which such information and analysis are presented, in consequence, are India, Turkey, Chile, Egypt, and Colombia.[8] For the first two countries, detailed procedures of allocation are set out and analyzed while the Chilean and Egyptian accounts are somewhat more sketchy. The Colombian study focuses rather more on a "revealed preference" analysis of the actual awards of licenses with the aid of a sample survey.

The evidence on criteria of allocation from the Indian study is the most pointed on the issue of the meaningfulness of economic terms thereof. While the reader can do no better than turn to the original discussion by the authors of the Indian study, their central conclusions are worth noting here. Distinguishing between the criteria used to award import licenses for raw materials, for example, among industries and among firms within the industries, these authors were forced to the view regarding interindustrial allocations that the "problem was Orwellian; all industries had priority and how was each sponsoring authority to argue that some industries had more priority than others?"[9] The result was that the bureaucrats tried to hold the overall allocations confidential and fell back in the interest of safety and objectivity on criteria of "fairness," which typically implied allocations *pro rata* to capacity installed, or employment, or shares defined by past allocations, or similar rules of thumb. The allocations within industries, among alternative claimants, were even more evidently governed by equal-shares criteria, related to capacity installed (in the main). It is evident from their analysis that these criteria were *not* intended to create more efficiency. Rather, they created sheltered existence for the firms and for the industries by assuring them of guaranteed and "equal" access to the scarce imports fetching high premiums in most cases, quite regardless of the efficiency of the firms and the industries.

The allocation of capital goods imports, on the other hand, was subject to both industrial and import licensing in India. The expansion of capacity by industry was governed by the actual exercise of such licensing machinery as also by the overall sets of targets laid down in the five-year plans for most industries. However, the industrial composition of expanding capacity was governed by macro-economic models which could, for obvious reasons, not take into account the detailed costs and benefits at the micro-level. In essence, therefore, one has to conclude that the targeting of industrial expansion by fairly minute detail was of a nature that militated against the reflection of opportunity costs in investment allocation among alternative activities. Hence, in principle the licensing of capital goods imports to buttress this pattern of industrial expansion was, in turn, counterproductive of economic efficiency.

The evidence on the allocation mechanism in Turkey, Chile, Egypt, and Colombia is not as detailed and focused on the meaningfulness of the criteria used as in the case of India. However, there is little about the allocation mechanism in these accounts of the import control regime that is more comforting. The only exception perhaps is the evidence produced by Krueger for Turkey that the import allocations by industry, once decided upon, were handled for interfirm allocations by the chambers of commerce. Perhaps this led to a more efficient intra-industrial allocation, but it could equally have led to an equal-shares approach among members for obvious reasons. The overall judgment of Krueger on the criteria again is that they did manage to ignore economic considerations, much as the Indian regime did, and that the inefficiencies she then documents are traceable to this neglect.

B. Evidence on Inefficient Allocation of Resources

The lack of economically meaningful criteria and the resort to practical rules of thumb—tempered, no doubt, by varying degrees of evasion (as discussed in Chapter 4)—imply a disregard of opportunity costs in the allocation of investable resources among alternative activities. In the immediately following analysis, we will discuss the evidence on such inefficiencies, postponing the discussion of the efficiency of factor use, *given* the investment pattern, to later analysis.

The marshalling of evidence on the misallocation of resources implied by exchange control regimes, as just described, requires the specification of a precise analytical framework plus measures of misallocation derived therein. While, in principle, such an analysis would require a general equilibrium model, with an explicit social utility function and information on the foreign trade elasticities for all tradeable commodities and on factor supplies and the production functions for all activities, plus knowledge of all the distortions in the system other than those resulting from the exchange control regime, such a task is clearly next to impossible to accomplish satisfactorily even if the resources for such an ambitious exercise were to be found.[10] In place thereof, we have resorted to a technique that the country authors recognize clearly as rather simple (and perhaps simplistic). The domestic resource costs (DRC) of earning a unit of foreign exchange in alternative activities have been computed, the analyst treating these costs as an approximate index of the differential returns that are being obtained from different activities, as observed at any point of time in the economy.

The DRC index, as applied in practice, measures the returns to domestic resources in foreign exchange by evaluating the tradeable inputs and outputs at international prices. In comparing any two DRCs for a pair of activities, then, we may argue that a marginal shift of domestic resources from the activity with higher DRC to the other would yield more value added at international prices with the input of domestic resources unchanged. Hence, the reallocation would be more efficient; or, in other words, the existing, initial allocation with differential DRCs in the two activities is inefficient.

This argument is clearly based on the main insight of static trade theory—that international prices, for a small country, represent opportunity costs. It also presupposes that the domestic resource costs should be measured at their "shadow" prices if there are distortions in the economy.[11] Hence, the analyst should work out the appropriate shadow prices of capital, labor, foreign exchange, and so on, that are to be used in evaluating the domestic resources used in each activity. In fact, as is now well known, this is precisely what divides the measure of effective rate of protection (ERP) from the DRC concept for, in the absence of such shadow pricing, the two measures will generally reduce to equivalence.

However, in practice, the shadow prices are not easily estimated.[12] Furthermore, it must be recognized that the demonstration of wide differentials in DRCs among different activities is not equivalent to arguing that the losses therefrom must also be correspondingly large: (1) the shift of resources from a higher DRC activity to a lower DRC activity may run into increasing costs; and (2) the expansion of output in the lower DRC activity may run into reducing output prices (as, for example, exports are increased to clear the supplies). In general equilibrium analysis, moreover, we should be prepared for three complications. First, as resources are shifted from a number of activities to other activities, in a shift to optimal equilibrium (e.g., free trade for a small country), the associated shift of prices may imply that, at the changed techniques, an activity that was higher DRC than another in the suboptimal equilibrium may become lower DRC than the other in the optimal equilibrium. Second, evaluation of the activity at, say, c.i.f. international prices in the suboptimal equilibrium may have to give way to its evaluation at f.o.b. prices in the optimal equilibrium.[13] Third, the relative expansion and contraction of different activities in the optimal equilibrium as compared to the suboptimal equilibrium cannot be forecast in general from the mere examination of the relative DRCs in the initial suboptimal equilibrium, in consequence.

Having thus set out what we *cannot* infer from the DRCs estimated in the country studies, we should then assert that they do give a reasonable clue to the wide variations in the social returns to different activities in the system, as of any time. Also, given the lack of attention to prices and costs in the exchange control regimes in many of our countries, such differences could be taken as evidence that these regimes have indeed brought about the inefficiencies that these variations in DRCs imply. However, even here we need to be somewhat cautious on both empirical and conceptual grounds. First, at the empirical level, only those economists who have tried to work with data on international prices will appreciate how difficult it is to estimate them meaningfully. In many exchange control regimes, which work with the principle of QR-conferred automatic protection, it is rather academic to interview traders and request reliable quotes on c.i.f. prices of comparable goods. The trade has been often eliminated too long for there to be anything but a "guesstimate" to be forthcoming at best. Second, as the pioneering work of Kravis and Lipsey has shown, the kind of input that is necessary to secure meaningful price quotations on imports of capital goods on a comparable basis for different sources (in this instance, between foreign sources and domestic production) is a conceptually tricky and statistically difficult exercise, lending itself to significant errors unless great care is exercised.[14] Third, the price quotations that may be obtained on actual imports are also subject to manipulation and deliberate error for the simple reason that the high premiums on imports are occasionally taken in undeclared income, a practice that certainly obtained in India and was possibly current in some of the other countries in the Project. In view of these difficulties in securing any, leave aside reliable, information on international prices from the market, the DRC calculations in some of the countries in the Project—Ghana and India being two major countries in this regard—had to rely on unit values plus premium estimates, each introducing degrees of error that are difficult to pinpoint with much accuracy. In assessing the DRC estimates in the various studies on which we report here, therefore, the reader should bear in mind that reading the fine print on the untidy methods used to derive the DRC estimates, appearing neatly in their tabulated form, is not merely a matter of scholarly curiosity but a useful corrective to the tendency to consider these estimates as yielding more than a rough-and-ready guide to differential returns among activities.[15]

Conceptually also there is need not to put too strong a weight on this kind of argumentation beyond the general inference of a broad pattern of misallocation of resources among different activities. Aside from the caveats already listed earlier—for example, that a shift to optimal equilibrium could well make an industry competitive and worthwhile with different techniques—we need to recognize that the view that all DRCs would be equalized in the absence of distortions, if only the foreign trade regime allowed international opportunity costs to be reflected in domestic decision-making, is not really convincing. This proposition is, after all, based on equilibrium theory. In practice, the economies with optimal policy frameworks (as defined from equilibrium theory) would experience disequlibrium and would be continuously adapting themselves to changing technological know-how, factor supply changes, variations in international prices, and so on. The variations in DRCs that would be observed in any one cross section at a single point in time cannot therefore be meaningfully attributed to the inefficiencies in the trade regime. This would be "economic overkill" and would at least fail to persuade the more sophisticated among the proponents of restrictionist exchange control regimes.

While therefore all these caveats need to be definitely borne in mind and the reader has been fairly forewarned against easy and facile deductions from the evidence on DRC variations about to be produced from the countries in the Project, it does not seem to us to be unreasonable to assume that the process of freer competition for imports under a more liberalized trade regime than that characterizing the Phase II regimes in many of our countries during the bulk of the period studied would have served to bring pressure to bear in reducing the wide variations in DRCs both within and between industries.

The process of careful qualification and skepticism should not be carried too far. In this instance, we feel that the weight of the evidence, when we recognize the documented lack of economic criteria in QR allocations, is certainly to create more than a *prima facie* case against Phase II type exchange control regimes.

We therefore proceed now to put together the evidence on DRC variations in alternative activities that has been gathered for the countries in the Project. The estimates of DRCs, adjusted for shadow prices or unadjusted (in which case they are essentially linked to ERPs, as already noted), in the different studies in the Project are described in Table 5-1 so that the reader can use the table as a guide to the country analyses. However, a few observations are called for here.

The use of only unadjusted DRCs, that is, ERPs, in certain countries (i.e., Ghana and India) has been justified by some of these authors primarily in terms of the inability to spend the necessary recources to devise a suitable methodology for computing meaningfully the shadow prices for intermediates and primary factors that would need to be derived in the presence of imperfections such as quotas, factor market distortions, and so on. On the other hand, other authors (such as Krueger for Turkey) did use shadow prices. However, it must be admitted that generally these were not derived in the context of a well-specified model, so that they should be regarded essentially as "sensitivity" estimates.

Moreover, the estimates are, strictly speaking, not comparable across the countries in the Project. The lack of standardization of the activity groups as also of the concepts in this regard reflected an appreciation of the fact that data availability, especially the procurement of reliable estimates of international prices, varied greatly among countries. Thus, given the large number of analytically more interesting and novel issues raised by the Project, several authors considered it undesirable to spend their limited time and resources on procuring such information at first hand, something that could at best have been attempted only in a rough-and-ready fashion in any event. Rather, most of them were willing to use such estimates of DRCs (and ERPs) as were already available in order to interpret them somewhat along the lines of the present discussion. Indeed, given the serious conceptual and empirical limitations already alluded to, attempts at manufacturing standardized DRC data for all the countries would have both been wasteful and lent a spurious sense of comparability to the resulting numbers.

Looking therefore at the adjusted and unadjusted DRC estimates, as described in Table 5-1 very summarily, and confining ourselves to a "structural" view of each country *taken by itself*, we note that there is indeed evidence of substantial interindustry variations in DRCs by different sectors. (For Egypt, this evidence obtains also within the agricultural sector, though we will say more on this presently since Hansen and Nashashibi do not rely exclusively on DRCs as an index of efficiency losses.)

Thus, for example, Krueger estimates intra-sector DRC variance for different industrial sectors in Turkey during 1968 and/or 1969 at values ranging from 6.26 for cement up to 278.88 for transport equipment and 890.49 for rubber products.[16] She concludes, in light of this evidence, that the "wide variation in DRCs on the import-substitution side is indicative of the degree to which encouragement of import-substitution has been indiscriminate."[17] Similar conclusions have been reached in other studies, including principally India and Ghana.

Recall, however, that inferences of "large" welfare losses from large variations in DRCs between industries are not persuasive in the face of such objections as: What would one do with the increased output from the expansion of the low-DRC industries? or, The factors utilized in one industry may be highly specific to that industry so that there may be rapidly increasing costs to expansion of outputs in the low-DRC activities. These objections however lose much of their force if the DRCs among alternative firms *within* the same industry show wide variations under Phase II type regimes. Evidence at this "micro" level is available from some of the Project studies. It is noteworthy that in these studies the interfirm variations in DRCs were almost as large as the interindustrial variations in DRCs[18] so that there is no easy way out of the conclusion that the pattern of investment allocations was less than optimal.

Next, while we have warned against making strong inferences from comparisons of dispersions in DRCs between countries, and possibly over time for the same country (given the relative unreliability of the underlying data), it is probably worth reporting that the South Korean study suggests somewhat low interindustrial ERPs dispersion during its Phase IV whereas the Indian study suggests that the dispersion may have fallen slightly soon after the Phase III episode in 1966.[19]

Table 5-1. Summary Information on DRCs and ERPs in Country Studies

Country	Measure used: ERPs; DRCs	Period	Nature of Period	Sectors Used	Methodological Remarks	Other Remarks
Chile	ERPs	1967	1961: Phase IV	92 sectors		
	ERP's DRC's	1961, 1967, 1968	1967 1968 Phase III	28 sectors		
	DRCs					
Colombia	ERPs	1969	Phase IV	29 groups of traded sectors, including primary products	Reliance principally on comparisons of domestic prices with export prices; non-traded inputs evaluated by both Balassa and Corden methods	"Large variance in the protection received by different sectors" (p. 226)
Egypt	DRCs (1)	1961, 1963, 1964		Agriculture		
	(2)	Before and after 1962	1962 devaluation	Selected manufacturing industries (cement, fertilizers, sugar, tires and tubes cotton textiles)		
	(3)	Various additional dates: 1954, 1957, 1969-1970		Ten industries: Above industries plus automobiles, paper, and iron and steel		

Egypt	ERPs (1)	1961, 1963, 1964		Agriculture		
	(2)	Same dates as DRCs above		Ten industries, as above		
Ghana	ERPs	1963 and 1970	Initiation of Phase IV	Industries from CBS Industrial Survey Classification	(1) Protection broken down by QRs and by Tariffs and Surcharges (including indirect taxes) (2) Nominal protection also available by some sectors	(1) A few cases of negative value added at world prices (2) Some cases where tariff was not redundant because of QRs (3) "Substantive and apparently random variation" in protection between industries and also at establishment level (p. 76)
	DRCs	Mid-1967 through mid-1968	End of Phase III and initiation of Phase IV	Sample of 41 manufacturing establishments		Wide variation in DRCs among different establishments
India	DRCs and ERPs	1963-1965 and 1968-1969	Phase II and relapse from Phase III into Phase II, respectively	(1) 69 industries (2) Also, aggregated by broad groups: consumer, intermediate, and capital goods, for 1968-1969 only	No adjustment made in DRCs for shadow factor prices; therefore the ERPs and DRCs are strictly related, as explained in text.	(1) Wide variation in DRCs and ERPs among different activities (2) ERPs lowest for primary consumer goods and highest for nonfood consumer goods.

Table 5-1 continued

Country	*Measure used: ERPs; DRCs*	*Period*	*Nature of Period*	*Sectors Used*	*Methodological Remarks*	*Other Remarks*
Israel	ERPs (1)	1956, 1957, 1958, 1959, 1960	Early part of Phase IV	80 industries	Computed for exporting and for import substitution; 1958 input-output coefficients used; effects of QRs were ignored	Variance was much higher for import substitutes than for exports (p. 101)
	(2)	1965	Later part of Phase IV	6 major industrial sectors	Domestic and foreign distinguished	
	"DRCs" and ERPs	1968	Phase IV; almost leading into Phase V	Textile industry	"DRCs" are basically ERPs adjusted for QRs and other restrictive measures not taken into account in ERP derivation; shadow prices *not* used	
Philippines	ERPs (1)	1965	Phase IV, close to Phase V	48 industrial categories	Estimates include effects of discriminatory sales or compensating tax but not of the margin fee on foreign exchange, the special import tax or the margin requirements for letters of credit	Some negative ERPs; disadvantageous position of exporting industries

	(2)	1949-1971	Varying Phases	Broad categories: imports (broken down by consumer goods, producer goods, etc.) and exports	Estimates include efects of several nontariff measures; estimation less careful than for 1965 estimates	Biases against exporting and essential goods industries
South Korea	ERPs	1968	Phase IV; following a mild tariff liberalization in 1967	Export and import-competing industries split into 11 sectors each; averages for these broad groups also	Both Corden and Balassa methods used for treating nontraded inputs; efects of quotas included *via* use of price comparisons but appear to be quantitatively unimportant (p. 195)	Variability in ERPs for different activities considered to be relatively low; variability for ERPs higher than for nominal protection; discrimination against exports minimal
Turkey	DRCs	Late 1960s, from 1965 to 1969, as available	Phase II	16 industrial sectors, with several product and establishment breakdowns	1965 and 1969 data were adjusted by using a shadow price for capital of 20 percent and also by assuming that all excess capacity had been eliminated	(1) Some examples of value subtracted at world prices (2) Wide variability in DRCs among and within industries

Sources: *Chile,* op. cit., pp. 138 and 325-329. *Colombia,* op. cit., pp. 225-233; based on T. Hutcheson's estimates. *Egypt,* op. cit., pp. 93, 100, 310-311. *Ghana,* op. cit., pp. 58-80; DRCs based on W.F. Steel's estimates. *India,* op. cit.; calculations made by V.R. Panchamukhi; pp. 179, 184. *Israel,* op. cit., pp. 91-104 and Appendix B. *Philippines,* op. cit., pp. 104-108; original 1965 estimates are by John Power; original 1949-1971 estimates are by Valdepenas. *South Korea,* op. cit., pp. 195-200. *Turkey,* op. cit., pp. 218-226.

Note next that the Egypt study additionally attempted to estimate, by fitting agricultural acreage response functions, the *actual* shifts in acreage that resulted from the distortions in *prices* away from international prices and from *quantitative* acreage restrictions, which were also practiced in the Egyptian case.[20] Hansen and Nashashibi could not estimate input-coefficient changes under their alternative assumptions and settled for estimating acreage allocations to different crops under three alternative conditions: (1) actual domestic prices and actual (short-term) response functions; (2) actual international prices and actual (short-term) response functions; and (3) actual international prices and hypothetical instantaneous long-term adjustment.[21] Using prediction (3) as an approximation to optimal allocation of land, they compared it with the actual allocation and used the difference A, column 4 in Table 5-2, as an indicator of misallocation due to *overall* price and quantity distortions. Comparing it, however, with prediction (1) yielded B, column 5, in Table 5-2. This was interpreted as a measure of the misallocation due to price distortions (*plus* market imperfections implying only short-term response/adjustment). Finally, a comparison of predictions (1) and (2) yielded C, column 6 in Table 5-2. This was interpreted as a measure of the short-term misallocation due to price distortions alone.

The Hansen-Nashashibi conclusions, based on these estimates plus estimates of DRCs and ERPs, are particularly interesting in their implication in this instance for the use of ERPs (and DRCs) for inferring the *direction* of misallocation of resources (a matter to which we turn more directly in the next subsection):[22]

> . . . there is no perfect rank correlation between ERP and DRC: nontraded outputs and inputs are included, and the DRCs are calculated on the basis of imputed factor prices to adjust for government controls over land rentals and to allow for normal profits on capital. It is also recalled that what disturbs the rank correlation between *A*, on the one hand, and *B* and *C*, on the other, is direct government interference with acreages, as well as random disturbances, while the lack of perfect correlation between *B* and *C* expresses differences between short- and long-term misallocation of land.
>
> As is to be expected, neither ERP nor DRC can be used as an indicator of the long-term misallocations related to both price distortion and direct acreage interference (including random disturbances). The correlation coefficients ERP-*A* and DRC-*A* are insignificant and very low in the latter case.
>
> The ERP could, however, be taken as a relatively reliable indicator of long-term and a weak indicator of short-term misallocation resulting from price distortions alone. The correlation coefficient ERP-*B* is significant at the 1 percent level, and that of ERP-*C*, at the 5 percent level.
>
> The DRC, finally, can be used as a weak indicator of long-term misallocation stemming from price distortion, with the correlation coefficient DRC-*B* significant at the 5 percent level.

Table 5-2. Ranking of Crops in 1963 According to ERP, DRC, and Alternative Measures of Acreage Misallocation: Egypt

			Rank in Decreasing Order		
Crop (1)	*ERP[a] (2)*	*DRC[a,b] (3)*	*A (Actual area – Prediction 3)/ Prediction 3[c] (4)*	*B (Prediction 1 – Prediction 3)/ Prediction 3[c] (5)*	*C (Prediction 1 – Prediction 2)/ Prediction 2[c] (6)*
Cotton	7	7	9	6	8
Rice	9	8	8	10	10
Corn	3	5	7	5	7
Millet	4-5	2	5	8	6
Wheat	6	3	10	4	5
Barley	4-5	4	4	3	4
Onions	8	10	2	7	9
Beans	1	1	1	1	1
Lentils	2	6	3	2	2
Cane	10	9	6	9	3

Note: Spearman's rank correlation coefficient works out as follows, with critical levels at 1 percent and 5 percent probability at 0.76 and 0.56, respectively:

ERP-DRC	0.75	ERP-C	0.57
ERP-A	0.45	DRC-C	0.50
DRC-A	0.10	A-B	0.41
ERP-B	0.84	B-C	0.67
DRC-B	0.59	A-C	0.45

[a]According to Table 7-1.
[b]DRC includes trade and transport margin.
[c]Predictions 1, 2, and 3 are explained in the text.
Source: *Egypt,* op. cit., Table 7-5, p. 189.

In conclusion of this subsection, note finally that, in the analysis so far, we have considered interindustrial variations in DRCs, thus essentially discussing the *pattern* of import substitution. Only in Chapter 7, where we discuss export performance, will we discuss the problem of the differential incentives against exports and in favor of production for the home market, that is, the problem of the *degree* of import substitution.[23]

C. Protective Structure and Industrial Expansion

Before we proceed to an examination of the other inefficiencies traceable to the exchange control regimes, we may digress briefly on the question, perhaps inevitable, whether there is any discernible relationship between the protective structure in the countries in the Project and the growth of specific industries.

It seems tempting to argue that industries when arrayed in descending order by their protective rates should also correspondingly be ranked in descending order by their growth rates or their import substitution ratios. In fact, there is some analysis in the Project studies, and elsewhere, of correlational type between the structure of protection by nominal or effective measure and indices such as growth rates or import substitution ratios, though the evidence seems to be very mixed.

Thus, Carlos Díaz-Alejandro reports on the earlier work of Hutcheson on Colombian protection that regresses growth rates successfully on effective protective rates[24] (using the Balassa method for treating non-traded goods as enjoying zero protection rather than as value-added a la Corden, although the two methods have a different analytical basis).[25] Similarly, Frank and others report on rank correlation coefficients between various measures of effective protection, and of effective "incentives" (defined so as to include the effects of tax rebates, credit preferences, and such incentives) and resource allocational indices such as import substitution ratios (or export shares for export industries) and "growth contribution."[26] Their results however are generally poor on the import side." Since the correlation between the share of imports in total supply and effective incentives is significant and positive, it suggests that import substitution had progressed the *least* in these sectors where the level of effective incentives to domestic sales was high and the "correlations between effective incentives to domestic sales and growth contributions are not significant, though they are negative."[27]

Additional cross-sectional analysis of this variety was also conducted for Chile by Jere Behrman to determine if "the price structures created by the international economic regimes were associated with growth across sectors."[28] He found a positive relation between growth in value added and in horsepower capacity between 1961 and 1967 and the *implicit* tariff rates (ITRs) for 1967 and also for the incremental ITRs between 1961 and 1967. But this relationship has little plausibility, as Behrman notes, and may be rationalized only by argument such as that the ITRs "perhaps . . . served as signals, however, of the government's intentions to favor particular sub-sectors."[29] Interestingly, Behrman found no evidence for a link between effective rates of protection and growth. In fact, the only significant non-zero correlation coefficient, using alternative estimates, was a negative one between effective rates and growth in production from 1953 to 1961.[30]

Going beyond the country studies in the Project, however, we may note two successful sets of regressions, one for Pakistan by Guisinger[31] and one for Nigeria by Oyejide.[32] The Pakistani analysis was unsuccessful for import substitution ratios but successful for growth rates for a twenty-three-industry study. The Nigerian analysis, for forty-two industries, resulted in successful regressions of import substitution ratios on effective rates of protection and changes therein.

While therefore the results for the different countries are fairly mixed, we also need to note that the construction of a *theoretical* rationale for a successful regression of import substitution ratios or growth rates in cross-section analysis is difficult and one many *reasonably* expect to find no relationships of the kinds postulated. It should be useful to the reader to spell out why this is so, taking the import substitution ratio as the dependent variable and effective tariffs as the independent variable.

1. First of all, since effective tariffs are the independent variable, a basic difficulty follows. The effect on the import-substitution (production to total supply) ratio is *not* uniquely determined by the effective tariff. The same effective tariff is compatible with different combinations of nominal tariffs on output and inputs and hence with different effects on production and consumption of the output. Hence, even if the partial-equilibrium supply and demand curves were identical across the industries, the relationship hypothesized would not follow unless the input-output structure and the structure of nominal tariffs on each industry's outputs and inputs were identical.

2. In general equilibrium analysis, furthermore, the hypothesis runs into trouble for the further reason that the theory of general equilibrium tells us unhappily that, in an n-output ($n>2$) economy, if more than one price changes, the direction of output changes cannot be predicted (qualitatively, in Samuelson's sense). One really has to work out the full general equilibrium solution.[33] This nihilistic conclusion carries over, of course, to a general equilibrium model with imported inputs as well.[34]

3. Finally, while the analytical points made above relate to the effects of the tariffs vis-à-vis the free trade situation with given resources, the exercises testing the postulated hypothesis relate often to a situation of *growing* resources. But, in this event, there is even less presumption theoretically in support of the hypothesis. Take a simple two-sector example, using the standard 2 × 2 model of trade theory. We know from Rybczynski's theorem that the supply curves of the two commodities will shift differentially rather than identically, so that even if the supply curves were identical in the initial situation across activities, they would cease to be so with economic expansion (unless all factors expanded uniformly). And hence any effect of the tariff structure on the import-substitution ratio would be "muddied" by this additional growth effect. This is clearly a pertinent point when one is relating the import ratios for 1967, for example, to effective protection in 1962 (as in the Nigerian exercise), a period over which the capital stock may have increased by nearly 30 percent (assuming a capital-output ratio of 3 : 1 and an average savings rate of 15 percent of GNP), and hence certainly in excess of the labor force.

Thus, even within the confines of our neoclassical economic theory, one would have difficulties with the hypothesis that higher effective tariffs lead to higher import-substitution ratios on a cross-sectional basis. In the context of actual LDC economies, these difficulties are accentuated indeed. The growth of industries is likely to reflect distortions arising from differential trade and domestic taxes and subsidies, industrial licensing and targeting, anticipation of tariff protection (as distinct from initial protection) once the industry has built up to size leading to an effective political pressure group, and so on.[35]

In addition, there are several major difficulties *specific to exchange control regimes* where QRs typically may dominate tariffs (as discussed for the countries in our Project in Chapter 2), with the notion that *observed* protective structures will tell the analyst anything conclusive about growth incentives. This is a most important and insufficiently appreciated point and the supporting reasons therefore need to be spelled out:

1. The translation of import premiums into implicit tariffs implies that one can treat tariffs and quotas as equivalent. This proposition is increasingly called into question. As noted in Chapter 2, non-equivalence will arise particularly under the presence of monopoly elements (not entirely absent from the scene in some of the countries in the project) and uncertainty (which is, of course, a fact of life).[36]

2. The import premiums are likely, except when entry domestically is totally free, to include elements of rent reflecting artificially controlled entry.[37] This is particularly true of countries with explicit industrial licensing (i.e., India, Pakistan) but also, in lesser degree, of the larger group of countries with QRs on capital goods imports (e.g., Ghana, Colombia, Turkey, and Egypt). Moreover, the problem arises partly also from QR-controlled access to imports of necessary raw materials. Unless entry enables a firm to get access to such imports, the absence of industrial or capital-goods-imports licensing will not be enough to get a truly free-entry situation. Thus the presence of licensing of imports of raw materials can, and does, serve to create rents that must be reflected in the premiums on imported inputs.

3. The fluctuations in the import premiums, which are evident in some of the countries, also make it somewhat meaningless to attach value to the cross-sectional translation thereof into one "incentives-determining" picture of the implicit tariff structure. Few of the entrepreneurs in an exchange control regime are likely to be ignorant of the fact of changes in incentives inherent in changing premiums, a fact that presumably accounts for the phenomenon of some industries actually going through the protective tariff-making process to have more secure, minimum protection conferred on them by tariff commissions and boards.[38]

4. Finally, we have already noted (in Chapter 2) that the Phase II type regimes in most countries operated with rules of "automaticity" in protection. QRs were used to grant protection as soon as domestic production was started. Once this "institutional" feature of the system is taken into account, it is easy to see that any *observed* (implicit) tariff structure fails to incorporate the in-

centive effects of guaranteed, "potential" tariff protection, which is clearly a significant factor on the scene. Thus, the incentive effects on resource allocation of an array of *n* observed (implicit) tariffs are surely not identical with the incentive effects of *n* observed tariffs plus *m* expected tariffs. This difference is further accentuated still when one must reckon with the fact that the *m* expected tariffs are not expected with certainty on their specific values but will depend on the precise extent to which the exchange control authorities would curtail imports in the face of domestic production.

It is for this set of reasons that the notion of relating tariffs, effective or nominal, to the pattern of industrial expansion—no matter how measured—may be lacking in sufficient rationale for countries in Phase II type exchange control regimes, as indeed our countries have been for the bulk of the period studied. This may well account for the mixed nature of the statistical results from various sources reported earlier in this subsection.

On balance therefore we are content to take the view, admittedly less ambitious, that the differential ERPs among different activities should be taken merely to indicate, *very broadly indeed*, the differential nature of the incentives that exchange control regimes tend to generate. This conclusion, in itself, is sufficiently interesting and important.[39]

III. UNDERUTILIZATION OF CAPACITY

We may now turn to the impact that the Phase II type exchange control regimes, heavily reliant on QRs, had on the returns from given investments, as distinct from the inefficiencies resulting from misallocation of investments. One of the major ways in which inefficiencies can arise is through the creation of excess capacity, which might have been avoided under a more liberal regime. There are several ways in which such a causal link between exchange control regimes and the presence of excess capacity can be established. We will detail these first and then consider the evidence for the countries in the Project in this regard so that some orders of magnitude can be indicated on the importance of such effects. Four types of such linkages may be spelled out.[40]

A. Incentives to Create Excess Capacity

The tendency to relate equity in allocations of licenses for imported inputs (directly to producers) to installed capacity should lead to an incentive to create capacity by linking the availability of premium-fetching imports with creation of more capacity. Thus, an entrepreneur, with given capacity, which was underutilized through lack of imported inputs, would not be able to expand output through additional utilization of capacity even if it were potentially profitable to do so. The only way he could respond to the profitability of the industry would be by getting more capacity installed and having some import quota allotted to him on basis thereof. But even if the entrepreneur could be allowed access to more imports at market prices,[41] so that this entrepreneur could expand utilization of existing capacity, the fact that he would have to purchase inputs at import-premium-inclusive market prices in order to do this, whereas expansion of capacity would enable him to expand output by access to premium-exclusive import allocations, would certainly bias his choice between these two courses of action toward more capacity creation.[42]

2. In addition to this effect of the methods of licensing intermediates and capital goods, there is another mechanism by which excess capacity could be accentuated in the system *via* the import-licensing mechanism. In an economic regime where the efficient firms can bid intermediates from the market away from the inefficient firms, the former will achieve greater utilization of their capacity whereas the latter will be forced out. This process, which is also efficient because all capacity is not desirable capacity and undesirable capacity must be scrapped to avoid larger losses, must necessarily lead to higher overall rates of capacity utilization than in a regime where inefficient firms automatically get "squatters' rights" to allocations of imported inputs.

3. An additional way in which the QR regime can affect capacity utilization is clearly *via* the bottlenecks it creates. Undoubtedly, bottlenecks would arise in *any* regime; but the ability to correct them is surely constrained for a number of firms by the difficulty with which remedial imports can be effected. And this difficulty varies of course with the degree of restrictiveness on the transferability of import licenses between commodities, firms, and sources. These bottlenecks add to excess capacity in two ways: (1) by preventing speedy availability of inputs into a process; and (2) by holding up the importation of critical spares and balancing equipment that would enable the existing capacity to be exploited more effectively. The former set of bottlenecks come from the restrictions built into the inputs-licensing system; the latter relate to both capital goods and industrial licensing procedures.

4. Yet another way in which the exchange control regime can affect capacity utilization is by inhibiting the employment of excess capacity for export markets. While, as we will argue presently, there is evidence that firms with substantial excess capacity can manage to improve capacity utilization through exports after liberalization policy changes, we will also note there that the export effort can be badly compromised, not merely by overvaluation of the domestic currency but also by the inability of the firms to exploit the intended liberalization of imports meaningfully. Severe restrictions on transfers of licenses and on permissible imports can prevent quick adjustments in production and capacity to respond to international orders. The substantial in-

flexibility of the import control regime can make it difficult for firms, when presented with export opportunities to reduce capacity underutilization at low marginal costs, to exploit these opportunities. If we are to reckon the full impact on capacity utilization from this cause, we should take the primary effect just discussed and add to it also the secondary effect that is implied by the fact that additional export earnings would ease the import situation and make more raw material imports available for further capacity utilization.

B. Evidence on Capacity Utilization

The evidence for these types of adverse effects of the import licensing mechanisms on the utilization of capacity in the country studies is mostly indirect. It consists of documentation of the allocation procedures and their likely impact, with some econometric evidence relating these institutional cum a priori arguments with excess capacity estimates. The major problem is the lack of reliable and conceptually clear data on capacity utilization. It is perhaps pertinent to note that, among the main reasons for the lack of reliable data on capacity, is the fact that these data are used for allocating premium-fetching licenses for (domestic and) imported materials on a *pro rata* basis, so that the governmental agencies maintaining the capacity data (as does the Directorate General of Technical Development in India) try to prevent upward revision of capacity data by firms whereas the firms try to do exactly the opposite. The final outcome depends partly or wholly on the relative ability of the two parties to offer and accept unlawful emoluments. Thus, ironically, here as in other areas, one of the casualties of exchange control systems is the ability to analyze the inefficiencies of such systems!

Such evidence and argumentation as there is for the countries in the Project relates to Turkey, India, Ghana, Colombia, Chile, and Pakistan. Of these, the Pakistan and Chilean analyses are perhaps the most comprehensive statistically so we may start with their results prior to a discussion of the other countries.

Gordon Winston has noted that, defining full capacity output as the single-shift maximum output, Pakistan had serious problems with capacity utilization in a number of industries.[43] Thus, in 1965 nearly half the industries worked at about half the capacity installed. Taking the average utilization rate for 1951-1966, nearly three-quarters of Pakistani industries had utilization rates below 60 percent of installed capacity, and nearly two-thirds had utilization rates below 40 percent. Winston sought to explain the capacity utilization rates cross sectionally by regressing these rates on a number of independent variables: ratio of exports to production (X), imports as a proportion of total supply (M), capital-income ratio (K/Y), average annual production per firm

(S), gross value added per man-hour (L), and number of firms in the industry (N). His result was as follows:

$$\begin{aligned} U = 29.26 &- \underset{(.069)}{0.366M} + \underset{(.067)}{0.234X} + \underset{(.871)}{2.40(K/Y)} + \underset{(.296)}{0.937S} \\ &+ \underset{(.012)}{0.034N} - \underset{(.704)}{1.256L} \qquad (5.1) \\ &R^2 = 0.90, \quad F = 20.5 \end{aligned}$$

This led him to conclude that utilization rates were positively related to exports (which increased demand), the capital-income ratio (because lower wages and low shift differentials in wages would lead to multiple shifts and hence to both power K/Y and U),[44] the number of firms in an industry (because a larger number stimulated competition and improved utilization rates),[45] and to size (because larger firms had economies of scale and political power to get more of the scarce inputs from the exchange control system). They were also negatively related to imports of competing products (because they competed with domestic production and/or may have encouraged investments in domestic capacity in the import-substituting climate of Pakistan), and to labor productivity (for the same reason as with the capital-income ratio).[46]

On working with the ratio of imported raw materials to total raw materials (RM), Winston found that:

$$\begin{aligned} U = 28.76 &+ \underset{(.103)}{0.241X} + \underset{(.957)}{2.838(K/Y)} + \underset{(.012)}{0.024S} - \underset{(.097)}{0.267RM} \qquad (5.2) \\ &R^2 = 0.70, \quad F = 9.95 \end{aligned}$$

indicating that the utilization rate fell as the dependence on imported materials increased.

What do these regressions imply for the questions we have posed regarding the relationship of the exchange control regime to underutilization of capacity? Few of the independent variables here are really plausible, and RM (raw materials) would seem to be the most convincing since, given Pakistan's regime, the extent of capacity utilization may well vary with the availability of imported raw materials. And, similarly, it is plausible that export promotion should help to utilize excess capacity in import-substituting industries.

If therefore these latter results are accepted as indicative of plausible connections between the independent and the dependent variables, then Pakistan's exchange control regime may well be considered to have contributed to excess capacity. For it is difficult to expect that any significant excess capacity could have endured over time, with growing investments *in face of shortages of imported raw materials*, unless the exchange control regime made such growth in capacity worthwhile by linking it to guaranteed equal-shares access to imported raw materials fetching high premiums. Similarly, by inhibiting growth of exports—a question discussed in depth in the next chapter—the regime again would have inhibited the reduction of excess capacity, both directly and by making less foreign exchange available for imports of raw materials.

The analysis so far has underlined the argument that the exchange control regime in Pakistan, as elsewhere, itself created the incentives to add to capacity despite initial excess capacity. But we may ask the different question: Why did the authorities *permit* such growth of capacity to occur despite excess capacity when in fact investment and/or capital-goods import licensing could have been used to *prevent* such expansion? Nurul Islam[47] argues that new firms were licensed while existing firms operated with excess capacity on the doubtful assumption that increasing the number of firms necessarily increased the degree of competition. Another motivation was the desire for a wider distribution of entrepreneurship and industrial capital. Moreover, new capacity was sanctioned with an eye to future demand. He further notes that the composition of foreign aid in terms of project and commodity assistance also had its effect on the creation of capacity ahead of the generation of current resources for the utilization of capacity. It was difficult to reject project assistance for fear that aid, if not accepted, would be lost forever, and a poor country could ill afford to forego aid. Moreover, there was always hope that the installation of new capacity might eventually enlarge the flow of commodity aid to enable the utilization of excess capacity. Note, however, that the *willingness* of the government to expand capacity in the face of excess capacity would not be a sufficient condition for such expansion by the private sector. Hence the critical role in explaining such capacity expansion must be assigned to the exchange control framework that made such expansion profitable in the first place.

The Behrman analysis of capacity utilization in Chile is far more thorough and addressed to the following three questions: (1) are there Phase associations of capacity utilization? (2) have capacity utilization rates been sensitive to foreign sector changes on a partial equilibrium basis? (3) what is the nature of general equilibrium reponse of capacity utilization to changes in the international economic regime per se?[48]

On the phasewise association, Behrman concludes that such an association is not evident for the reason that the significant determinants of capacity utilization are domestic in nature. "Much of the importance of the foreign-sector in the determination of capacity utilization, moreover, has been due to wars and export market fluctuations. These phenomena are beyond Chilean control. They clearly are not caused by any changes Chile might make in her international economic policy regimes."[49]

In fact, Behrman's careful econometric, partial equilibrium analysis of the determinants of capacity utilization in eight sectors (agriculture, mining, construction, industry, transportation, utilities, housing, and services) during 1947-1965 shows strikingly the importance of several micro and macro domestic factors such as credit availability, relative output-input prices, and the state of economic activity in explaining underutilization of capacity. At the same time, the foreign sector factors of importance include the stringency of QRs. However, the signs of the coefficients in this factor go in both directions, indicating that the beneficial effect of reduced import-competing supplies on capacity utilization may or may not offset the adverse effect of reduced imports of intermediates, spare parts, and so on.

While therefore the Chilean partial equilibrium analysis seems to yield results that suggest a general lack of links between the exchange control policies and the rate of capacity utilization, we can argue (as we did in the case of the Pakistani analysis) that, *as between Phase II and Phase IV on a sustained basis*, the effect of Phase IV *via* improved foreign exchange availability *could* have been to *reduce* the capacity underutilization through increased availability of imported inputs for the industry and mining sectors. But, clearly, we cannot go beyond this for, as the Chilean analysis underlines, there are several other factors that significantly influence capacity utilization in the different sectors (including industry and mining). Moreover the improved availability of foreign exchange could have been used also to increase imports of *competing* products (a factor perhaps of some importance, as discussed above, in some cases in Behrman's analysis), thus *increasing* excess capacity.[50] It is perhaps useful to note also that, unlike in the Pakistani case for example, the Chilean procedures of import allocations do not appear to have created significant incentives to add to capacity in the face of excess capacity. Hence the effect of the exchange control regime on the emergence or accentuation of excess capacity (for several of the reasons discussed at the outset of this section) is likely to have been minimal and this may therefore also help partially to account for the general lack of any link between the Chilean phases and the capacity utilization rates.

Finally, we may note that Behrman's *short-run* general equilibrium simulation runs for devaluation and for equi-proportionate increase in imports through relaxed QRs yield the conclusion that capacity utilization through production change would *drop* from such policy changes. However, these results follow from macro price and income changes built into the model under the devaluation simulation and, in the QR-change simulation, from the fact that "the protective effects of quantitative restrictions on competing final goods apparently dominate effects on imported input supplies."[51] This set of short-run results however is of interest essentially in the analysis of the transition to Phase IV and does not bear directly on the issue whether, as between

Phase II and IV on a sustained basis, one may expect lower capacity utilization in Phase II for many of the reasons set out earlier.

The evidence for the other countries is more qualitative and, for some of them (e.g., Colombia and Turkey), the authors again assign only a rather modest magnitude to the effects under consideration. Thus, Carlos Díaz-Alejandro cites relatively high utilization rates in Colombia, compared to some other countries, and further argues that underutilization rates have been linked by other analysts to "long-term" factors such as management quality "which are influenced by trade policy only indirectly. Stop-go cycles related to the foreign exchange bottleneck have influenced capacity utilization, particularly during 1956 through 1967, and excess capacity in the 'horror stories' of import-substitution can also be found, but no strong general link appears to exist between import licensing as practiced in Colombia and excess capacity."[52] The link, weak as it is, can only be inferred from the fact that the willingness to add to capacity in the face of excess capacity would have been higher under the direct allocations of imported inputs by INCOMEX, much as in Pakistan and India, to Colombian firms on some fair-share basis. Also the underutilization of capacity, linked to a shortage of imported raw materials, provides empirical evidence in support of the pertinence of such an argument.

For India, the evidence of the links between the import control regime and underutilization of capacity is more considerable. This is *not* to say that the bulk of the substantial excess capacity in the Indian economy can be explained in this way. Recent micro-studies have highlighted the role of factors such as labor problems, mismanagement, and so on, in many industries. However, the institutional work on import allocation procedures, combined with interviews and examination of corporation reports, confirms the role of bottlenecks resulting in substantial shortfalls in production in different firms from time to time. Similar evidence on the inhibiting of exports by firms with underutilized capacity is also available. And, as with Pakistan and Colombia, the evidence of underutilization due to shortages of raw materials points to the importance of the argument that guaranteed access to fair shares in such raw materials imports, combined with sheltered markets for the output under the policy of automatic protection from imports *via* QRs, would make the expansion of capacity in the face of underutilized capacity more attractive than otherwise.

Thus, in regard to bottlenecks, it is clear that the Indian import control regime could not have been better designed for creating such bottlenecks! The AU (actual user) licenses (for raw materials and intermediates) were specified in great detail by composition and by source and were besides non-transferable between firms and, in principle, even between plants within a firm. There was no legal provision for resale of the AU imports either.[53] The creation of bottlenecks, with no legal redress, was thus almost guaranteed! Redress through appeals to the import control authorities was possible but time-consuming.

The normal, bureaucratic delays were compounded by the policy of using QRs to protect domestic producers that was embodied in the rather sacrosanct rule of "indigenous non-availability" as the critical factor in permitting imports. The resulting bottlenecks were, to some extent and only with lapse of time, eased by the growth of illegal resales of import licenses and imports and, with the growth of the export-promoting import entitlement schemes, by the imports legally made available thereunder.

The bottlenecks did not arise merely from the inflexibility endemic to AU licensing. The strict control over CG (capital goods) and industrial licensing also extended to regulating the composition and level of output by detailed specification. It was therefore not infrequent to find firms that could have technologically and profitably switched to new products, with capacity licensed for a different product, but were prevented from so doing by the rules of licensing. Nor was it infrequent to find firms with unbalanced equipment, seeking to add marginal equipment that could have multiplied output disproportionately, unable to secure permission to do so from the licensing authorities.[54]

The difficulties raised by the rule of indigenous non-availability extended also to exports. Thus, the effect of the 1966 liberalization policy package on exports by industries with excess capacity (and hence on their capacity utilization) was partly blunted by the inflexibilities of the control system. One of the important side effects of the principle of indigenous availability was that exportable items that therefore had to be manufactured with inferior-quality domestically produced inputs and capital equipment were, in turn, faced with enhanced difficulties in the highly competitive international markets. This was particularly the case with the new exports in the engineering industries, which in any case faced serious difficulties in cultivating foreign markets almost from scratch. Further, since there was little flexibility for getting more inputs through bidding in the market, in view of the restrictive character of the import policy, and capacity also could not be expanded (without prior licensing) owing to controls on entry, industries that needed flexibility in production in order to get hold of large foreign orders, whenever available, found themselves unnecessarily handicapped.[55]

There is some evidence on capacity underutilization in the Ghana study as well, but it is somewhat inconclusive. Leith does record the presence of excess capacity during the 1960s owing to shortages of imported raw materials and spare parts. This phenomenon was particularly acute during the late Nkrumah period, in 1964 and 1965, and after the coup as well. Thus, in setting out its plea for additional aid required for 1967, the NLC government put as its goal the attainment of "roughly some 50-55 percent of the theoretical 100 percent capacity on a one-shift basis." According to a study by Steel, interviews in 1968 of the forty-one manufacturing firms in his sample showed that capacity utilization rates for 1967-1968 ranged from 10 percent to 100 percent, with an average of less than 50 percent. Leith's own data from the CBS 1968 Industrial Survey also showed a range of capacity utilization rates as broad as Steel's, with an unweighted mean of 57 percent and a standard deviation of 32 percent.[56]

Therefore there was indeed significant capacity underutilization in Ghana, and Leith records that shortages of imported inputs and spares were present. So we can infer reasonably that the exchange control regime must be assigned some role in the phenomenon of capacity underutilization. In particular, (1) increased exchange earnings would have increased imports of raw materials to improve capacity utilization; and (2) expansion of capacity in the face of underutilized capacity would have been less likely if the exchange control system had not effectively linked access to producer-licenses of scarce imports to capacity installed.[57]

Finally, Anne Krueger has also discussed the problem of excess capacity and the exchange control regime for Turkey. She notes for Turkey,[58] as other authors did for India and Pakistan, that "import licenses were allocated among industrialists on the basis of their capacity. Thus incentives were created by the import-licensing system to build additional capacity even if existing capacity was underutilized." At the same time, she records the Union of Chambers of Commerce data on capacity underutilization for 1966, 1967, and 1969, suggesting rather serious underutilization rates while also noting (as did the India study authors) that there was an incentive to overreport capacity to get more import allocations. Her conclusion, based on a detailed AID field study plus her own interviews with businessmen during these years, was to discount these high estimates and conclude, rather cautiously, that the "import regime led to some overbuilding of capacity and idle capacity in some heavily import dependent sectors" but that the magnitude of this phenomenon was not substantial.

In conclusion, it seems reasonable to argue that several specific aspects of the exchange control operation during Phase II, in some of the countries in the Project, created definite inducements to the creation or accentuation of excess capacity. However, we cannot really establish plausibly the magnitudes of these effects. Moreover, in many cases, there were enough other, purely domestic, factors that significantly influenced capacity utilization as well. Hence, even in the cases where Phase II procedures may be expected to have accentuated the creation of excess capacity, a time-series investigation of Phase II and others would not, and in fact does not (in Chile, for example), reveal any association between the phases and the rates of underutilization of capacity. The only important *statistical* link between Phase II regimes in general (as distinct from that resulting from allocational procedures of particular types encouraging excess capacity) and excess capacity that can be argued finally seems to come down to regressions of capacity utilization on indices of dependence of the industry on imported raw materials. This enables us to argue that Phase II regimes, by adversely affecting the growth of export earnings (as discussed in Chapter 7), are likely to have consequently accentuated excess capacity in the industries using imported materials.

IV. EXCESS HOLDINGS OF INVENTORIES

The exchange control regimes can also be argued to have led to increased holdings of inventories of raw materials and intermediates, thus increasing the social cost of production beyond what it would otherwise have been. The basic argument centers on the fact that the exchange control regimes are characterized by frequent changes in the assignment of imports of specific commodities among different categories of restrictiveness and in the expected delays on grant and disposal of licenses, phenomena that *add* to the uncertainty inherent in the act of importation under any exchange regime. The *increased* uncertainty then leads to the holding of additional inventories to reduce the risk of losses from sudden bottlenecks in production.[59] In addition, there is the interesting argument that a general shift in import licensing from traders to industrialists—documented in Chapter 3 for many of our countries—also implied that there would be a general increase in inventories held as the economies of centralized holding by traders would be lost.[60]

The argument about individual firms holding increased inventories under exchange control regimes however relates strictly to the firms' *desire* to hold larger inventories. It may still be that the exchange control authorities may deny to the firms the ability to hold these inventories by refusing to allocate new import licenses unless the inventories are reduced. Hence any empirical examination of this thesis becomes tenuous and difficult.

The evidence on excess inventory costs, in the country studies in the Project, is mostly indirect—that is, citing the frequent changes in import policies and classifications—but there is *some* direct evidence of excess holdings.

The evidence of frequency of import policy changes for specific items is compelling for many countries. But the most detail will be found for Turkey and India.[61] There is ample documentation there of the transition of specific items from category to category (e.g., for Turkey, items moved from the liberalized list to quota list and back), of changing quantities of permissible imports (within the quota list), of the inclusion and withdrawal of the item under export-promotion licensing (e.g., under the import entitlement scheme, or the scheme for importing at international prices, in India), and so on.

As for the direct evidence on inventory holdings, there is some evidence, using international comparisons for similar industries, that suggests that there were unusually large inventory holdings in India,[62] though time-series analysis on individual industries' inventory holdings has failed to show, so far at least, any relationship between the stringency of the QR regime and increased inventory holdings (presumably because stringency implies reduced imports and hence this tends to pull in the direction of reduced inventory holdings).

The international comparison route has been taken also by Anne Krueger for Turkey to supplement interviews. In particular, taking a sample of thirty-two Turkish firms' balance sheets, as of the close of each firm's 1969 fiscal year, she calculated the value of raw materials and other goods used in production, excluding semi-finished and finished products. The weighted average ratio of inventories of inputs to net fixed assets was then calculated as 0.4655, and the unweighted average at 0.5175, implying that inventory investment was approximately half as large as the investment in fixed assets. Comparisons with various countries tended to confirm impressions from the sample and from interviews. Table 5-3, utilizing data on national accounts, contains Krueger's estimates of the ratio of investment in inventory to fixed capital investment for a sample of countries (including Turkey). Turkish investment in stocks averaged 15 percent of investment in fixed capital, a ratio that was more than twice that of all countries in the sample except that of Japan and Spain. Krueger concluded that although this high Turkish ratio "cannot be attributed entirely to the trade regime (domestically produced goods were part of inventory accumulation, too) there can be little doubt that the import regime was a

Table 5-3. Ratio of Investment in Stocks to Fixed Investment, Various Countries, 1966 to 1968

Country	*Ratio*	*Country*	*Ratio*
Australia	0.080	Israel	0.030
Belgium	0.036	Italy	0.038
Brazil	0.074	Japan	0.135
Chile	0.081	Korea	0.060
Denmark	0.049	Netherlands	0.054
France	0.069	Spain	0.107
Germany	0.025	Turkey	0.152
Greece	0.021	United Kingdom	0.030
		United States	0.065

Note: a) Data for Brazil are for the 1965-1967 period.

b) These data cover *all* inventory investments in all sectors and are therefore not comparable with data from firms' balance sheets.

Source: SPO data for Turkey; *Yearbook of National Accounts Statistics*, United Nations, 1969, country tables for other countries; from Table VIII-2 in Krueger, *Turkey*, op. cit.

contributing factor in Turkey's high figure. . . . Nonetheless, the very high Turkish figure combined with interview impressions and sample data suggests that inventories were probably substantially higher as a result of the trade regime than they would otherwise have been.''[63]

Finally, we should note that, for Ghana, Clark Leith regressed, using cross-sectional data for Ghanaian industries for 1968, the material stocks at the beginning of the period as a percent of materials used during the period (*ST/USE*) on the percent of imported material used in total material purchases (*IMP/TOT*). He found the relationship:

$$ST/USE = 25.48 + \underset{(1.480)}{0.805}\, IMP/TOT \qquad R^2 = 0.075, \quad DF = 27 \tag{5.3}$$

where the explanatory power of the equation was very low.[64] Leith, in discussing the failure of his estimation exercise to reveal the link between inventories and the exchange control system, notes that ''while the restrictive regime may shift the demand for inventories outward, it may also prevent the satisfaction of that demand.''[65] A further reason that could imply lack of a significant relationship is that, in a *cross-section* analysis, the requisite assumptions to put all industries in one regression are not necessarily satisfied to begin with; any ''prevention'' of the satisfaction of demand for more inventories should affect all industries. It seems much more likely that the cross-section analysis fails to allow for critical differences among alternative industries and firms that affect the dependent variable. For example, a high ratio of import dependence on raw materials may be correlated with larger size of firms (because larger firms are associated with the modern import-substituting sector that is characterized by high imports of raw materials and intermediates) and larger firms may also be better able to break bottlenecks arising from critical shortages of inventories just because they have better access to the licensing authorities (as has indeed been discussed in Chapter 2), so that they would need to hold less inventories, *ceteris paribus*, on that account. Cross-sectional regressions are thus likely to yield poor results for reasons different from those that afflict time-series analysis of this question.

Basing ourselves largely on the international-comparisons type of evidence and the institutional evidence on licensing procedures that would seem to create the need for holding added inventories, we may then conclude that exchange control regimes are prone to lead to increased social costs on this account.

V. EFFECTS OF CHEAP IMPORTS OF CAPITAL GOODS AND RAW MATERIALS

One of the major aspects of the overvalued exchange rate systems in many of the countries in the Project was that intermediates and capital goods, when imported from abroad by producers under import licensing, were imported at premium-exclusive prices and at relatively low tariffs. Hence, compared to the situation where the parity would have been allowed to adjust, it can be argued that such imports were artificially cheapened by these exchange control regimes. Another aspect of the same phenomenon is that (producer-) imported intermediates and capital goods were cheaper for the favored firms under these exchange control regimes than were domestic substitutes.

Hence it is clear that the choice of technique by producers could be distorted if there was substitution between domestic and imported inputs. There is in fact plenty of evidence that, in addition to substitution between capital goods and labor, raw materials also substitute with capital and labor. For example, the loss of raw materials in production may be reduced by more expensive equipment costing more capital, rejects may be reduced by better supervision costing more salaries, and so on. Raw materials further substitute with one another as in the Egyptian analysis of Hansen and Nashashibi where low-quality imported and high-quality domestic raw cotton are considered as alternative inputs in the cotton textile industry. There are both specific examples of such substitution in the literature and econometric studies, incorporating raw materials in the specification of the production function (for gross output rather than for value added), which allow successfully for such substitution.[66]

However, in determining the resultant impact on choice of techniques and relative outputs of alternative sectors, it is important to distinguish between micro-effects and macro-effects. Assuming that the overvalued exchange rate system reduces available imports and that this translates into a lower quantity of capital goods imports, for example, we then see readily that while each micro-producer would have an incentive to shift his choice of technique toward cheaper imported equipment, the reduction in the total availability of such imports must reflect itself in the final equilibrium. It is clear then that, given the direct allocation system, we can think of each individual choice being biased in this way but the total demand for imported equipment being rationed to what is feasible, so that the additional demand will be addressed to *domestic* equipment (where available), which is both more expensive than imported equipment *and* costlier than under a more liberal trade regime. We must think therefore of a set of techniques where the imported equipment has been used at lower prices and another where the domestic equipment has been used at higher prices—than under a more liberal regime. Each set of choices is distorted and suboptimal, in consequence. It also follows that the activities, firms, and industries that are allowed access to cheaper imported equipment (or raw materials, for that matter) will also expand relative to those that are not so fortunate.

Evidence on such effects in the countries in the Project is found in Ghana, Turkey, and Pakistan and points in direction of the conclusion that such distortions were significant. For Ghana, the argumentation is confined to micro-effects and extends to raw material imports. Basically, Leith has estimated Cobb-Douglas production functions for three industries, using cross-section data on establishments where gross output is defined on capital, labor, domestic materials, and imported materials.[67] He then proceeds to estimate the implicit subsidy on imported raw materials for each industry—by assuming that this can be defined as the proportionate cheapening of imports relative to the average cost of importation in all industries, inclusive of import premiums.[68] Using the equilibrium factor-reward conditions, the shift in technique following from such a subsidy, given the prices of all other factors, can be readily worked out. However, output levels are indeterminate unless some additional assumption such as diminishing returns to scale or increasing supply price of at least one factor, with given output price, is made. Thus Leith, who intends to consider not merely the shift in technique but also the expansion of output following the implicit subsidization of the imported inputs, assumes that labor or domestic materials are subject to increasing supply price.

Using the observed prices of inputs and outputs, the estimated Cobb-Douglas production functions and implicit subsidy on imported inputs,[69] and illustrative elasticities of supply of the factor whose supply price is assumed to be increasing, Leith works out alternative estimates of the impact of the cheapened imports of the inputs on supply of output in the industry and on relative factor proportions.

The resulting empirical estimates, thus based on Ghanaian reality as far as feasible, are nonetheless stated by Leith to be "nothing more than illustrative of the general type of response exhibited by Ghanaian industries." However, they suggest a significant response of output in Ghanaian industries to subsidies on imported inputs and a fall in the ratio of output to these inputs, conclusions that carry over *also* to subsidized capital use as well, and hence presumably to any cheapening of capital goods imports that results from the exchange control regime (as discussed already).[70]

The evidence from Turkey is focused on the substitution between imported and domestic equipment, rather than on imported *versus* domestic raw materials as in the case of Ghana. But this evidence is somewhat inconclusive, revealing no link between the relative price of imported and domestic equipment and their relative quantities. Thus Krueger cites the earlier study of McCabe and Michalopoulos, which yielded for all of Turkey during 1950-1963 the following regression:

$$\log (I_m/I_d) = \underset{}{2.40} - \underset{(0.04)}{0.03} \log (P_m/P_d) + \underset{(2.57)}{0.26} \log (R_e/R_d) - \underset{(-6.51)}{1.60} D \qquad (5.4)$$

$$R^2 = 0.89, \quad F = 28$$

where I_m/I_d was the ratio of investment in imported to domestic capital equipment, P_m/P_d the ratio of the prices of the two kinds of equipment, R_e/R_d the ratio of external to internal credit (the volume of bank loans) and D was a dummy for the post-devaluation years (1959-1963).[71]

The McCabe-Michalopoulos hypothesis was that the availability of foreign credits (official and private) largely determines total capital goods imports and that the relative price of imported to domestic equipment also influences their relative use. The regression result did not, however, bear out the latter link. This may very well have been due to the fact that the (significant) devaluation dummy picked up this price effect. The evidence thus remains somewhat inconclusive, especially if we further note that the indices of capital goods prices, imported and domestic, are likely to contain more than the usual complement of errors, that the two independent variables P_m/P_d and R_e/R_d are likely to be correlated, and that external credits do not account for all capital goods imports while internal credits would generally not match the value of purchases of domestic equipment.

No output-expansion and contraction effects can be deduced from the above exercise. By contrast, the Leith exercise for Ghana did produce estimates of output expansion in specific industries in response to the implied subsidy on imported inputs in a partial-equilibrium framework for each industry. However, they rested somewhat heroically on an assumption about the presence of "diminishing returns" from one or more (arbitrarily specified) factors with rising supply price and the further assumption that the supply of the imported factors would be perfectly elastic to the favored firms up to the amount necessary to support the increased output at the new technique.

Evidence on compositional shifts in output or investment, linked to the trade regime, is available for Turkey. Phase II periods there are associated with relative expansion in the import-unintensive investment in construction relative to investment in import-intensive machinery and equipment. As Krueger notes, "the timing of the changes in importance of construction in total investment coincides remarkably closely with the delineation of Phases of the trade regime in Turkey. During Phase II, in both the 1950's and 1960's, investment became increasingly oriented toward those sectors requiring relatively few imported capital goods. During Phase IV of the early 1960's investment shifted toward plant and machinery. . . ."[72] Evidence of compositional shifts linked to changes in international economic regimes is to be found in the Chilean study as well.[73]

Further evidence of the impact of the trade regime on choice of techniques comes from Pakistan. The cheap importation of capital goods under the overvalued exchange rate to the agricultural sector has been shown to have accentuated the tractorization of Pakistani agriculture in the Panjab, in the work of Bose and Clark.[74] Comparing the relative price of tractors to output (e.g., wheat and rice), at landed and domestic prices, these authors show that, in the domestic market, owing to the ability of the farmers to secure imports of tractors at landed (premium-exclusive) prices, the relative price of tractors was considerably more advantageous than it would have been if the exchange rate had been unified for imports of both tractors and agricultural outputs.

Citing Bose and Clark, Nurul Islam has argued that capital available to the large farms in agriculture was underpriced not only because they had access to the imported agricultural machinery at relatively low price, but also because the large farmers had access to borrowed capital from credit institutions at a rate of interest of about 6.5 percent per annum. This low rate of interest compared with the shadow price of capital, which was estimated to be between 10 percent and 15 percent. The opportunity cost of agricultural machinery such as a stationary thresher, after correction for the overvaluation of the domestic currency and for underpricing of capital, was estimated to be 40 percent to 60 percent higher than the market price at which it was available substantially below its opportunity cost.

The combined result of the above factors was that from the private point of view, mechanization in agriculture was profitable. However, its profitability was in serious doubt from the social point of view. According to one estimate, the social cost of tractor mechanization (evaluating all inputs including prices of tractors in world prices and labor at zero social cost) exceeded social benefit by 43 percent to 60 percent, depending upon the intensity of tractor use varying between two acres and three acres per horsepower. The social benefit consisted of output (evaluated in world prices) and of the opportunity cost of fodder that would be saved consequent on the replacement of the bullock by the tractor. However, private costs were not much higher than social costs evaluated in world prices because tractors were available until recently at the official rate of exchange with little or no duty. While the social rate of discount used was 10 percent, the big farmers who were using tractors could borrow at 6.5 percent. The only significant element of private cost not included in social cost was the cost of labor. Total private costs in domestic prices were about 14 percent higher than social costs, excluding labor, in terms of world prices. But private returns were considerably higher than social returns. The evaluation of agricultural output in domestic prices was 30 percent higher than world prices, and hence private returns from output were 30 percent higher than social returns, excluding the additional value of output released from the production of fodder. Furthermore, there was the saving of labor costs, especially in the displacement of sharecroppers or tenant farmers, who received a larger share of output than wage labor. Nurul Islam therefore concludes that while the precise calculations of private versus social costs and benefits of mechanization would require further studies, the broad orders of magnitude are clear and show that "the price structure for scarce inputs, i.e., capital and foreign exchange, had the effect of increasing the private returns of mechanization above the social returns."[75]

The weight of the evidence in the countries in the Project then is in support of the hypothesis that exchange control regimes, by cheapening the cost of intermediates and capital goods, influence and distort both the choice of techniques within activities and the relative composition of outputs and investments among activities.

VI. MISCELLANEOUS EFFECTS

Before we proceed, in Chapter 7, to discuss their additional allocative effect in the shape of discrimination against exports, we need to complete the present analysis by reference to yet other effects of exchange control regimes.

A. Reduced Competition

The availability to domestic producers of protection against imports was a major aspect of Phase II type regimes, as we have already noted. It should also be noted, however, that this form of QR-generated protection could take extreme forms, as in the Indian rule that importation of an item generally required the production of "non-availability" certificates from indigenous suppliers, or be operated somewhat less drastically as in Turkey or Colombia. Moreover, over time, there is evidence that both the pressure from user industries, who were forced to use costly and/or inferior substitutes, and also the independent realization that automatic protection with QRs could lead to extremely high protection, led to the establishment in many countries of modified procedures and practices to reduce the incidence of automatic protection. Thus, in Israel, ceilings were established on the amount of price differential that domestic import substitutes were entitled to. In India, the possibility of securing imports of materials despite the law of indigenous availability was, *de facto*, made somewhat easier after the recession following the 1966 liberalization had given way to improved levels of activity, and a cell was established in the Ministry of Industry to monitor foreign-domestic price differentials. In Brazil, the law of similars, parallel to the Indian law of indigenous availability, was also progressively eased. And in South Korea, automaticity in domestic protection was progressively dismantled through the 1960s. For both Israel and South Korea, furthermore, the use of QRs was progressively reduced and (relatively moderate) tariff protection took over, implying that protection was no longer total and that the import-substituting firms had to face a relatively elastic supply of imports at the tariff-inclusive price. During the bulk of the Phase II regimes, however, the effect of the QRs was indeed to confer fairly automatic protection to domestic production in nearly all of the countries in the Project. Two negative consequences of this elimination of foreign competition must be noted.

1. The lack of foreign competition could imply that the domestic firms had less reason to be conscious of reducing costs. As Hicks once remarked, a monopolist's chief revenue is leisure. This effect does not necessarily follow insofar as free entry of domestic firms into production could serve to eliminate excess costs. However, in many of the countries in the Project, such free entry was generally not possible because of either industrial licensing or capital-goods-imports licensing. Given raw-material-imports licensing *pro rata* to capacity, efficient firms could not expand and compete effectively with the inefficient firms either. Hence, domestic entry was not free and the restriction or elimination of foreign competition through use of QRs for conferring automatic protection meant that the prospect of having effective competition was often reduced to negligible levels. The only substantial exceptions to this situation were to come from fortuitous overexpansion of capacity by all firms taken together or the possibility of competitive expansion by firms using domestic inputs and equipment outside of the control framework. Such exceptions were therefore generally not important.

2. The lack of attention to cost reduction was not the only consequence of the elimination or significant reduction of competition. One could also have monopolistic restriction of output. In fact, given the relatively small (economic) size of the market and the possibly large economies of scale in many modern industries, it is clear that the elimination of foreign competition could leave the domestic field open to successfully collusive behavior on the part of the few firms that could supply the (small) market. The welfare losses from such growth of domestic monopolies, in the sheltered markets created by QRs, may be quite significant even if we rule out the cost-raising inefficiency discussed immediately prior to the present point.[76]

Both the above effects are difficult to quantify in practice and there is therefore scant, direct evidence on them in the country studies in the Project, an excellent example being provided, however, by the case of the tire industry in Egypt.[77] However, there is considerable institutional evidence of the automaticity of protection, and the methods of allocation of raw material and capital goods licenses, to support the contention that the exchange control regimes in many of these countries did manage to blunt competition seriously and thus to make the economy liable to the inefficiencies of the two types just detailed. The only systematic analysis of the effect of the reduced competition in the Project is in regard to possible reduction in the incentives to conduct research and development or improve quality matters taken up in Chapter 7 later.

B. Delays, Administrative Costs, and Resource Loss

The process of getting licenses allocated under the exchange control regimes requires resource input that is likely to exceed the corresponding demands made under a market system. This is because the bureaucratic regimes that oversee and administer the license allocations are characterized by varying degrees of delays arising from bureaucratic procedures, which are unlikely to exist on the same scale in a market-oriented system. The authors of the study of India, for which serious delays have been amply documented, argue as follows:[78]

> The working of any system of allocation will take a certain amount of time. Even if a free foreign exchange market were to operate, the participants in the market would have to expend time, for example, in acquiring information about availabilities of different kinds of foreign exchange. In principle, the administrative system of allocations need involve no significant increase in time, and hence in "delays," over a price system under which scarce foreign exchange is rationed out in the market: the introduction of priorities would, in principle, be equally time-consuming in both cases, though the procedure would be different, since the price system would involve administrative decisions as to tax and subsidy incentives whereas the control system would involve administrative decisions as to quotas.
>
> In practice, however, the exchange control system seems to degenerate into an inordinately time-consuming allocational device. There are essentially three reasons for this. (1) In a situation of general scarcity of foreign exchange, the definition of priorities becomes exceptionally difficult. . . , and the system ends up having to accommodate all conceivable demands on some "equitable" basis, while making a pretense of administering priorities, this pretense frequently taking the form of collection of yet more information from applicants and time taken in "scrutinizing" it and "arriving at an informed decision." Delays become, sociologically, the "conspicuous" substitute for exercise of priorities by

> the bureaucracy. (2) Equally important, the multiplication of the bureaucratic apparatus leads inevitably to files failing to move quickly and decisions being delayed because procedures are time-wasting. . . . much of the delay to which the Indian import-control system was subject can be put down to the inefficiency of administrative procedures. For example, where indigenous clearance had to be obtained by the DGTD [Directorate General of Technical Development] from two or more other directorates, these were to be sought sequentially rather the simultaneously. (3) Finally, some significance must be attached in explaining delays under the Indian allocation system, to the fact that, with files often moving from the bottom to the top in the Indian administrative system, they often fail to move until suitable graft is paid to the lower-level clerks. If all graft were paid promptly, there should be no delay on this account; but newcomers and honest applicants are unlikely to conform readily to this widespread practice, hence delays occur on this count in the system as well.

These delays (which are also documented for restrictionist periods in Chile[79]) mean, of course, that it (privately) pays firms to engage in hiring resources (e.g., contact men) to expedite the moving of licenses and, where corruption arises, to secure for themselves the licenses that should have gone to others (the case of normal corruption) or licenses that should have come their way anyway but which were being held up merely for collecting bribes (the case of "ultimate" corruption). In short, the exchange control regimes are likely to wind up using real resources, which could well have been utilized productively under alternative regimes, merely in order to minimize delays and to deflect licensed allocations in desired directions.

In addition to these losses, we must reckon the *direct* costs of administration that exceed the market system's costs. Not merely are the administrated exchange allocations costly in inducing firms to expend resources in minimizing delays and maximizing access to licenses, they also are likely, in practice, to cost more administrative resources per se. In the absence of the constraint provided by the profit motive, the bureaucracy is likely to proliferate beyond the optimal level necessary to administer.

Little hard evidence can be produced on these resource effects, and practically none is available for the countries in the Project. Again, however, the evidence is inferential and relates to the great delays in licensing, the growth of resources devoted to tackling the licensing system (in the shape of air travel to centers of bureaucratic allocations, hiring of contact men, etc.), and the growth of the bureaucracy in general in some of the countries in the Project, especially India, Egypt, and Turkey, during their Phase II years.

C. Other Effects

Finally, although the evidence on them is somewhat scant and sporadic, it is worth noting a few additional effects. Thus, Hansen and Nashashibi note for

Egypt that the import-licensing policy typically failed to allow for sufficient imports of spares for maintenance of equipment.[80] This was a problem with the Indian policy as well, and it also arose in Chile, requiring attention *via* appropriate modifications permitting freer access to foreign exchange for the importation of spare parts. Identical problems arose, of course, with the imports of equipment for replacement.

The desire to enforce investment controls strictly was responsible for such a policy. It also led, as in India, to preoccupation with the prevention of imports of "balancing" equipment to augment capacity at low marginal cost. The licensing authorities would frown on these as attempts to get around controls on capacity. The result was often to inhibit low-cost additions to capacity. The prevention of expansion of capacity by working more shifts, and hence economizing the use of capital, also could follow (though, as with underutilization of capacity given the number of shifts, the factors affecting the lack of multiple-shift working are numerous).

Then, we must also note the effect of source-tying of aid and source restrictions *via* bilateral agreements on the choice of technique. Artificially high prices of capital goods, as a result of purchases forced from more expensive sources, should shift the choice of technique toward labor-intensive goods. But in densely populated countries such as India, Pakistan, and Egypt, where labor's shadow wage *might* be considered to be lower than its actual wage, this may not necessarily be an adverse effect. On the other hand, such source-tying could also mean importation of capital-intensive technology. For example, U.S. machinery (imported with U.S. aid) may be more automated then Japanese machinery. Similarly, Kidron has noted how source restrictions have often led to strange amalgams of disparate components from different sources into a working whole, giving the visitor to a plant in India the recurrent impression that he was visiting a museum.[81] Needless to say, in such cases, the productivity of the plant, so assembled, cannot have been as high as when the equipment was put together without source restrictions in the most economical way.

In conclusion, we may close this chapter with the judgment that, while part of the evidence is inferential in deducing effects from the observed institutional features of the exchange control regimes of the Phase II variety and only part is direct, the overwhelming bulk of it is consistent with the view that the static efficiency effects of such regimes have been adverse in practice.

NOTES

1. If we take "structural" models (e.g., the Feldman-Mahalanobis type of model discussed in Chapter 6), the current allocation of investments may critically affect growth. We leave out this and other such problems (e.g., second-best savings arguments) from the present analysis.

2. Of course, it is possible to show that the long-run rate of growth *asymptotically* may be independent of such a productivity loss: as in R. Solow, "A Contribution to the Theory of Economic Growth," *Quarterly Journal of Economics* 70 (February 1956):65-94.

3. Allocative inefficiency resulting from bias against *exportation* is discussed, however, in Chapter 7.

4. Ghana, op.cit., Section 2. For the supporting statistics, see Table IV-2 on p. 84. Leith also has a rough Kendrick-type calculation for Ghana; ibid, p. 82, footnote 6.

5. *Israel*, op.cit., Chapter 6, Section (3), pp. 159-163.

6. *Israel*, ibid., p. 163.

7. *Chile*, op.cit., Chapter 12, pp. 276-280.

8. *Chile*, op.cit., Chapter 4; *Colombia*, op.cit., Chapter 6; *Egypt*, op.cit., Chapter 2; *India*, op.cit., Chapter 2; and *Turkey*, op.cit., Chapter V.

9. *India*, op.cit., p. 38.

10. However, as we note below, Hansen and Nashashibi have attempted a more ambitious analysis than DRC computation for Egypt with care and ingenuity.

11. However, as noted in the next footnote, the shadow prices will equal the market prices of factors under *ad valorem* trade and product market distortions.

12. While it is relatively straightforward to argue that the appropriate shadow prices on factors should be used for calculating DRCs, their derivation is not an easy matter, either analytically or empirically. Thus, for example, in the context of project analysis, Srinivasan and Bhagwati ("Shadow Prices for Project Selection in the Presence of Distortions: Effective Rates of Protection and Domestic Resource Costs," *Journal of Political Economy* 86 (February 1978):97-116 have shown that the valuation of factors used in the project in question must be such as to reduce the DRCs in the *existing*, trade-distorted activities to unity! On the other hand, if DRCs are computed for the purpose indicated in the text above, that is, to indicate disparities in economic returns arising from existing allocations in a regime of trade distortions, then the DRCs would have to be computed at existing *market* prices of primary factors; but, to anticipate later discussion in the text above, the DRC ranking would not generally reflect the relative expansion or contraction of activities vis-a-vis their optimal level. It might be added that, for the latter questions, the computation of DRCs when distortions other than trade distortions are present, for example, under factor market distortions, would presumably require *some* shadow pricing of factors but, as of the present date, no theoretical exercise that does this explicitly seems to have been undertaken.

13. For this reason, Hansen and Nashashibi make their DRC estimates using *both* c.i.f. and f.o.b. prices for a number of commodities in Egypt. Cf. *Egypt*, op.cit.

14. I. Kravis and R. Lipsey, *Price Competitiveness in World Trade* (New York: National Bureau of Economic Research, Columbia University Press, 1971).

15. This corrective is perhaps essential as there is ample evidence elsewhere of enthusiastic inferences from these arrays of ERPs and DRCs about which industries should be expanded and which contracted, and where a planning commission is wrong in its choice of targets, and so on. Rather we plan to use these estimates much more "weakly" as a broad piece of evidence pointing to the general misallocation that can be inferred as likely to result from the operation of a foreign trade regime that pays little or no attention to economic costs and benefits, without pretense that the numbers tell you anything more than that.

16. *Turkey*, op.cit., pp. 219-222. A still higher variance—43,737.12—is reported for iron and steel products, but Krueger notes (p. 224) that this result is dominated by an extreme observation for bolts and nuts.

17. Ibid., p. 225.

18. See *India*, op.cit., Chapter 13, Tables 13.3 and 13.4, in particular. *Turkey*, op.cit., Chapter VIII, pp. 216-226, including Table VIII-1, also has some factory- and firm-level DRC estimates, suggesting significant variability.

19. Cf. *South Korea,* op.cit., p. 201; and *India*, op.cit., pp. 178-182. On South Korea, note that the low rates of dispersion apply to estimates of effective protection after deleting all activities with ERP rates over 500 percent; and that "the degree of dispersion increases as the measure of protection includes more of the incentive policies" (pp. 200-201). Note also that the Korean study reduces a number of quantitative measures to *ad valorem* "equivalents" and that the resulting statistical picture of low dispersion rates probably hides substantial differences and selectivity in effective incentives to different industries: a point to which we return in Chapters 7 and 8.

20. Cf. Hansen and Nashashibi, op.cit., pp. 167-194.

21. *Egypt,* op.cit., p. 169. They argue that:

> A comparison between prediction 1 and actual crop areas will yield an estimate of the extent to which the government's interference has forced cultivators to deviate from the cropping pattern they would have chosen at the given domestic prices without government area interference.
>
> A comparison between prediction 2 and actual crop areas will tell us whether or not government area interference has forced cultivators to adopt a crop pattern similar to what they would have chosen themselves had the domestic prices been equal to international prices. Should this happen to be the case, the government has performed as well as the market forces would have done at the given international prices without area controls.
>
> A comparison between predictions 2 and 1 will show the difference between the result of private market forces at actual domestic prices and at perfectly free trade and thus illustrate the effects of price distortion.
>
> A comparison between prediction 3 and actual crop area will indicate the distance of the actual pattern from the optimal crop pattern—assuming that the cultivators' long-term response is optimal. If the government could instantly accomplish a cropping pattern according to this prediction, area allocation would be optimal and perhaps better than what the cultivators could accomplish under free trade. It should be understood that such perfect planning would require that there be no extra (social) costs involved in instantaneous adjustment, and that the government be capable of making perfect forecasts of both prices and yields for the crops to be sown. We assume that these conditions are fulfilled.

22. Ibid., pp. 189-190.

23. This distinction between the pattern and degree of import substitution, as two separate aspects of the analysis of the efficiency of import substitution, was developed earlier in J. Bhagwati, "Trade Policies for Development," in G. Ranis, ed., *The Gap Between the Rich and the Poor Nations* (London: Macmillan), Proceedings of the International Economic Association Conference at Bled, Yugoslavia, August 27 to September 2, 1970. Note that "interindustrial" includes "intercommodity" or "interactivity."

24. *Colombia*, op.cit., p. 226.

25. The superiority of the Corden technique has been demonstrated in general equilibrium theory by A. Ray in his excellent contribution to the *Symposium* on the Theory of Effective Protection in the *Journal of International Economics*, 3, 3 (August 1973). For a fuller and more definitive treatment, see also H. Suzuki, "Nontraded Inputs and the Effective Rate of Protection," *Journal of International Economics*, 1978, forthcoming. Note however that, in the case of Chile at least, the distinction between the two measures is not empirically important. Cf. *Chile*, op.cit., Appendix B, p. 375.

26. *South Korea*, op.cit., Chapter 10, pp. 206-208.

27. *South Korea*, op.cit., Chapter 10, pp. 207-208.

28. See J. Behrman, *Chile*, op.cit., Chapter 12, for full details of this analysis.

29. Ibid., Chapter 12, page 271.

30. Nor, for that matter, did Behrman manage to find any significant association between DRCs and growth indices.

31. S. Guisinger, "The Characteristics of Protected Industries in Pakistan," in H.G. Grubel and H.G. Johnson, eds., *Effective Tariff Protection* (General Agreement on Trade and Tariffs, Geneva: 1971).

32. "Tariff Protection and Industrialization via Import Substitution: An Empirical Analysis of the Nigerian Experience," *Bangladesh Economic Review* 1, 4 (October 1973):331-340.

33. However, Alan Deardorff has recently shown, in R. Dornbusch and J.A. Frenkel, eds., *International Economic Policy: Theory and Evidence* (Baltimore: Johns Hopkins Press, 1978), that when *n* prices change as a result of $n > 2$ different tariffs, a *correlation* will exist between the tariff rates and the changes in the *n* activities' outputs.

34. In fact, for predicting *output* changes, as distinct from "value-added" changes, in models with imported inputs, the effective protection measures run into trouble *even if* we confine ourselves to *two* goods. This problem was first raised by V.K. Ramaswami and T.N. Srinivasan, "Tariff Structure and Resource Allocation in the Presence of Substitution," in J. Bhagwati, et. al. eds., *Trade, Balance of Payments and Growth* (Amsterdam: North-Holland, 1971) and is extensively analyzed in the contributions of M. Bruno and J. Bhagwati and T.N. Srinivasan in the symposium on the theory of effective protection in general equilibrium in the *Journal of International Economics*, 3 (August 1973).

35. Thus, the causal relationship may well run from the growth and size of an industry to the magnitude of its tariff protection. In fact, it is only recently that economists have begun to concern themselves with the question of why tariff structures are what they are, as distinct from what they should be. At an institutional-analytical level, the work of Padma Desai on the criteria used by the Indian Tariff Commission in granting tariff protection represents one approach of interest and importance (cf. her *Tariff Protection and Industrialization: A Study of the Indian Tariff Commission at Work*, Delhi: Hindustan Publishing Corporation, 1970). At a statistical-econometric level, the work of Travis, Basevi, et. al. on examining the factor intensity of protected industries in the United States represents a different, and equally useful, approach; for an interesting analysis of the relationship between the labor force characteristics of an industry and the degree of exemption secured by it from the across the board 50 percent tariff cut in the Kennedy Round, see John Cheh, "United States Concessions in the Kennedy Round and Short-Run Labor Adjustment Costs," *Journal of International Economics*, 4 (November 1974):323-340.

36. See J. Bhagwati, "On the Equivalence of Tariffs and Quotas," op.cit.; and G. Fishelson and F. Flatters "The (Non-) Equivalence of Optimal Tariffs and Quotas under Uncertainty," op.cit.

37. In consequence, a high import premium may merely reflect the fact that *both* imports and domestic production are controlled, so that the correspondingly high ERP, instead of reflecting the excessive growth of domestic production, may indicate the opposite, namely, that domestic production has been severely curtailed!

38. Evidence on this is available for India and Pakistan. See Padma Desai, *Tariff Protection. . .* , op.cit. (1970); and Nurul Islam, *Pakistan*, op.cit.

39. This view, of course, has its parallel in the view expressed earlier that the differential DRCs among activities must be taken also to imply, only in a broad and rough manner, the differential *returns* to different activities in the system, stemming from the presence of the exchange control regime.

40. The discussion below follows closely the detailed argumentation in *India,* op. cit., Chapter 13, Section 2. The effects on multiple-shift working are discussed later.

41. This could happen, to some extent, through illegal purchases in the black market, as discussed in Chapter 4.

42. Needless to say, this incentive becomes relevant only if the gain from import-premium-exclusive access to materials exceeds the cost of installation of yet more capacity. Hence, the likelihood of the bias leading to installation of yet more capacity (despite current underutilization) increases with the import premium and the proportion of imported inputs to value added and decreases with the cost of capacity installation.

43. G. Winston, "Capital Utilization in Economic Development," *Economic Journal* 81 (March 1971):36-60.

44. This argument has subsequently been shown to have an analytical weakness; see the discussion in Mary Ann Baily, *Capital Utilization in Kenya Manufacturing,* Ph.D. dissertation submitted to M.I.T. (February 1974).

45. This argument is not persuasive as it equates increased numbers with increased competition: an issue that is well recognized in the theory of imperfect competition.

46. This argument is also therefore not persuasive.

47. Islam, *Pakistan*, op.cit., Part IV, Chapter II, pp. 30-31.

48. Cf. *Chile*, op.cit., Chapter 9, pp. 231-236 for full discussion.

49. Ibid., Chapter 9, p. 231.

50. Behrman refers in this regard to "frequent policies of increasing food imports as part of the anti-inflationary strategy" and notes that such imports may have had a negative impact on capacity utilization in agriculture (Behrman, op.cit., p. 234).

51. Ibid., Chapter 9, p. 236.

52. *Colombia*, op.cit., Chapter 8, pp. 118-119.

53. For detailed evidence, see Bhagwati and Desai, op.cit., pp. 321-323.

54. In both cases, the authorities not merely wished to constrain the pattern and level of output but were occasionally unwilling to relent because they felt that the firms were trying to dodge the rules.

55. *India*, op.cit., Chapter 2, p. 46; see also Chapter 8 and 11.

56. *Ghana*, op.cit., pp. 154-156.

57. But, again as with most other countries, Leith found no meaningful regression link between capacity utilization and other variables. For details on some regressions that he tried, see ibid., pp. 105-108.

58. *Turkey*, op.cit., p. 230.

59. To the extent therefore that firms do so, the bottlenecks experienced will be reduced: hence excess capacity costs discussed in the preceding section, (only) insofar as they result from such bottlenecks, are less the greater the excess inventory costs.

60. This argument becomes yet more cogent in the case of exchange control regimes that prevent legal resale of imports.

61. Cf. Krueger, *Turkey*, op.cit., Chapters V and VIII; and Bhagwati and Desai, op.cit., Chapters 15 and 16.

62. Among several contributions, see A.K. Sen, "Working Capital in the Indian Economy," in P.N. Rosenstein-Rodan, ed., *Pricing and Fiscal Policies* (London: George Allen & Unwin, 1966).

63. *Turkey*, ibid., pp. 228-229.

64. *Ghana*, op.cit., pp. 106-107.

65. Ibid., p. 107.

66. Cf. Z. Griliches and V. Ringstaad, *Economies of Scale and the Form of the Production Function* (Amsterdam: North-Holland, 1971), for such estimates using Norwegian data; Padma Desai, "Technical Change, Factor Elasticity of Substitution and Returns to Scale in Branches of Soviet Industry in the Postwar Period," paper presented to the Reisenberg Symposium, *On the Measurement of Factor Productivities: Theoretical Problems and Empirical Results*, (June 23-27, 1974, Munich), published in the series: *Mathematical Studies in the Social and Behavioral Science*, F.L. Altmann, O. Kyn, and H. Wagener, eds. (Gottingen-Zurich: Vandenhoeck and Ruprecht, 1976), for Soviet Union; and D.F. Burgess, "Production Theory and the Derived Demand for Imports," *Journal of International Economics* (May 1974), for Canada.

67. *Ghana*, op.cit., pp. 97-105. The estimation uses value data rather than deflated data owing to lack of information on quantities; and for a fourth industry (radio/TV), the Cobb-Douglas form is merely assumed rather than estimated, the exponentials being estimated from the shares.

68. Leith is therefore assuming that a liberalized regime would have been characterized by an import parity equivalent to that obtained by looking at the import EER (*inclusive* of the import premium). This however would be an overstatement if, as argued in the text, foreign exchange earnings would improve under a liberalized regime, *ceteris paribus*.

69. Leith also adds in the cheapening of capital that follows from low real interest rates.

70. See, in particular, Tables IV-9 and IV-10 in *Ghana*, ibid. The methodology underlying the calculations is also spelled out more fully in Appendix D in that volume.

71. *Turkey*, op.cit., pp. 236-238.

72. Ibid., p. 237.

73. Cf. *Chile*, op.cit., Chapter 6.

74. S.R. Bose and H.H. Clark, "Some Basic Considerations in Agricultural Mechanization in West Pakistan," *Pakistan Development Review* (Autumn 1969); cited in Nurul Islam, *Pakistan*, unpublished manuscript (NBER).

75. *Pakistan*, op.cit., Chapter II on "Choice of Techniques, Capital Utilization, Scale and Productivity." Footnotes have been omitted from the quotes.

76. The work of Arnold Harberger, "Monopoly and Resource Allocation," *American Economic Review Proceedings*, 44 (May 1954):77-87, has contributed to the notion that such welfare losses are generally small. However, doubt has been effectively raised on this issue by A. Bergson, "On Monopoly Welfare Losses," *American Economic Review* 63 (December 1973):853-870.

77. Cf. *Egypt*, Chapter 9.

78. *India*, op.cit., pp. 41-42.

79. *Chile*, op.cit., Chapter 4, pp. 14-16.

80. *Egypt,* op.cit., Chapter 5. Earlier, we discussed the *separate* point that delays characterized the *access* to (given) spares.

81. Cf. Michael Kidron, *Foreign Investments in India* (London: Oxford University Press, 1965).

Chapter 6

Saving: Domestic and Foreign

We now address ourselves to a somewhat more difficult set of questions, relating exchange control regimes to saving formation. The analysis is complex, partly because we must distinguish between domestic and foreign saving, and hence we must examine not merely how the trade regime may influence each of these two types of saving but also how they interact with each other (as indeed they do, as we shall see below). But the complexity also follows, and mainly, from the numerous possible linkages between the foreign trade regime and domestic saving formation. In the analysis that follows, we will initially discuss these linkages between trade regimes and domestic saving (Section I-III) and then between those regimes and foreign saving (Section IV).

The analysis of possibilities and of the empirical evidence in regard thereto does not lead to strong *generalizations* in support of either Phase II type, retrictionist exchange control regimes, or, for that matter, of Phase IV type, liberalized regimes.[1] It does however undermine the occasional claim that restrictionist exchange control regimes, while creating static inefficiencies (as discussed in Chapter 5), are "dynamically" efficient *via* their beneficial effects on capital formation. Such a *generalization* is just not supportable, in theory owing to a multiplicity of possible linkages between the trade regime and saving and in practice owing to conflicting empirical evidence on these linkages.

As recommended at the outset of the volume, therefore, the present chapter is best read for its value as a manual (i.e., as a reference for ideas, hypotheses, statistical evidence, and techniques for economists planning to analyze the interaction of trade policies and saving formation for *their* country), rather than as a source of strong cross-country or time-series generalizations on how restrictionist or liberalized trade regimes would affect saving formation.

I. POSSIBLE LINKS BETWEEN DOMESTIC SAVING AND FOREIGN TRADE REGIMES

We begin with a purely theoretical analysis of possible linkages between the foreign trade regime and domestic saving. It should be noted at the outset that the linkages that we will discuss in terms of alternative "model" types relate to the exchange control mechanism essentially in two ways. (1) We may argue that Phase II type exchange control regimes imply, for example, the relative expansion (or contraction) of sectors, regions, functional incomes, and hence (owing to differential saving propensities) smaller or larger savings. These and similar other arguments focus essentially on the fact that Phase II regimes are characterized by overvalued exchange rates. (2) On the other hand, we can also produce arguments that relate to differences *within* Phase II regimes. For example, the tax revenue, and hence overall saving, effects of the Phase II regime could differ depending on whether tariffs are in operation to mop up (partly or overwhelmingly) the import premiums in the Phase II situation. The former set of arguments embraces many more possible linkages and is also probably the most significant. Hence the main focus here will be put on those arguments, though our (taxonomic) analysis will naturally extend to both sets of arguments. Note however that we will *not* be discussing whether the saving so resulting from any specific trade regime, whether larger or smaller than in alternative trade regimes, is socially *optimal*; this issue is deferred until later.

A. Income Distribution and Saving

The link of saving in an economy to its foreign trade regime, *via* the income distribution associated with that regime, has been well recognized as a possibility in trade-theoretic literature. This argument was noted many years ago and has been resuscitated by a number of trade theorists in recent years.[2] In principle, there are a number of models that could be constructed to analyze such saving linkages with specific foreign trade regimes. We discuss here a few of them to suggest the kinds of arguments that may be relevant to examine in empirical analysis.

1. Saving and Functional Income Distribution.

One approach is to assume with the Cambridge (U.K.) school that there are specific and significant differences between the "wage earners" and the "capitalists" in their saving propensities. As the trade regime alters the distribution of income between these two classes of income earners, it correspondingly alters total saving and hence the rate of saving (the latter depending also on the effect of the trade regime on the income level).[3]

The neatest model along these line has been developed by Pattanaik.[4] He works with two commodities (1 and 2) and two factors (L and K) in a small economy (with given international prices). Commodity 2 is the importable and commodity 1 the exportable; one of them must be a capital good and the other a consumer good. The symbol z represents the K/L ratio, with the subscripts 1 and 2 denoting the commodity and the superscripts A and F representing autarky and free trade, respectively. The policy shift from autarky to free trade—which is welfare improving for this small country—is analyzed. The average propensity to save from labor income (i.e., $L \cdot w$ where w is the price/wage of labor in terms of commodity 2) is s_w, and from capital income (i.e., $K \cdot r$ where r is the price/rental of capital in terms of commodity 2) is s_r; and, *a la* Cambridge school, it is assumed that $s_w < s_r$. S and Y are total savings and income, measured in units of commodity 2. The model is then essentially of the Heckscher-Ohlin variety except for the introduction of the two saving function; the new wrinkle essentially is that one is deploying a certain type of demand function (as the total savings generated represent demand for the capital good).

Assume now that commodity 1 (the exportable) is labor intensive ($z_1 < z_2$). A shift from autarky to free trade in raising the (relative) price of the exportable then lowers national income measured in terms of *exportables* (given the concavity of the production possibility curve to the origin). Thanks to the Stolper-Samuelson theorem, it also raises the share of labor in income and lowers the share of capital; and, given $s_w < s_r$, this implies that the *average* (weighted) propensity to save must also fall. Hence *total* saving in terms of exportables will necessarily fall. But, since Y (measured in terms of *importables*) rises with the rise in the price of the exportable with free trade, one cannot conclude that saving measured in importables (S) will also fall.

Pattanaik, however, establishes the necessary and sufficient conditions for s to fall by showing that:

$$s^F - s^A < 0$$

that is, saving under free trade will be less than under autarky, that is

$$\left\{ s_w \cdot L(w^F - w^A) + s_r \cdot K(r^F - r^A) \right\} < 0 \text{ if } \frac{s_w}{z \cdot s_1} < \frac{r^A - r^F}{w^F - w^A}$$

In conjunction with his derivation:

$$\left\{ \frac{1}{z_2^A} \geqslant \frac{r^A - r^F}{w^F - w^A} \geqslant \frac{1}{z_2^F} \right\}$$

it is then easy to see that a change in the trade regime from autarky to free trade will reduce s (i.e., saving measured in terms of importables) if $z/z_2^F > s_w/s_r$ and only if $z/z_2^A > s_w/s_r$. [Since $z_2^F > z_2^A$ (i.e., the capital-labor ratio in the capital-intensive commodity 2 must rise under free trade, which reduces the relative commodity price of 2), it follows that $z/z_2^F > s_w/s_r$ implies $z/z_2^A > s_w/s_r$.] Since savings will necessasrily fall, measured in terms of exportables, it is clear that when $z/z_2^F > s_w/s_r$—a condition that would be necessarily satisfied if $s_w = 0$ or negligible—we would have an unambiguous decline in total saving with a change in the trade regime from autarky to free trade.

This Heckscher-Ohlin-Pattanaik type of model thus makes saving very clearly a function of the functional distribution of income that results from the resource allocation associated with a specific trade policy. This model is directly relevant to the analysis of exchange control regimes as well, since a Phase II type restrictionist exchange control regime can be identified in such a model with a "real" situation where there is a tariff.[5] This is because under such a regime exports are domestically priced at the exchange parity and imports at the parity plus the import premium. When the Phase II type exchange control regime is also characterized by some export subsidies, this argument must be modified but is not reversed as long as we plausibly assume that the average rate of export subsidization is below the average import premium. Moreover, if tariffs or exchange auctions are introduced to mop up the import premium, we merely substitute the average tariff or auction premium for the import premium in the argument above. The only difference, with subsidies and tariffs being introduced, is that revenue effects would have to be considered. Thus, if revenue is gathered in lieu of import premiums, public saving could rise and may exceed the private saving that may have resulted from the "rents" earned on import licenses. On the other hand, a profligate government and accumulating rentiers could continue to make the net effect adverse to the overall savings rate (more on this later).

It is sufficient to note that the model—which deliberately ignores revenue effects—does suggest the possibility that overall saving may fall unambiguously if an overvalued exchange rate is replaced by a unified exchange rate in a developing economy that exports labor-intensive goods, where the saving is exclusively a function of market-determined wages and profits and where the propensity to save out of profits exceeds the propensity to save out of wages.

On the other hand, possibly the only statistical estimation of saving functions along functional-income-distributional lines in the project by Behrman for Chile (reported in Table 6-3 below) suggests that "shifts from nonwage to wage income and from the rest of the economy to agriculture would both increase savings."[6] Behrman notes that this result, which is anti-Kaldorian in inverting the relative rankings of labor and non-labor saving propensities, may be due to the inclusion in labor income of income from self-employed proprietors.[7]

2. Saving and Sectoral Income Distribution

There are also a number of hypotheses that could be advanced about the link between, *not* functional distribution, but the sectoral composition of value-added and the overall saving in the economy assuming, of course, that the sectoral propensities to save are reasonably stable and it is meaningful to define, for predictive analysis, the overall saving propensity as a weighted sum of the sectoral saving propensities. In the literature on trade and saving, it is possible to detect, though not always in the formalized models of economic theorists, the following four varieties of such sector-specific arguments:[8]

a. The Export Sector vs. the Rest. Maizels, in particular, and several other economists following him,[9] have argued that the relative growth of the export sector in the economy is conducive to greater saving. It is best to quote Maizels on this, as the writers that follow him have usually fitted regressions linking saving to exports with a nod in the direction of Maizels for the underlying rationale of their procedure:[10]

> . . . variations in exports might well result in associated variations in domestic savings. This could occur either because the propensity to save is higher in the export sector than elsewhere or because government savings rely heavily on taxes on foreign trade. In Malaya, for example, the ratio of savings to income of the tin and rubber companies is no doubt considerably higher than that of companies producing for the home market (and certainly much higher than for peasants), while in 1963 Customs duties were estimated to bring in over 40 per cent of total tax revenue. It seems probable that in countries like Malaya a close relationship exists between changes in exports (and thus in the net income of the export sector) and changes in gross domestic savings.

The relationship of export growth to overall saving is then based on two underlying functions. One relates exports to taxation and thence to public saving and the other links exports to higher corporate saving via the higher propensity to save of the corporations in the export sector. These links will be well to remember when we examine the evidence that is produced in support this export-sector linkage to saving.

In turn, however, this linkage ties trade regimes to saving performance, of course. Let us take again the two-sector (exportables and importables) model of traditional trade theory. An overvalued exchange rate then implies a relative overexpansion of the importable sector and underexpansion of the exportable sector. Consider, however, the theory of overvaluation in terms of the familiar Salter-Pearce model of two traded goods and one non-traded good.[11] The analysis of this model is rather complex when overvaluation is considered as distinct from the traditional question of whether a devaluation will improve or worsen the trade balance. However, it is known from the standard trade-theoretic analysis of this model that, under certain plausible assumptions, we *could* deduce that overvaluation would adversely affect the production of the exportable sector (even though the relative expansion of the importable sector does not follow with the same degree of plausibility in the [three-good] Salter-Pearce model as in the traditional [two-tradeable-goods] Heckscher-Ohlin model). In fact, as the *empirical* analysis of Chapter 7 strongly indicates, overvalued exchange rate regimes in Phase II *are* generally associated with relatively poor export performance (and hence presumably with relative underexpansion of exportable production).

It then follows that, insofar as overvaluation does lead to such relative underexpansion of the exportable sector, the Maizels hypothesis would imply that overvaluation *adversely* affects the saving generated in the economy (except insofar as we can assert that the changed composition of investment and output leads to an overall increase in national income to offset the falling, weighted, propensity to save in the economy) for, part of the Maizels argument relates to the size of the exportable sector.

However, the other part of Maizels's argument depends on exports increasing, as distinct from the exportable sector expanding: increased exports are supposed to lead to increased tax revenue and hence increased public saving. It is also seen from Chapter 7 that, under fairly plausible assumptions, the volume of exports (and hence also value, if international prices are given) will also fall with overvaluation: so that this second element in Maizels' overall hypothesis would also be sustained, and overvaluation would lead to reduced saving, *ceteris paribus*

b. The Corporate Sector vs. the Rest. A quite unrelated argument on saving arises from the observation that the major contribution, certainly at the margin, to overall domestic saving may come from the corporate sector. It may both have a larger propensity to save *and* be more readily taxable and at higher rates than other sectors. If therefore overvaluation leads to the relative expansion of those production sectors that have a larger incidence of the corporate sector within them, the net result could be to increase corporate, and hence total, saving.

While this argument is, in principle, of interest, note that it is not necessarily linked to any one of the production sectors. Thus it is perfectly possible in a developing country of the Salter-Pearce variety (with exportables, importables, and non-traded goods) that the incidence of the corporate sector is highest in the importable sector because non-traded goods are services and the exportables are agricultural goods produced in the traditional organizational molds, *or* highest in the exportable sector because it is characterized by plantations that are virtually corporations (as in Maizels' Malayan example) whereas the importable sector has smaller sized concerns and the non-traded sector consists of services. Thus, even if one assumes that the non-traded sector has the least incidence of the corporate form of organization, an overvalued exchange rate, as under the Phase II type of exchange control regime, which (under suitable restrictions) leads to a relative expansion of the importable and reduction of the exportable sector, may be associated with a change in either direction in the average propensity to save and in the tax revenue gathered.

c. The Urban Sector vs. the Rural Sector. Yet another link between the foreign trade regime and the saving performance of the economy may be asserted in the form of the impact of the regime on the relative sizes of the urban and the rural sectors. Two aspects of this link need to be discussed: (a) the relationship between the relative size of the two sectors and the overall propensity to save; and (b) the relationship between the foreign trade regime and the relative size of the urban and rural sectors.

Regarding the former, there is some evidence for India (to be shortly discussed), for example, that the urban sector may be a better saver than the rural sector. This comes about not merely because of the presence of the corporate sector in greater degree in the urban sector (which reduces the argument to that just discussed in the preceding subsection) but also because urban households may have a higher average propensity to save than the rural households. It also occurs because the tax net of the government on urban incomes may be more effective and/or feasible than the tax net on rural incomes. These parameters are also related to the degree of inequality of (earned and unearned) incomes. These are not identical between urban and rural sectors and greater inequality would, *ceteris paribus*, be associated with higher propensity to save on the average within a sector if the poor tend to dissave and the rich to save much.

With regard to the impact of the trade regime on the relative size of the rural and urban sectors, this in turn can be related to the expansion and contraction of the production sectors (i.e., exportables, importables, and non-traded goods), *if* each of the latter tends to be predominantly located within the rural or the urban sector. Thus the underexpansion of exports, brought about by overvaluation, could well imply for a specific developing country (e.g., undivided Pakistan) the underexpansion of the rural sector and a decline in its relative share within total national income.

Given these arguments, it would appear that overvaluation could lead to more saving by relatively expanding the importable sector and inhibiting the growth of the exportable sector, thus increasing incomes in the urban and depressing them in the rural sector if the average propensity to save and the taxability in the urban sector were higher than in the rural sector.

d. Regional Income Distribution. Finally, we may note the argument that the foreign trade regime may increase saving by expanding production sectors and incomes[12] in high-saving (geographic) regions. This asymmetry in saving propensities between regions may come from the differences in income inequality among them, or from income differentials between them (such that, for example, the more affluent region has a higher propensity to save).[13] This argument is clearly akin to, though different from, the rural-versus-urban type of argument that we have just discussed.

B. Tax Revenues and Saving

Our analysis so far has *not* ignored the effects of trade regimes on saving *via* their effects on tax revenues. However, the only effects systematically considered have been those associated with the relative expansion and contraction of sectors of production. Hence we have really been contrasting (restrictionist) Phase II with (liberal) Phase IV regimes. For the same type of comparison, we should now also note that an overvalued rate (vis-à-vis a unified exchange rate) implies, when there is a trade deficit reflecting absorption of foreign capital as in a typical developing country, that the government is losing net "revenue". This is merely the other side of the proposition, now well understood, that a devaluation from a position of trade deficit has a built-in deflationary impact.[14]

We should also note that, even as *among* Phase II regimes, those that rely less heavily on QRs and relatively more on tariffs will also generate correspondingly more tariff revenue and hence more (overall) revenue (since the loss in revenue from taxing the profits implied by the import premiums should be less than the tariff revenue as long as import premiums were not taxed at a marginal rate of 100 percent). Hence, we should consider the possibility of greater public saving and hence greater overall saving (allowing for offset by reduced private saving) under an exchange control regime with greater reliance on tariffs during Phase II.

The arguments just advanced are generally unfavorable to overvalued exchange rates, and hence to exchange control regimes of the Phase II variety.

We may next consider, however, a different type of revenue argument that might work in favor of QRs. Thus one may argue that the exclusion of items of conspicuous consumption by QRs or prohibitive tariffs could help the tax effort. It is difficult to sustain a broad-based tax effort when conspicuous consumption makes economic inequalities more offensive and taxation of one's (inevitably) modest income more intolerable.[15] However, this argument applies only to conspicuous consumption imports. It is moreover virtually irrelevant when only imports, and not domestic import-substituting production, are moderated or eliminated.

C. Foreign Trade Constraint and Saving

The arguments linking the trade regime to saving that have been developed so far are essentially within the "flow"-analytic framework of the Harrod-Domar type growth models—*ex-ante* saving automatically translates into *ex-post* investment. But it is equally possible to construct "structural" models where the ability to raise saving *ex-post* depends critically on the capacity to transform *ex-ante* saving into investment.

The latter is the case with the well-known Mahalanobis-Feldman models. Here, there are two sectors: capital goods and consumer goods, and a closed economy. The division of the output of capital goods into two classes of capital goods, those producing capital goods and the others producing consumer goods, fixes the productive capacity for the *next* period in the two sectors. This capacity is not transferable, once installed, between the two sectors. It is then easy to see that if one wishes to raise the rate of saving (the ratio of capital goods output to total output) in the future, one must accordingly plan for the investment allocation between capital goods and consumer goods *now*. Alternatively, such allocation now will freeze the feasible rates of saving in the future. Thus, take the customary formulation of the Mahalanobis model.[16] Divide current investment flow I_t into two parts, $\lambda_k I_t$ and $\lambda_c I_t$ where λ_k is the proportion going to the capital goods sector and λ_t to the consumer goods sector. Then:

$$I_t - I_{t-1} = \lambda_k \beta_k I_{t-1}$$

and

$$C_t - C_{t-1} = \lambda_c \beta_c I_{t-1}$$

where β_k and β_c are the output-capital ratios in the capital and consumer goods sectors, respectively, and I and C represent investment and consumption goods outputs, respectively. From the first equation, we can write:

$$I_t = I_0 (1 + \lambda_k \beta_k)^t$$

and the second equation can be rewritten as:

$$\sum_{r=1}^{t} (C_r - C_{r-1}) = \sum_{r-1}^{t} \lambda_c \beta_c I_{r-1}$$

which can be shown to lead to:

$$\sum_{r=1}^{t} (C_r - C_{r-1}) = \frac{\beta_c \lambda_c}{\beta_k \lambda_k} I_0 \left[(1 + \lambda_k \beta_k)^t - 1\right]$$

Since $(I_t - I_0) = I_0 \left[\left\{1 + \lambda_k \beta_k \right\}^t - 1 \right]$, we get by adding it to $(C_t - C_0)$ from the preceding equation, the complete solution for output at time t:

$$Y_t = Y_0 \left[1 + \frac{I_0}{Y_0} \left(\frac{\beta_c \lambda_c + \beta_k \lambda_k}{\beta_k \lambda_k} \right) \cdot \left\{ (1 + \lambda_k \beta_k)^t - 1 \right\} \right]$$

Now, in this result, $\beta_k \lambda_k / (\beta_c \lambda_c + \beta_k \lambda_k)$ is nothing but the share of incremental investment in incremental output: and, of course, this is also the share of incremental savings in incremental income, the marginal saving ratio. Thus the saving ratios, marginal and average,[17] are functions of λ_k, β_k, and β_c. The *ex-ante* behavior of saving units such as households plays no role in determining the savings that emerge in the economy. Just as the Harrod-Domar model, concentrating on the latter, totally ignores the structural factors, the Mahalanobis model does the exact opposite.

Basically the same idea of a "structural" constraint on the ability to raise savings underlies the numerous "two-gap," open-economy models of the type used intensively by Hollis Chenery and his associates. The simplest way to understand the two-gap models is to take the stylized picture of an economy that produces only corn (the consumer good) with tractors (the capital good) that are wholly imported with corn that is saved and exported for this purpose. Assume that, in this economy, the government decides to increase capital formation. The finance minister will raise taxes and create the additional savings in the form of corn (not consumed). But this incremental saving must be transformed into tractors through foreign trade. If this is a small country in Samuelson's sense—that is, the terms of trade are given to it—then the saved corn can be turned into tractors. The "savings constraint," that is, the ability of the finance minister to get the economy to save corn, is the only constraint then on raising savings and investment. But assume instead that the country faces unitary elasticity of demand for corn in international markets. In this case, the saved corn buys you no more tractors. There is now a "foreign exchange" constraint on raising savings and investment for the finance minister can raise savings through fiscal policy, only to have them dissipated (in terms of trade loss in this instance).[18]

The two-gap models essentially build variations on this theme. Later, when we discuss the interaction between foreign aid and domestic savings, we will have occasion to state and analyze the resulting economic issues at greater length. Presently, however, it is enough to note that, *if* foreign transformation presents a constraint on raising savings *ex post*, then clearly an improvement in export performance would help to increase savings and an overvalued exchange rate, in inhibiting exports, would reduce them.[19]

Yet another argument of a "structural" variety must be noted here. It carries the Mahalanobis-type argument to its extreme in arguing that, even if the finance minister is unwilling to raise savings through fiscal policy and if the investment allocation is designed so as to raise the ratio of investment to consumer goods in the system, there would be no choice except to have a higher savings ratio: "you cannot eat steel, so more steel production must imply more investment/saving." A trade regime that promotes or permits greater production of steel must therefore be more productive of saving. This argument however is surely simplistic. In practice, the resulting excess demand for consumer goods, unless fiscal policy is also geared to raising saving to match the higher ratio of investment goods to total production, would surely spill over into the balance of payments, steel would pile up for lack of demand, and so on. It is more sensible to think of the Mahalanobis model as rather providing a rationale for planning investment allocations so as to *permit* the transformation of *ex-ante* saving into *ex-post* investment.

The simplistic version of the Mahalanobis-type argument above has its counterpart also in the earlier argument, familiar from the standard discussion of import restrictions, that the elimination of consumer goods imports would lead to "forced saving" as incomes cannot be spent on these goods. Since, as we have seen, nearly all the developing countries have drastically reduced consumer goods imports, can we infer that this must have led to higher saving? Clearly the argument is fallacious except in a short-run framework. Once we permit domestic adjustment in expenditure patterns and in the production of import substitutes to occur, the argument loses substance.

D. Money, Trade Regimes, and Saving

The final set of arguments that we may consider in relating trade regimes to saving center round the effects of monetary phenomena associated with the trade regimes. We cite and analyze here the most influential argument in this area.

Thus, assume that the willingness to use QRs to suppress the balance of payments deficit that would accompany internal inflation leads to an "ill-disciplined" government that then can inflate more than would be the case if the fixed rate of exchange were maintained without QRs (causing a deficit) or if the exchange rate were adjusted downward (causing the political difficulties associated with devaluations). If then the system of overvalued exchange rates permits greater inflation, what can we infer about saving performance from this possibility?

If we assume, as in recent discussions initiated by Edward Shaw and Ronald McKinnon,[20] that there is a tendency for the money interest rates to be sticky in developing countries, the greater the inflation, the lower the real interest rate. If then the saving performance is positively associated with real interest rates, the net effect of the overvalued exchange rate system would be to lower the saving performance of the economy.

The argument, as presented above, already suggests some doubts. Should we necessarily assume that money rates of interest would remain sticky at levels invariant to the rate of inflation? Moreover, the argument about lower real interest rates leading to lower saving applies, at best, to non-governmental saving, and ignores the real possibility that governmental saving may be inversely related to non-governmental saving (as it represents a policy variable, and tax revenues and public saving therefrom may be raised precisely to offset lower private saving). Besides, it is not at all clear that inflation is not accompanied by income distribution in favor of the richer, higher propensity to save classes at the expense of the less-saving poor classes, so that the weighted propensity to save may rise even if each component propensity to save falls thanks to the real-interest-fall effect. It is also not evident that those whose real incomes are adversely affected by the inflation do not wind up saving more because they are Champernowne men: whose objective is to provide for a certain target level of saving.[21]

II. EMPIRICAL EVIDENCE ON LINKS BETWEEN DOMESTIC SAVING AND FOREIGN TRADE REGIMES

We now review the evidence in support or refutation of these alternative, possible links between saving and foreign trade regimes, drawing upon both the evidence in the country studies in the Project and, where relevant, on the evidence from other analyses.

A. Income Distribution

1. Functional Income Distribution.

As before, we begin with functional income distribution. There is no systematic evidence on this in any of the country studies. However, some support for the view that the savings out of wage and non-wage income are systematically different is available from cross-sectional analysis across countries as also from time-series analysis. Thus, Houthakker[22] has analyzed twenty-eight countries (including DCs) and estimated the following linear regressions:

$$S_{pers} = \underset{(2.35)}{-1.09} + \underset{(0.011)}{0.081}\, Y_{pd} \tag{6.1}$$

$$S_{pers} = \underset{(0.011)}{0.080}\, Y_{pd} \tag{6.2}$$

where S_{pers} is personal saving *per capita* per year and Y_{pd} is *per capita* disposable income per year in U.S. dollars at 1955 prices and official exchange rates.[23] The intercept in Equation 6.1 is smaller than its standard error; hence Equation 6.2 is estimated and yields a marginal propensity to save of 0.08.

However, when Houthakker distinguished between *per capita* income from employment and transfers (L) and other personal income (P), he obtained the following equation:

$$S_{pers} = \underset{(0.022)}{0.043}\, L + \underset{(0.041)}{0.120}\, P \tag{6.3}$$

and it is clear that the marginal propensity to save from wage (and transfer) income is about a third of that from non-wage income.

Houthakker's result on this differential propensity to save out of wage and non-wage income has been reinforced by Williamson's later analysis of Asian LDCs (including Japan).[24] He distinguishes between wage and salary income, and non-labor income, and separates out transfers. Writing

$S_{i,t}$ = Personal saving in nation i at time t
$Y^{P}_{i,t}$ = Personal income
$Y^{w}_{i,t}$ = Wage and salary income
$Y^{e}_{i,t}$ = Non-labor income (including property and entrepreneurial income)
$Y^{T}_{i,t}$ = Direct taxes on households *minus* net transfers to them
$Y^{d}_{i,t}$ = Disposable income

he then postulates a linear savings function of the type:

$$S_{i,t} = \alpha + \beta Y^w_{i,t} + \gamma Y^e_{i,t} + Y^T_{i,t} \tag{6.4}$$

He then distinguishes between a "short-period" and a "long-period" formulation of the estimating equation by expressing all variables as deviations from their means ($t = 0$ representing means over a given national time series), to write:

$$(S_{i,t} - S_{i,0}) = \beta(Y^w_{i,t} - Y^w_{i,0}) + \gamma(Y^e_{i,t} - Y^e_{i,0}) + \lambda(Y^T_{i,t} - Y^T_{i,0}) \tag{6.5}$$

for the short-period saving function and, treating the country observations as deviations from the Asian average taken as a group (such that $i = 0$, $t = 0$ represents a mean for the whole Asian sample):

$$(S_{i,0} - S_{0,0}) = \beta(Y^w_{i,0} - Y^w_{0,0}) + \gamma(Y^e_{i,0} - Y^e_{0,0}) + \lambda(Y^T_{i,0} - Y^T_{0,0}) \tag{6.6}$$

for the long-term saving function.

Williamson finds extremely good fits for these equations, using the Asian data. "The parameters of the long-run saving function are less than those of the short-run savings function. Furthermore, the coefficient attached to non-labour income in all tests far exceeds that of labour income. . . ."[25] In fact, the former lies between 0.25 and 1.47 whereas the latter ranges between zero and 0.10.

While, however, the functional shares hypothesis is useful and important in explaining personal savings behavior, the question as to whether a country's trade regime will significantly influence it in any one direction, and if so in which direction, is a separate question. The evidence on the latter issue is not compelling in the country studies in the Project.

Thus, it appears more likely that the impact was probably on the distribution between different labor groups, as distinct from the impact on profits versus wages. As Krueger has argued for Turkey:[26]

> . . . the import-substitution industries generally paid higher wages, required skilled workers, and offered fewer employment opportunities than did the traditional and export-oriented industries. Minimum wage legislation also contributed, since the import-substitution firms, being large and visible, could evade it less easily than the smaller, relatively labor-intensive traditional firms.

The consequent increase in demand for skilled workers undoubtedly raised the wages of those men relative to those of the unskilled. The fact that demand for unskilled labor rose more slowly than under an alternative trade regime probably meant fewer employment opportunities, rather than lower wages, in the presence of minimum wage legislation.

The incidence of fewer employment opportunities for unskilled workers was on the urban unemployed and those in rural areas who would have migrated if employment had been available. Insofar as there would have been more migration, per capita incomes in the agricultural sector might have been higher had urban employment increased more rapidly. Regardless of whether it was the urban unemployed or potential migrants who were adversely affected, the income-distributional effect was to increase the labor income accruing to one group and reduce the labor income going to another. Without quantitative evidence to estimate the magnitude of the increase in skilled workers' incomes and the elasticity of demand for unskilled workers, it is not possible to estimate whether labor income increased or decreased. With the two changes in offsetting directions, however, it is likely that any change in aggregate labor income was relatively small.

On the other hand, for Philippines, it seems that the devaluation and decontrol, characterizing a shift from Phase II to Phase III, may well have resulted in a rise in the saving ratio, thanks to income distributional change in favor of profits and against wages. Thus, Williamson[27] has argued that this led to an upward shift in the saving function after 1960, income having been redistributed from the urban wage earners, in Manila, to entrepreneurs and property owners in the export sector. Note that this evidence goes *against* the proponents of exchange control regimes who contend that they must lead to *greater* savings.

Interestingly, in the Chilean case, Behrman's short-run general equilibrium simulation runs indicate that devaluation would have a negative impact on labor's share in national income while increasing the share of agriculture, the latter helping and the former *reducing* (in an anti-Kaldor fashion) saving formation.[28]

Finally, we may recall here the classic study of devaluation by Díaz Alejandro for the Argentine economy, which explicitly built into the formal and empirical analysis of the 1958 devaluation of the Argentine peso the redistributive effect thereof in favor of the rural producer-exporters who had a higher marginal propensity to save than the wage earners.[29]

2. Sectoral Income Distribution.

The more substantial evidence however relates to the sectoral distribution and there, in turn, to the possible relationship between exports and savings.

a. Exports and Saving. As we shall see, however, the cross-country regressions support the hypothesis of exports leading to saving while the evidence in the countries in the Project, which probes below the apparent relationship to test the underlying rationale, is not so conclusive and seems to suggest caution until further research along these lines has been undertaken.

The work of Maizels, as we noted, was the pioneering one in this area. His regression results, which embrace only eleven countries, are reproduced in Table 6-1. It is seen that the coefficient (b') of exports is positive in nearly all cases. If we (heuristically) add together ($b' - c$), where c is the coefficient on GDP minus exports, as the "net" export coefficient—we would have to re-estimate its significance, of course—the coefficient declines to extremely low levels, however, for Rhodesia/Nyasaland as a whole, Jamaica and Iceland, and is almost halved for South Africa.

The Weisskopf results are based on a time-series analysis of seventeen countries, all LDCs, and (as with Maizels's data) relate to total (as distinct from per capita) savings and real variables.[30] These results, based on a regression that "explains" savings as a (linear) function of income, capital inflow (defined as imports *minus* exports), and exports, turn up generally negative coefficients on capital inflow and positive on exports, so that if we subtract the coefficient on capital inflow from that on exports, we get a "net" export coefficient that is even more pronounced than the "gross" coefficient in Weisskopf's results.

The analysis by Papanek, embracing only LDC observation in 1950s and 1960s, confirms the high correlation between exports and savings. However, he uses *per capita*, real variables, and also distinguishes between primary and other exports. He gets positive, statistically significant coefficients for both types of exports in this cross-section analysis.[31]

The evidence on this issue in the country studies in the Project however is not so clear-cut. In particular, for the India study, the authors specifically tested one underlying hypothesis that is held to account (as we noted in Section I) partly for the relationship between exports and savings, namely, that the corporation savings propensity in the export sector exceeds that in other sectors. Noting that the corporate savings is not an important saver in the Indian economy, the authors tested to see whether the industries favored by the import-substitution policies were relatively better savers.[32]

A number of alternative relationships between retained earnings (RE) and profits after taxes (PAT) for public limited companies were estimated, of which the following were reported on:

$$RE = \alpha + \beta(PAT) + u \qquad (6.7a)$$

$$\frac{RE}{N} = \alpha + \frac{\beta}{N} + \gamma\left(\frac{PAT}{N}\right) + u \qquad (N \text{ is net worth}) \qquad (6.7b)$$

$$\frac{RE}{N} = \alpha + \frac{\beta}{\sqrt{N}} + \gamma\left(\frac{PAT}{\sqrt{N}}\right) + u \qquad (6.7c)$$

Table 6-1. Summary of Results of Regressions of Gross Domestic Saving on GDP and Exports: Several Countries and Periods

	Period	Coefficient of[a] *Q*	*X*	*Q–X*	R^2
More Developed Countries					
Australia	1950-62	0.28 (0.07)	–	–	0.588
		–	2.85 (0.68)	–0.42 (0.19	0.831
South Africa	1950-60	0.32 (0.02)	–	–	0.974
		–	0.57 (0.36)	0.24 (0.12)	0.966
Iceland	1950-61	0.24 (0.03)	–	–	0.896
			0.26 (0.23)	0.23 (0.08)	0.896
Ireland	1950-62	0.20 (0.05)	–	–	0.625
		–	0.49 (0.13)	0.00 (0.09)	0.756
Less Developed Countries					
Burma	1950-61	0.20 (0.03)	–	–	0.789
		–	0.59 (0.19)	0.12 (0.05)	0.858
India	1950-60	0.32 (0.05)	–	–	0.809
		–	2.23 (0.99)	0.30 (0.05)	0.874
Rhodesia/Nyasaland	1952-62	0.47 (0.02)	–	–	0.982
		–	0.51 (0.08)	0.42 (0.09)	0.983
Malawi	1954-63	–0.27 (0.07)	–	–	0.660
		–	–0.62 (0.25)	–0.13 (0.12)	0.741
Rhodesia	1954-63	0.34 (0.04)	–	–	0.892
		–	0.57 (0.23)	0.21 (0.13)	0.906
Zambia	1954-63	0.57 (0.07)	–	–	0.895
		–	0.75 (0.34)	–0.15 (0.37)	0.932
Jamaica	1953-60	0.15 (0.03)	–	–	0.840
		–	0.24 (0.31)	0.11 (0.12)	0.843
Trinidad and Tobago	1951-61	0.22 (0.03)	–	–	0.888
		–	0.38 (0.05)	–0.05 (0.09)	0.951

[a]Based on regressions of annual data at constant prices. The equations used were:

$$S_t = a + bQ_t \text{ and } S_t = a' + b'X_t + c(Q_t - X_t),$$

where S = gross domestic saving, Q = gross domestic product and X = merchandise exports.
Source: Maizels, op. cit., p. 95.

The relationship in Equation 6.7a is straightforward and needs no explanation. The relationship in Equation 6.7b was suggested by the fact that the Reserve Bank publishes only pooled data relating to the companies operating in different sectors of the economy and *not* individual company data. Since the number of companies in each sector had changed over time, it is possible that some heteroskedasticity may be present in Equation 6.7a. Equation 6.7b, with

$\alpha = 0$, would then correspond to Equation 6.7a with correction for heteroskedasticity if one assumed that the residual variance in Equation 6.7a was proportional to the square of net worth. Similarly, Equation 6.7c, with $\alpha = 0$, would be the correct estimating equation if the residual variance in Equation 6.7a was proportional to net worth. Note, however, that the coefficient α in the equations estimated was *not* specified to be zero so that the *data* could determine whether it indeed was significantly different from zero. Also, a positive (negative) α (in Equations 6.7b or 6.7c) would imply that for any given level of profits after tax, retained earnings would be higher (lower) the larger the net worth. The regression results relating to ten industries, for the years 1950-1958 and 1960-1961 to 1968-1969, are reproduced here in Table 6-2.

The first four industries in Table 6-2 are, by and large, long-established and "traditional" industries. The first two are also major exporters, and none can be considered to have been "helped" by the foreign trade regime. Industries 5 to 10 did certainly "benefit" from such controls, however. Looking at the results obtained by estimating Equation 6.7a, the authors then note that while two out of four traditional industries had marginal propensities to save exceeding 0.50, the corresponding figure was four out of six in the case of the remaining industries. The correction for heteroskedasticity (Equations 6.7b or 6.7c) improves the goodness of fit and Equation 6.7c seems to yield a better fit to a certain extent in almost all cases though in none of the cases is the increase in R^2 very large.

Confining their attention to estimated Equation 6.7c, in Table 6-2, the authors then concluded that, keeping net worth constant, an increase of a unit in profits after taxes would have increased retained earnings by more than 0.75 unit in all cases except jute for which the figure is 0.74. Thus their analysis suggested that all the ten industries considered were good savers regardless of whether they were export oriented or import substituting in structure.

In order to examine rigorously, however, whether the "non-traditional" (mainly import-substituting) industries were (on the average) better or worse savers than traditional industries, they ran a number of statistical tests. These tests were performed as follows. A common marginal propensity to save (i.e., β of Equation 6.7a, γ of Equation 6.7b and Equation 6.7c), was estimated for the two *groups* of industries while allowing the other parameters to vary among industries, using an appropriate (slope) dummy variable technique. It turned out that the coefficient of this dummy variable (i.e., a variable that had the value zero for all the observations relating to traditional industries and the value of PAT [for Equation 6.7a], PAT/N [for Equation 6.7b], and $PAT\sqrt{N}$ for Equation 6.7c] corresponding to each observation relating to non-traditional industries) was negative in each case (i.e., for Equations 6.7a, 6.7b, and 6.7c), suggesting that non-traditional industries on the average had a lower marginal propensity to save (MPS). However, the "t" values of these

Table 6-2. Corporate Saving Regressions in Selected Industries: India

	$RE = \alpha + \beta(PAT)$			$\frac{RE}{N} = \alpha + \frac{\beta}{N} + \gamma(\frac{PAT}{N})$				$\frac{RE}{\sqrt{N}} = \alpha + \frac{\beta}{\sqrt{N}} + \gamma(\frac{PAT}{\sqrt{N}})$			
	α	β	R^2	α	β	γ	R^2	α	β	γ	R^2
1. Cotton Textiles	−707.43 (−7.3)	0.77 (11.4)	0.890	−0.05 (−26.7)	245.64 (7.4)	0.86 (76.2)	0.997	−14.48 (−25.4)	1227.07 (16.4)	0.85 (73.5)	0.987
2. Jute Manufactures	−139.77 (−17.85)	0.73 (33.15)	0.986	−0.01 (−1.03)	−71.27 (−1.09)	0.74 (29.27)	0.986	−2.07 (−1.08)	−2.38 (−0.02)	0.74 (29.74)	0.986
3. Cement	−73.40 (−2.12)	0.48 (7.37)	0.773	−0.06 (−11.32)	7.74 (0.96)	0.90 (17.72)	0.957	−7.13 (−10.83)	225.27 (8.68)	0.86 (18.54)	0.960
4. Electricity Generation & Supply	−57.29 (−3.42)	0.50 (11.83)	0.897	−0.05 (−3.34)	−2.16 (−0.13)	0.91 (6.60)	0.798	−6.06 (−5.30)	183.73 (4.08)	0.94 (10.56)	0.938
5. Aluminium	−16.83 (−1.64)	0.59 (18.40)	0.955	−0.05 (−4.47)	21.21 (2.75)	0.80 (9.75)	0.924	−4.77 (−7.68)	84.40 (6.73)	0.96 (18.40)	0.984
6. Iron and Steel	−103.73 (−0.99)	0.63 (6.68)	0.736	−0.04 (−6.83)	−73.50 (−2.43)	0.98 (17.56)	0.964	−6.88 (−6.25)	238.31 (3.75)	0.94 (13.85)	0.929
7. Transport Equipment	−21.93 (−0.84)	0.48 (13.25)	0.917	−0.04 (−5.45)	31.88 (5.36)	0.79 (12.25)	0.939	−4.87 (−5.93)	142.01 (5.78)	0.78 (13.74)	0.969
8. Electrical Equipment	−29.80 (−1.48)	0.57 (15.13)	0.934	−0.02 (−2.14)	3.91 (0.90)	0.67 (8.16)	0.853	−4.95 (−7.82)	103.28 (7.08)	0.89 (18.57)	0.982
9. Other Equipment	−96.41 (−2.45)	0.65 (7.81)	0.793	−0.03 (−2.93)	22.70 (1.10)	0.67 (10.21)	0.874	−4.30 (−5.23)	150.98 (3.77)	0.76 (13.99)	0.929
10. Basic Chemicals	−19.92 (−0.82)	0.44 (10.26)	0.868	−0.05 (−4.46)	21.21 (2.75)	0.80 (9.76)	0.931	−7.21 (−7.93)	196.47 (7.42)	0.93 (14.53)	0.977

Note: Figures in parentheses are t values. Variables are explained in the text.

Source: *India*, op. cit., Chapter 16, Table 16-5, p. 237.

coefficients turned out to be insignificant so that the average MPS of non-traditional industries was not significantly different (at 1 percent level) from that of traditional industries (except in the case of Equation 6.7a).[33]

After comparing the average MPS of the two groups of industries, these authors also examined whether there was any significant difference between the MPS of industries *within* each group. This was done through an analysis of variance test, which compares the increase (after dividing by the appropriate degrees of freedom) in the residual sum of squares brought about by estimating a common slope for the group in relation to the sum of the residual sum of squares of the industries in the group when a separate regression is estimated for each industry. It turned out that the MPS of the non-traditional industries did not differ significantly (in a statistical sense) regardless of the form of the relationship (Equations 6.7a, 6.7b, or 6.7c) estimated. The traditional industries had, however, significantly different (at 1 percent level) MPS except in the case of Equation 6.7a.[34]

They concluded therefore that it was not possible to argue on the basis of the available and analyzed evidence that any systematic differences in the marginal propensity to save could be discerned by different industries, or by traditional as against non-traditional industries. In fact, the only significant differences within any group of industries that were observed belong to the limited group of traditional industries.

A note of skepticism about the relationship between exports and saving, indicating that it may well be spurious, is also suggested by the Turkish study of Anne Krueger. This study does not contain any systematic examination of Turkish saving behavior. But it is interesting that, in her discussion of the income distributional impact of the Turkish exchange control regime, Krueger notes that, on the issue of "export versus import-competing interests," the effects of the trade regime were swamped by *other* policies:[35]

> In an exchange-control regime with currency overvaluation, theory predicts that potential exporters will be adversely affected relative to those whose interests lie in import-competing production. In Turkey, however, the major exporting interests are in agriculture and mining. The effect for agriculture of any redistribution away from exporting interests that might have resulted from currency overvaluation was largely offset by the government's price policies towards agriculture. . . . price intervention by the various state agencies and cooperatives resulted in severing the relations between the real exchange rate and the price received by farmers for wheat, tobacco, figs, raisins and hazelnuts. For those commodities, which constitute the bulk of agricultural exports, the chief determinant of prices was the nature of the price support program, and not the real exchange rate. . . .
>
> The second export sector in which adverse income distributional consequences might have been expected was the mining sector. There can be little doubt that mining activity was stagnant and even declining in response to the ero-

> sion of the real exchange rate. However, in terms of the personal income distribution it is not clear that there would have been any effect: most mining enterprises are state-owned. During the 1950's, Central Bank credits covered most of the SEE [State Economic Enterprises] deficits, with the result that the incidence of the losses was spread over the entire community.

Clearly, in the Turkish case, it would not have been meaningful to link exports directly to saving, for the simple reason that the impact of changed exports on domestic income shares could not have been predicted by merely looking at exports.

We should thus conclude cautiously that, while there *is* much empirical evidence in support of a statistical association between exports and saving, there is little evidence so far for some of the hypotheses that could provide a *rationale* for such an association implying a causal relationship running from exports to saving. At the same time, it is clear that there is evidence of neither kind in support of the opposite contention that an overvalued exchange rate regime (i.e., a Phase II exchange control regime) would provide more saving, so that there is little comfort in the statistical evidence examined so far for those who would seek to excuse the static inefficiencies of a restrictive exchange control regime on the ground that it contributes to growth by increasing domestic saving.

b. Corporate Sector and Saving. Next, we may consider the linkage between domestic saving and foreign trade regimes *via* the relative size of the corporate sector. Quite aside from the fact that the corporate sector is potentially more taxable than other sectors in many LDCs, it is also a sector that probably saves better than other sectors.

While the early, cross-sectional work of Houthakker again suggested that this is the case, evidence of a more persuasive type is available in the Chilean study of Behrman's. Since we will refer to his econometric estimates fairly frequently and as they are fairly rich in variables and hypotheses, we have reproduced here as Table 6-3 his results on the real consumption-saving functions for households and non-profit institutions, business, and the government during 1945-1965.

A principal statistic of direct interest to us in Table 6-3 is that the marginal saving propensity for the business sector is indeed substantially greater than for the household and non-profit institutions sector, though it is below that for the government. Thus, *after adjustment* (for households for permanent income considerations), the point estimates of marginal saving propensities run from 0.04 to 0.38 for households and non-profit institutions, 0.55 to 0.63 for business, and 0.67 to 0.73 for the government. It follows that income shifts within the private sector from households to business and income shifts from the private sector to the government would tend to increase real saving.[36]

Table 6-3. Real Consumption-Saving Functions for Chilean Households and Nonprofit Institutions, Business, and the Government 1945-1965[a]

Dependent Variable		*Per Capita Real Disposable Income*	*Rate of Inflation*		*Per Capita Real Monetary Balances*	*PLD NER for the Black Market*	*Inverse of GDP Deflator*	*Real Foreign Savings*	*Standard Deviation*		*Non Wage Income/ Total Income*	*Agric./ Total GDP*	*Constant*	*R^2 SE DW*
									Rate of Inflation	*PLD EER*				
		Z1[b]	*Z1[b]*	*Z2[b]*	*Z1[b]*									
		(1)	*(2)*	*(3)*	*(4)*	*(5)*	*(6)*	*(7)*	*(8)*	*(9)*	*(10)*	*(11)*	*(12)*	*(13)*
Real per capita Private Consumption	I	−0.623 (6.5) [0.6]	2.24 (6.9) [−0.0]	−0.418 (6.2)		13.6 (2.9) [0.0]	−1.04 (4.9) [−0.0]		3.65 (3.7) [0.0]	−61.9 (1.6)[c] [−0.0]	508.0 (4.0) [0.1]	−2083.0 (4.0) [−0.2]	798.0 (3.8)	0.98 18.5 2.4
	II	−0.674 (5.8) [0.6]	2.32 (5.4) [−0.0]	−0.439 (4.8)	−9128. (2.0) [1.2]		−1.11 (4.6) [−0.0]		4.75 (3.6) [0.0]	−72.0 (1.5)[c] [−0.0]	512.0 (3.5) [0.1]	−1841.0 (3.0) [−0.1]	572.0 (2.0)	0.98 20.9 2.5
	III	−0.961 (24.6) [0.9]	1.94 (4.7) [−0.0]	−0.371 (4.4)		15.0 (2.3) [0.1]		0.837[d] (4.3) [0.0]	2.0 (1.6)[c] [0.0]		790.0 (4.7) [0.1]	−591.0 (1.1)[e] [−0.0]		0.96 26.9 2.4
		Real After Tax Non-Wage Income	*PLD EER*		*Real Monetary Balances*									
			Z1[b]	*Z2[b]*										
Real Business Savings	I	0.633 (13.4) [0.3]	26.0 (5.5) [−0.2]		−0.627 (5.1) [−1.5]		4.55 (4.7) [0.4]						664.0 (2.5)	0.94 89.9 2.1

	II	0.554	108.9	18.9	−0.767		−0.178			650.0	0.91
		(10.9)	(2.4)	(2.1)	(4.4)		(1.6)[c]			(2.0)	110.0
		[0.3]	[−0.2]		[−1.9]		[−0.0]				2.4
		Real Government Revenues					*Real Foreign Savings*				
							Z1[b]	*Z2*[b]	*Z3*[b]		
Real Government Consumption	I	0.331				−0.667				516.0	0.94
		(11.0)				(1.1[e]				(4.9)	94.5
		[0.6]				[−0.0]					1.7
	II	0.275				1.25	0.400	−0.252	0.0372	758.0	0.96
		(7.0)				(1.2)	(1.5)	(1.6)	(1.4)	(4.8)	80.0
		[0.5]				[0.0]	[0.1]				2.2

[a]The absolute value of the t statistics are given in parentheses beneath the point estimates. All point estimates are significantly nonzero at the five percent level unless otherwise noted. Long-run elasticities at the point of sample means are given in brackets beneath the t statistics.

[b]The Hall-Sutch [1969] polynomial method with the tail constrained to zero is used for this variable. Zi (i = 1 or 2) is the order of the polynomial. The implied lag structures are as follows:

			Lags (no. of years)				
			−0	*−1*	*−2*	*−3*	Σ
Real Per Capita Private Consumption	I	Income	0.249	0.187	0.125	0.063	0.623
		Rate of Inflation	−227.0	−44.5	53.9	68.8	−148.0
	II	Income	0.270	0.202	0.135	0.067	0.674
		Rate of Inflation	−225.0	−37.4	62.9	75.4	−125.0
		Monetary Balances	0.3651	0.2738	0.1826	0.093	0.9128
	III	Income	0.385	0.288	0.192	0.096	0.961
		Rate of Inflation	−183.0	−25.7	−57.0	65.6	−85.8

Table 6-3 continued

		Lags				
Real Business Savings: Real Cost of Foreign Exchange Adjusted for Import Taxes	I	−10.4	−7.80	−5.20	−2.60	−26.0
	II	−13.3	−42.9	9.3	23.6	−23.3
Real Government Consumption: Real Net Foreign Savings	III	0.065	0.250	0.153	0.004	0.465

[c]Significantly nonzero at the ten percent level.

[d]Per capita for real household-and-nonprofit-institutional savings estimates.

[e]Significantly nonzero at the 15 percent level.

$\hat{R}^2$ = Coefficient of multiple determination adjusted for degrees of freedom.

SE = Standard error of estimate.

DW = Durbin-Watson statistic.

Source: *Chile*, op. cit., pages 282-284.

For Chile, Behrman also argues that differentials in saving propensities of the different sectors were important because the foreign trade regimes did affect (though not in any clear direction) the distribution of resources among the sectors. He focuses however on the distribution between the private sector as a whole and the government sector. Hence we will revert to his specific arguments later when discussing the tax revenue effects.

The other country in the Project for which the corporate sector is important is South Korea. Frank and others sought to estimate corporate saving (*SC*) as a function of non-agricultural value added (*YNA*), the expected real rate of interest, and the average rate of subsidy on exports. Their results were significant only for the value added and the nominal rate of interest on savings deposits (*RD*):[37]

$$SC = \underset{(-0.16)}{-0.5689} + \underset{(10.51)}{0.0730\, YNA} + \underset{(4.13)}{115.2640\, RD} \qquad (6.8)$$

Regression technique: Ordinary least squares
Sample: 1960 to 1970

$R^2 = 0.9827$
$d = 1.6131$

The household and government saving functions however were successfully estimated with other independent variables: for example, government expenditure was assumed exogenous, and government income explained by tariff revenue functions that distinguished among direct and indirect (trade and domestic) taxes. The three sectors therefore had divergent behavioral relationships for their saving, and hence the effect of alternative foreign trade regimes on overall saving turned out to be a most important ingredient of the general conclusions that emerged from their simulation exercises on alternative trade regimes.[38]

In conclusion, there is little doubt that wherever the corporate sector manages to make a non-negligible contribution to the country's saving formation—and this does not seem to be the case with many of the other countries in the Project, as seen from Table 6-4—we must contend with the possibility of an impact of the foreign trade regime on domestic saving. However, the net direction of this impact, for restrictionist, Phase II type exchange control regimes for example, is not necessarily favorable or unfavorable. We might merely note, however, at a somewhat *a priori* level, that the inefficient pattern of resource allocation *within* the import-substituting sector as also the occasional inducement to excess capacity (and related phenomena documented in Chapter 5) may well result in a reduced growth of the industrial, corporation-

Table 6-4. Estimated Shares of Government, Corporate, and Personal Saving in Total Domestic Saving in Countries in the Project

		Percentage Share in Total Domestic Savings		
Country	*Period*	*Government*	*Corporate*	*(Other) Private*
Brazil	1960	29		71
	1970	8		92
Chile	1960	30		70
	1970	49		51
Colombia	1960	24		76
	1970	31		69
Egypt	1965 1973	Negative		–
Ghana		N.A.		N.A.
India	1960-1961	23	9	68
	1970-1971	18	5	77
Israel	1960	16		84
Philippines	1960	14	19	67
	1970	12	34	54
South Korea	1960	104	27	Negative
	1970	61	11	28
Turkey	1965	29		71

Sources:

1. The Indian estimates are from *National Accounts Statistics, 1960-1961 to 1974-1975,* Central Statistical Organization, Government of India, New Delhi, October 1976; net savings estimates are utilized here.
2. The Philippines and South Korean estimates follow U.N. definitions and come from *The Yearbook of National Accounts Statistics, 1975,* United Nations, New York, 1976.
3. The estimates for Brazil, Chile, Colombia, Egypt, Israel and Turkey come from *World Tables, 1976,* I.B.R.D., Washington, D.C., 1976.

intensive sector below what a liberalized, Phase IV type exchange control regime would lead to. Hence, the result may well have been to make the Phase II regimes of the 1950s and early 1960s marginally harmful to growth of saving and capital formation if, as seems to be the case for countries such as Chile, the marginal propensity to save of the corporation sector is higher than in other private sectors.

c. Urban vs. Rural Sectors. In addition to its corporation intensity relative to the rural sector in nearly all of the countries in the Project, the urban sector may also be a better saver because of a higher propensity to save by urban households. The only evidence in support of this possibility seems to be from the India study.

The authors of the India volume argue that:[39]

> The National Council for Applied Economic Research conducted two household savings surveys, the first in 1960, covering urban households, and the second in 1962, covering rural households. The Council has also conducted another survey in the early 1970s, the results of which are yet to be published. The earlier surveys, however, showed that the marginal propensity to save (MPS), net of rural households, was 0.168 when savings in the form of currency, consumer durables and livestock were included, and 0.145 if these were excluded. The MPS of urban households was higher, at 0.34, coming down to 0.24 if the top and bottom 10 percent of income groups are excluded on assumption that their incomes are affected by transitory factors, influencing excessively the estimated MPS.

The authors note that the urban sector is also a better contributor to the direct tax revenues because agricultural income is hardly taxed in India.[40]

It may be contended that the Phase II type foreign trade regime in India helped the urban sector grow relative to the rural sector by discriminating against the exportable rural sector. But this argument must be put into perspective by noting that many of the agriculture-based exports were in oligopolistic markets, to which the optimum tariff argument may reasonably be applied and that the main discrimination against exports was really *within* the manufacturing, and hence largely urban sector.[41] Moreover, if one associates increasing (relative) urbanization with income expansion in the low-income countries and if (as per our arguments in Chapter 5) the Indian foreign trade regime reduced income expansion from given investments, *ceteris paribus*, the result would be to reduce urbanization and thus militate *against* the growth of saving.

On the other hand, for Pakistan, the evidence on urban and rural saving propensities seems to suggest that the latter is higher than the former in contrast to the Indian estimates. Thus, for 1963-1964, the rural ratio of gross saving to gross personal income was estimated at 12.00 percent for East Pakistan and the urban ratio at 9.9 percent; the corresponding ratios for West Pakistan were 9.2 and 6.7 percent.[42] With calculations of implicit exchange rates for "rural" exports and "urban" (manufacturing) imports then suggesting that the rural sector would have had better terms of trade under a liberalized regime with domestic prices closer to international prices, it has been argued that the result under the Phase II type exchange control regime was to shift income away from the rural to the urban sector and hence actually to *retard* domestic savings and capital formation.[43] The effect of this particular chain of arguments is then again to undermine the position of those who would justify restrictionist exchange control regimes on the ground that they add to domestic saving by turning their argument on its head.

Finally, we may note that, for Chile as well, Behrman's econometric analysis suggests that the rural sector may be a better saver than the urban sector. However his analysis of the relationship between the foreign trade regimes and saving formation does not build exclusively on this particular sectoral difference in saving propensities.[44]

d. Regional Income Distribution. The case of Pakistan again illustrates the regional wrinkle in the argument. With East Pakistan more heavily agricultural, the region lost income to West Pakistan (as just argued). Since East Pakistan had also a higher saving rate, both urban and rural, compared to West Pakistan,[45] it could be argued that this *regional* shift in income distribution, thanks to the Phase II exchange control regime, also adversely affected domestic saving.

B. Tax Revenues and Saving

Before we discuss the evidence on the relationship of the foreign trade regime to domestic saving *via* tax revenues, let us first look at the evidence on the relationship of tax revenues to saving. The latter must clearly relate to both the possibly adverse saving effect on those taxed and the possibly favorable effect on public saving.

There is some cross-sectional evidence in Houthakker's study[46] that governmental saving is positively related to governmental tax revenues, with some indication that there may be a positive intercept, implying that governments with low revenues have higher saving ratios. But clearly the net effect must allow for the possible decline in personal and corporate saving that could result from the tax revenues. Nothing systematic is available on this in Houthakker's own analysis. However, Williamson (who used *direct* taxes as an explanatory variable in his personal saving regressions) generally found an insignificant effect (except for only one regression where the coefficient was large and negative), and if one may contrast (as one really cannot) this result he obtained with Houthakker's coefficient on government tax revenues (at 0.017), it would appear that the latter will approximate the net effect of taxes on savings, thus indicating a net, favorable effect on overall saving from tax revenues.[47]

As elsewhere, the analyses of a time-series variety in the countries in the Project are far more thorough and persuasive on this issue. Thus, for Chile, Behrman's work on estimating saving propensities (which we have already noted) led him to the conclusion that the marginal propensity to save of the Chilean government (during 1945-1965) was higher than that of the private sector and, furthermore, that the restrictive exchange control regimes did influence, though not in any clear direction, the division of resources between the government and the private sector:[48]

> More restrictive regimes have shifted resources to the government in at least two important ways. First, government imports have been given high priority at substantially overvalued EER's. . . . In 1971, for example, the government share of imports increased to 45 percent mainly because government imports were exempted from the 10,000 percent prior import deposit requirement introduced in May of that year. Second, the government netted substantial revenues from its operation of the multiple exchange-rate system because of the large differential. . .between the escudo price it paid to large-scale mining enterprises for dollars and the price at which it sold such dollars. . . .
>
> On the other hand, greater restrictiveness worked in the opposite direction: First, it reduced the quantity of foreign trade, a relatively easy source of tax revenue. . . . Tax revenues related to foreign trade as a proportion of total taxes have dropped secularly, from a mean of 0.83 in 1908-1927 to a mean of 0.18 in 1965-70. . . . Second, at times it lowered the effective average import tax rates since restrictions usually were applied more stringently to commodities with higher legal tax rates. The intensity of restrictions also has had some relation to the availability of loans to the government from foreign sources. . . .
>
> Partially as a result of these counterbalancing effects, the share of the government in GNP, savings, and investment does not indicate any strong phase association.

In addition to the kinds of interactions noted by Behrman in the foregoing quote, we should also note here the important point that governments lose revenue when import premiums accrue to import licenses in a QR regime and hence, *ceteris paribus*, a Phase II regime that relies heavily on QRs is losing revenue and hence—assuming, as we just argued, that increased public savings would dominate reduced private saving from the premiums—reducing aggregate saving. As it happens, the import premiums that were lost to tax revenue under restrictive exchange control regimes could amount to large sums indeed. For India, the authors of that volume produce the following estimate:[49]

> If we allow for an average premium of 40 percent on imports, and assume an average import bill of Rs. 18 billions (which is the approximate average for the import bill for the first four years of the Third Plan) and assume, in turn, that half of this could have been subject to this premium-siphoning exercise, we would have had an annual tax revenue collection of Rs. 350 billions on this account alone, representing nearly 10 percent of the tax revenue in India during 1969-70 of Rs. 39.9 billions. Thus, even if nothing else had been changed in the Indian economic regime, a shift to an exchange rate regime which eliminated this premium, by devaluation or by the use of adjustable tariffs or exchange auctions suitably designed, would have helped generate greater savings.

However, the authors also add that all the increase in taxation would not have implied a corresponding increase in savings in the economy. This is because, aside from the reduced private saving from the premiums, other factors needed to be taken into account: (1) the bulk of the imports went to the corporate manufacturing sector as the AU import licensing became more important, and the profits of that sector were subject to the 50 percent corporation tax anyway,[50] and also (2) the corporate sector in India had a rather large propensity to save out of incremental retained earnings.

For Pakistan also, similarly large estimates of revenue loss from QRs have been made. Thus, citing Papanek's earlier work, Nurul Islam argues that.[51]

> The importers earned the excess, windfall profits on the landed cost of imports, arising from import restrictions. The windfall profits amounted to 40% to 50% over the landed cost of imports during the sixties. During the early fifties, when the exchange restrictions were at their peak, the scarcity margins on the landed cost of imports were probably in the neighborhood of 60% rather than 40%. Total private imports in the fifties were about Rs. 800 million annually, yielding total annual profits of about Rs. 480-500 million to the private traders engaged in import trade. The order of magnitude of the profits on import trade can be gauged from the fact that it constituted about 5% of the annual income from the non-agricultural sector in the fifties.
>
> During the sixties, imports on private accounts were about Rs. 2000 million annually and profits at the rate of 50% over the landed cost amounted to Rs. 1000 million. This was about 6% of the annual non-agricultural GNP in current prices during the sixties. Similarly, high profits were earned throughout the period, by the industrialists producing import substitutes for the domestic market. Profit rates of about 50 to 100% were reported in the fifties, but had declined to about 20-50% by the sixties.

Similarly, Krueger's data on import premiums in Turkey for 1968 provided her with an estimated "average windfall gain, or premium, of TL 23.11 per TL 9 of licenses received," indicating again a very sizeable loss of revenue to the government.[52]

Aside from the above type of argument, Michaely has noted another interesting aspect of this phenomenon for Israel:[53]

> . . . the government of Israel is a major recipient of capital imports, mainly in the forms of sales abroad of Independence and Development bonds, the reparations payments from Germany (during 1953-63), and grants and loans from foreign governments (mainly the United States). To this should be added the income of the Jewish Agency from the United Jewish Appeal, which for the present purpose is almost equivalent to a government income. A rule of behavior to which the government has normally adhered is that government receipts from abroad are

allocated to the development budget. Since capital imports are recorded in the government's accounts at the formal rate of exchange, maintaining a rate below the equilibrium level leads to a *reduction* in the size of these receipts as expressed in local currency. This would be so even if the *effective* rate for foreign trade purposes were not below its equilibrium level: maintaining a rate higher than the formal rate by means of duties on imports and subsidies to exports implies, in effect, a net result in which part of the potential revenue in the development budget (from capital imports) is diverted, as revenue from tariff duties, to the current budget.

In Table 6-5, column 1 contains one possible, and arbitrary, estimate of this revenue loss. The estimate is initially based on the assumption that the *average* effective exchange rate (EER) for value added in exports is the equilibirum exchange rate. This assumption facilitates the computations involved, but there is

Table 6-5. Effect of Exchange Rate on the Development Budget, 1951-1968: Israel

	Loss of Revenue in Development Budget	Column 1 as Percentage of	
Year	(IL mill.)	GNP	Net Domestic Investment
	(1)	(2)	(3)
1951	5	0.8	3.3
1952	7	0.7	2.6
1953	36	2.6	12.2
1954	70	3.9	19.0
1955	3	0.1	0.5
1956	32	1.3	6.2
1957	59	2.0	8.9
1958	85	2.5	11.8
1959	104	2.6	13.1
1960	111	2.5	13.0
1961	156	2.9	13.8
1962	0	0	0
1963	8	0.1	0.5
1964	13	0.1	0.6
1965	18	0.2	0.9
1966	51	0.4	3.4
1967	87	0.7	10.3
1968	133	1.0	7.2

Source: *Israel,* op. cit., Table 6-3, p. 157; original for explanatory notes.

> almost no doubt that it *under*estimates the level of the equilibrium rate and thus also the results in column 1. The figures shown . . . are derived by multiplying the excess of the EER for exports over the formal rate by the amount (in foreign exchange) of the capital inflow recorded as revenue in the development budget. The results are then put in perspective by comparing them with GNP (column 2) and net domestic investment (column 3). Although the size varies markedly in different years (naturally, it is smallest immediately after a formal devaluation and then rises gradually), it is as a rule rather significant. This impression is strengthened if the downward bias just pointed out is borne in mind and if it is noted that the estimate in column 1 is based only on the budget of the government proper, and not on the accounts of the Jewish Agency, in which a similar element is contained.

Michaely thus concludes that the maintenance of a below equilibrium formal exchange rate was of some consequence in reducing governmental saving.[54]

C. Foreign Exchange Constraint and Saving

Recall that, in the presence of a foreign exchange constraint, increased availability of foreign exchange, *via* export expansion or (better still) foreign aid, enables *ex-ante* saving to be translated into *ex-post* saving. But so does any policy that reduces the imports "required" to sustain any given amount of investment and/or income.

While therefore increased exports under a liberalized trade regime may help realize greater *ex-post* saving, aside from possibly increasing *ex-ante* saving as discussed earlier, we could argue that an overvalued exchange rate may—by increasing inventories and capacity underutilization, biasing choice of technique toward "subsidized" imports of equipment, and so on—increase rather than reduce the import-requirement coefficients for investment and/or income and hence actually retard the growth of *ex-post* saving.[55] Since there is certainly evidence in the country studies for the latter effect of exchange control regimes, the question then is whether one can plausibly argue that these or other LDCs can be characterized as being subject to a binding foreign exchange constraint. Here, we may cite the work of Luis Landau on Latin American countries, and of Thomas Weisskopf on a wider range of LDCs, which attempts to devise tests to classify countries mainly according to savings and foreign exchange constraints.[56] Landau concludes that eight countries (Bolivia, Chile, Colombia, Dominican Republic, Guatemala, Nicaragua, Panama, and Uruguay) were on a binding foreign exchange constraint, with six others (Costa Rica, Honduras, Argentina, Ecuador, El Salvador, and Mexico) alternating between trade and savings gaps. Weisskopf, whose model and analysis are somewhat different, also finds that as many as eight countries had a clear foreign exchange gap (Brazil, Cyprus, Dominican Republic, Guatemala, Ireland, Pakistan, Paraguay, and Peru), with six others being "hybrid" cases characterized by both trade and savings constraints.

We may therefore conclude that, taking the evidence on the import requirements increasing effects of exchange control regimes and on the possibility of certain LDCs being characterized by a binding foreign exchange constraint, it is arguable, with some plausibility, that exchange control regimes may be harmful to achieving higher saving.

D. Capital Markets and Saving

The final argument to be evaluated now is that relating exchange control regimes to lower saving *via* their ostensible effect on lowering real interest rates. The evidence on this issue is far from clear-cut, with several cross-sectional and time-series studies outside the Project showing negligible, or even negative, coefficients and with two analyses in the Project, for South Korea and Chile, showing some form of significant relationship of personal saving either (positively) to the (real or nominal) interest rate or (negatively) to the rate of inflation.

In his cross-sectional study mentioned earlier, Houthakker in fact found it distressing that "the rate of interest was not found effective as an explanatory variable" and went on to speculate that perhaps he had not used the correct measure and that the rate of return on the non-financial assets of manufacturing industries might have produced better results.[57]

Williamson's examination of Asian LDCs was more definitive but consistently turned up a negative coefficient on real interest rates.[58] This led him to speculate that this was probably because "savings and investment decisions are highly interdependent in the Asian household sector," that is, presumably higher interest rates inhibit investment and hence the saving that is undertaken to finance the investments.[59]

Serious evidence in favor of the *positive* relationship between real interest rates and saving however comes from South Korea.[60] Thus, Frank and others have shown that business saving in Korea was moderately responsive to interest rates, the elasticity of response (to *nominal* interest rates) being estimated at 0.34. Household saving was even more sensitive, showing response to both the rate of inflation and the interest rate on time deposits.[61] This result, however, seems to have been heavily influenced by the major interest rate reform of 1965. Prior to that, the real interest rates actually were so low that, for instance, the real rate of return on time deposits had been −10 to −15 percent. The interest rate reform changed the situation dramatically, so that "from 1964 to 1966, the real rate of return (deflated by movements in the wholesale price index) rose about 11 percentage points on demand deposits, and rose about 26 percentage points on time deposits of longer maturities."[62] The steep rise in household saving, from practically negligible levels during 1960-1964, to nearly a quarter of total saving during 1965-1970,[63] was thus quite a dominant fact on the scene. One may therefore still entertain a reasonable skepticism whether a finding dominated by a steep rise of the real interest rate from negative to high, "normal" levels, and an associated rise in personal saving from negligible to "reasonable" levels has anything illuminating to offer if one is interested in the effects on saving of variations in real interest rates within narrower bounds and in the positive-values range. The analysis by Behrman of the Chilean saving function for households (Table 6-3 above) also indicates a significant (negative) response to the rate of inflation, but not to real interest rates directly.

III. OVERALL PHASE RELATIONSHIPS

The evidence on the possible links between foreign trade regimes and domestic saving is thus not as clear-cut as the proponents or opponents of restrictionist exchange control regimes would wish. But the weight of our evidence seems to throw serious doubt on the view that such exchange control regimes, while they are inefficient on static tests (of the kind undertaken in Chapter 5), offset this inefficiency through their beneficial effects on domestic saving and capital formation. If anything, the evidence indicates the opposite for many possible linkages, taken each in turn.

When we consider overall associations between restrictionist and liberalized phases and the behavior of the overall saving rate, the conclusions are no more favorable to the proponents of restrictionist exchange control regimes. Thus Behrman notes the lack of any systematic relationship between Chilean phases and domestic saving. Similarly, Bhagwati and Srinivasan also discuss at some length this issue for India.[64] They begin with the simple relationship:

$$S_t = \alpha_0 + a_1 Y_t + u_t \tag{6.9}$$

where S_t is total saving, Y_t is national income, and u_t a random disturbance term, all relating to year t. The period of the analysis being 1951-1952 to 1969-1970, they divide the period into 1951-1952 to 1959-1960 and 1960-1961 to 1969-1970, roughly approximating the fact that the latter period had a rather more stringent exchange control regime than the former, on the average. Thus the problem is to see if any significant change in saving behavior could be observed between the decade of the fifties and that of the sixties.

While they work with four alternative measures of real saving—the combination of superscripts I and II, and the subscripts 1 and 2 to S giving the relevant measure used, as explained in their work—the best fits alone are reproduced here, in Table 6-6. It is then clear that there is little evidence in the Indian case for the argument that greater stringency of exchange control during the 1960s was associated with a significantly higher marginal propensity to save (except in one regression).[65]

IV. POSSIBLE LINKS BETWEEN FOREIGN CAPITAL FLOWS AND FOREIGN TRADE REGIMES

So far, we have been considering links between foreign trade regimes and domestic saving and have found little firm evidence that restrictionist exchange control regimes can be rescued from the judgment (reached in Chapter 5) that they are inefficient by pointing to beneficial effects regarding domestic saving. We may well ask, however, whether any links can be established between *foreign* capital and foreign trade regimes.

In assessing this question, we need to distinguish between official and private capital flows. The motivating forces governing the two are surely not identical (except in the pure Marxist-Leninist model where foreign aid is being dispensed for imperialist reasons by a donor government exclusively controlled by the capitalist interests) and therefore we should not expect to be anything but misled by failing to distinguish between them.

Table 6-6. Saving Regressions for India: 1951-1952 to 1959-1960 and 1960-1961 to 1969-1970

	1951-1952 to 1959-1960		*1960-1961 to 1969-1970*	
1. S_1^I =	$-815 + 0.18\,Y$ (520) (0.04)	$R^2 = 0.73$	$-592 + 0.18\,Y$ (698) (0.04)	$R^2 = 0.73$
2. S_2^I =	$-1087 + 0.21\,Y$ (607) (0.05)	$R^2 = 0.72$	$-1271 + 0.22\,Y$ (560) (0.03)	$R^2 = 0.87$
3. S_1^{II} =	$-532 + 0.16\,Y$ (563) (0.05)	$R^2 = 0.63$	$-834 + 0.19\,Y$ (610) (0.03)	$R^2 = 0.80$
4. S_2^{II} =	$-804 + 0.18\,Y$ (600) (0.05)	$R^2 = 0.67$	$-1514 + 0.24\,Y$ (741) (0.03)	$R^2 = 0.91$

Note: Figures in parentheses are standard errors. Refer to the text for explanation of the regressions.

Source: *India*, op. cit., Table 16-2.

A. Private (Long-term) Capital Flows

A few basic arguments relating exchange control regimes to private capital flows may be set out here.

1. With exchange control regimes leading to sheltered markets—under varying degrees of automaticity of protection furnished thereby—it is evident that private investment in these import-competing activities could become profitable. Indeed, "tariff-jumping" investment is among the best known forms of private foreign investment. There is little doubt, though no econometric way of supporting this assertion, that much of the foreign investment in Phase II of the countries in the Project was of this variety, although its magnitude and composition would have reflected other factors such as the overall host country policies toward such investments.

2. On the other hand, as compared with tariffs and an equilibrated exchange rate without exchange controls, the exchange control system may be considered to be less effective as an inducement to invest. The repatriation of profits and the principal may be suspended, and this risk may be greater in the investor's calculus than the risk of exchange depreciation.[66] Furthermore, as Michaely has noted, exchange control is likely to lead to "a large measure of bureaucratic intervention in capital flows from abroad and in investment decisions" and may also result in uncertainty about the degree of protection granted to the industry in which investment is intended.[67]

3. The difficulty of reaching overall judgment on this issue is well illustrated in the Israeli case where Michaely describes both the tenuous character of private investment data and the judgment concerning the possibly adverse effect of the exchange control regime on such inflows.

Thus, Michaely could not test directly the proposition that QRs attract foreign capital to the protected industries because of lack of data about the allocation of foreign investment by industries. However, he noted that in the mid-1950s (and presumably in earlier years as well), the total size of foreign private investment was very small—about $10 million to $20 million annually or roughly 5 percent of total investment in the economy. He therefore concluded that even if the grant of QR protection attracted foreign investment, the amount could not have been large enough to have had a significant impact on growth.

Foreign investment did start rising, and assumed substantial proportions, in the late 1950s. In both absolute size and as a ratio to total investment, it was many times larger in the 1960s than in the 1950s. This could perhaps be explained by the process of liberalization, since the effect of the largely liberalized exchange system of the 1960s was to reduce the obstacles to private capital inflow presented by the exchange control system of the earlier period. However, Michaely thought that various other explanations could be given for the phenomenon. Thus, for instance, the size of private foreign investment is without any doubt correlated with the country's security position. In the early and mid-1950s Israel's position was considered insecure; only since late 1957 or early 1958 did expectations of relative peace start to prevail. Moreover, the greater heterogeneity of the economy as time progressed, the higher income level, larger and more varied supply of skills, and so on, may all have induced greater inflow of foreign investment. Michaely concluded therefore that: "(a) during the era of stringent exchange controls and QRs, private foreign investment was negligible; and (b) in later years, private capital inflow increased very substantially, an event which may be explained by several economic factors and circumstances, one of which is the policy of liberalization."[68]

Among the countries in the Project for which there is systematic information on the volume of inflow of private foreign investment is South Korea. Indeed, the inflow of such capital into South Korea has partially taken over, since the mid-1960s, the critical role that official aid played until then in maintaining high rates of gross investment, the share of foreign saving being as great as almost 40 percent of gross investment and over 10 percent of GNP on the average during 1966-1970.[69] There is little doubt that continued liberalization of the exchange control regime has been associated in South Korea with a sizeable increase in the inflow of private long-term investment and that the relationship between liberalization and such capital inflow has been of a two-way variety.

For Chile, the relationship between phases in the trade regimes and variations in the inflow of capital has been extensively analyzed by Behrman.[70] He shows that, for net *direct* investment, there are indeed striking associations, such that the mean net inflows increased in every more liberal phase and decreased in each more restrictive one. A substantial share of these investments went into large-scale mining; but, even in recent years when other sectors have come to play an increasing role in this inflow, the flows have shown the strong association just noted. Behrman notes that this relationship was in response to both "the perception of a 'favorable investment climate' caused by the overall stabilization *cum* liberalization programs" *and* the fact that such programs were accompanied by loosened restrictions on capital entry and repatriation. Even when the outflow of income from direct investments is subtracted from the net direct investment, Behrman finds that "for all but one of the recent phases, the short-term command over foreign exchange rose in liberalization and fell in more restrictive periods."[71] However, *other* private *long-term* investment shows little phase association.[72]

4. The Korean case also suggests qualification to the argument that exchange control, through its protective effect, may be an inducement to inflow of foreign investment for yet another reason: foreign, direct investment may well be attracted into *exporting* industries, essentially to take advantage of the

presence of cheaper factors (mainly labor) under a regime that discriminates less against exports than an exchange control regime. The QR or tariff-jumping investment for domestic markets is only one major "type"; local raw material using investment for exporting intermediates or finished goods is another; local cheap factors using investment is yet another.[73] Aside from the effect on total inflows, it is likely therefore that foreign trade regimes that are more "liberalized" will also attract relatively more of the export-oriented foreign direct investment. It might even be contended, as discussed later in Chapter 8, that such inflow may be more sizeable than that induced by the protection of the domestic market, though evidence on this is difficult to come by. In any event, the export orientation of the foreign investment may, in turn, affect the political and cultural effects of the capital inflow, a hypothesis for which there is little evidence so far.

5. We may next consider the possibility, discussed in Chapter 4, that the exercise of exchange control may induce capital flight—a reverse outflow of private capital. Evidence of such a phenomenon was considered at length there,[74] indicating rather strongly that capital flight from several LDCs was evident from the partner country, trade-data comparisons that implied faked invoicing of transactions. More detailed and careful analysis, as of Turkey and Pakistan, has also indicated serious underinvoicing that seems related to QRs and, to some extent, to tariffs.[75]

Can we argue that exchange control regimes necessarily lead to greater capital flight than regimes under which the exchange rate is adjusted more freely? It would seem that this can be asserted insofar as exchange control regimes create high incentives for holding foreign exchange, beyond that legally available, by leading to high import premiums. But this may only lead the illegal foreign outflow to come back to finance the underinvoiced imports (induced by the import premiums) and does not necessarily result in net flight of capital. The argument has finally, it would seem, to turn on the fact that the high premium attached to the access to foreign exchange creates an inducement to hold portfolio investments in the form of (*illegal*) foreign exchange that would not obtain equally under an alternative system with more ready *legal* access to foreign exchange. Against the inducement, if any, provided for private foreign capital inflow by exchange control regimes, we would thus be wise to put the inducement likely to be provided for capital flight by such regimes to arrive at the *net* effect on private capital flows.[76]

6. We may finally note the question of the optimality of the capital inflow. Thus, even if exchange control regimes, on balance, reduce such inflow and liberalized regimes increase it, can we argue that the "more the inflow, the better for the economy"? This is a much-debated question, indeed. While the monotonicity of the relationship between capital inflow and economic welfare generally tends to be accepted without question by international monetary

economists, and interference with the free flow of capital among the countries constituting the international economy is generally considered as inefficient,[77] there is a clear absence of such a consensus among developmental economists and also the "pure" theorists of international trade. Since the arguments for and against the unrestricted (by level and composition) inflows of private foreign capital are well known,[78] we merely remind the reader about them and note here two arguments that are not so commonly encountered, while referring the reader to further discussion of the issue in Chapter 8.

First, if private foreign investment can affect foreign aid flows, this may be considered a benefit or a loss, depending on the view taken of the effect of foreign aid on the recipient countries. Thus foreign investors may become a lobby for increasing aid so that they are treated better by the host country. Alternatively, they may be a lobby against foreign aid because they think that the latter enables the host country to continue restricting inflow of private capital. On the other hand, it may be that, like trade, investment follows the flag. Hence investment may follow where foreign aid, and presumed political influence therefrom, flows. As it happens, Papanek's cross-section regression analysis, using eighty-four observations for the 1950s and 1960s, indicates that aid flows and private investment flows are not substantially correlated.

Second, private foreign investment may be held to substitute for domestic saving and thus impair the domestic effort at reaching "self-sustaining take-off." This argument is examined, with evidence, in subsection B below.

B. Substitution Between Foreign Capital and Domestic Saving

We must now consider a question of some importance, which links the present analysis of foreign capital with the preceding analysis of domestic saving. Can the two be treated as exogenous to each other; or are there any functional links between them?

Although the net result of the latter possibility would be to compound the difficulty of assessing the impact of foreign trade regimes on domestic saving and on overall investment, it must be admitted that there *are* possible links here and that some evidence is also available in support thereof. Note, at the outset, that the links between foreign capital and domestic savings can, in principle, be in both directions.

1. Aid Inflow as a Function of Domestic Saving.

A rising domestic saving ratio may be "rewarded" by aid donors with greater aid inflows on a "matching" principle of the kind often discussed by aid agencies. It may equally lead, at higher saving ratios, to lower aid flows as aid agencies may feel that aid is no longer "necessary" to supplement domestic savings effort. One may therefore hypothesize a reverse U-shaped curve, linking the (independent variable) domestic saving ratio to the (dependent variable) foreign savings (either as ratio to GNP or in absolute magnitude).[79] While there is some evidence in the literature on the pronouncements of donor agencies and aid proponents for the "matching" principle in aid "awards," and some supporting evidence in the aid deceleration to South Korea and Taiwan (which were relatively "successful" in achieving an economic take-off) for the other half of the postulated argument, it should be noted that little support for this type of aid-allocational decision-making process has been found in the cross-sectional analysis of the *ex-post* aid flows among different recipients.[80]

On the other hand, evidence for this bell-shaped relationship may well be detected through a time-series analysis that introduces additional explanatory variables such as shifts in political alliances, growing availability of private foreign capital, and so on. Alternatively, such a relationship may be, not between domestic saving *in toto* and foreign aid, but rather between public savings or tax effort (which are far more reliably measured than total savings and are also a more direct, if incomplete, measure of recipient-governmental effort at raising domestic resources for investment) and foreign aid, at least for the recipient countries with lower saving ratios. Further econometric analysis may thus well rescue some of the hypothesized effect of domestic saving performance on foreign aid inflow.

2. Private Capital Inflow as a Function of Domestic Saving

It is rather more difficult to argue a relationship between domestic saving and private inflow. It may be argued, however, that a higher domestic saving rate, *ceteris paribus*, would imply a higher growth rate (in a Harrod-Domar framework) and that the latter may induce greater private capital inflow. This would yield a monotonic increase in capital inflow with rising saving rates, contrary to the possibly U-shaped relationship that we just discussed for foreign aid.[81] Again, however, as with the latter, there seems to be little supporting evidence for any such systematic relationship between private capital inflow and domestic savings.

3. Domestic Saving as a Function of Capital Inflow.

The most influential hypothesis recently has however been that postulating that domestic saving is rather the dependent variable and foreign capital inflow the independent variable, and that foreign capital substitutes for domestic saving. Thus, we may write:

$$S = a + bY + cF \tag{6.10}$$

where S is saving, Y income, and F the foreign capital inflow, the parameters having the following "normal" signs: $a < 0$ (the Keynesian assumption), $b > 0$, and $c > 0$.[82] The underlying rationale for this hypothesis is that, as an economy gets more foreign capital, this supplements its available resources, so that it is reasonable to assume that part of this will be expended on increasing current, and part on augmenting future, consumption. With current consumption rising, at given income, the current domestic saving would then fall.[83]

A voluminous amount of cross-country and time-series statistical analysis has been turned up on this issue, essentially regressing domestic saving (as the dependent variable) on income, foreign capital inflow (rarely distinguishing between private and official capital),[84] and at times, supplementary independent variables (e.g., exports, as already discussed in the previous section).

The results of several regression studies are summarized here in Table 6-7 and indicate strongly the recurrence of a negative impact, of varying magnitudes, of foreign inflows on saving. The signs are almost always negative. What are we to conclude from this mass of regressions? First, as Papanek has correctly stressed, some caution is necessary in interpreting these results. While it is true that no systematic regression can be fitted that explains low saving ratios as a cause of higher aid flows, this is not the same as ruling this out for some countries (e.g., South Korea after the Korean War's devastation) as a complicating factor that *alternatively* may account for the inverse association between external capital inflows and domestic saving ratios.

Next, the method of computing domestic saving is usually the "residual" type whereby the payments deficit is subtracted from the estimated investment. If therefore the payments deficit (and hence capital inflow) is overestimated, the saving will be underestimated. Thus the bias in errors of estimation runs systematically in favor of supporting the negative relationship that emerges from the regressions.

But major doubts and difficulties in interpretation also come from other directions. In particular, we could reformulate the saving equation:

$$S = a + b(F) \cdot Y + cF$$

$$b = d + eF \qquad (b, e > 0)$$

so that

$$S = a + dY + cF + eFY \tag{6.11}$$

Table 6-7. Results of Major Analyses Regressing Saving on Foreign Capital Flows

Author	*Cross-Country (C) Time Series (T) Pooled (C, T)*	*Number of Observations*	*Form of Equation*	*Deflated Variables (D) Nominal Variables (N)*	*Effect of Foreign Inflow on Saving*
Griffin and Enos	*C* *C*	32 13	$\frac{S_d}{Y} \cdot 100 = a + b \frac{S_p}{Y} \cdot 100$	*N* *N*	−0.73 −0.82
Griffin	*T*	13	$\frac{S_d}{Y} \cdot 100 = a + b \frac{S_b}{Y} \cdot 100$	*N*	−0.84
Rahman	*C*	31	$\frac{S}{Y} = a + b \frac{F}{Y}$	*D*	−0.2473
Areskoug	*T*	(22 countries) ≈13-14 observations per country	$I = aB + bY + cF'$	*D*	−1.53 to +4.30
Weisskopf	*T, C*	(17 countries) 9-12 observations per country	$S = a\ \mathrm{b}Y + \mathrm{c} \frac{E}{Y} + dF$	*D*	−0.227
Chenery	*T*	(16 countries) 13-14 observations per country	$S = a + bY + c \frac{E}{Y} + dF$	*D*	+.64 to −1.15[a]
Chenery	*C* }	90	$\frac{S}{Y} \cdot 100 = a + b \log Y + c(\log Y)^2 + dN + eT + fF$	*D*	−0.4894
	C }		$\frac{I_d}{Y} \cdot 100 = a + b \log Y + c(\log Y)^2 + dN + eT + fF$	*D*	−0.8892
Papanek	*C*	85	$S = a + bA + cI_p + dF_0 + eE_p + fE_0$	*N*	*b* −1.00, *c* −0.65, *d* −0.38

			$S = a + b \log \frac{Y}{N} + d \log N + eF + fEp + gE_0$		−0.64
			$S = a + b \log \frac{Y}{N} + c \log N + dF$		−0.73
Clark	C, T	(33 countries)	$\frac{S}{Y} \cdot 100 = a + b \log \frac{Y}{N} - c \frac{F}{N} \cdot 100 + dP + eW + fD$	D	−0.58

[a]12 of 16 negative.

List of Variables:

Y = GDP.
S_d = Domestic saving.
S_f = Foreign saving.
S = Gross domestic saving.
I = Investment.
B = Net government external borrowing.
F' = Net private capital outflow *plus* change in government foreign reserves *minus* net transfer receipts from abroad.
F = Net foreign inflows.
N = Population size.
T = Time.
I_d = Gross domestic investment.
A = Net transfers received by government plus official long-term borrowing.
I_p = Private investment.
E_p = Primary exports.
E_0 = Other exports.
F_0 = Other capital inflows.
P = Decadal rate of population growth.
W = War damage expressed as multiple of 1938 NNP at factor cost.
D = Dummy variable: 0 pre-1955; 1 post-1955.

Sources: Griffin, K.B. and J.L. Enos. "Foreign Assistance: Objectives and Consequences," *Economic Development and Cultural Change* (April 1970). Griffin, K.B. "Foreign Capital, Domestic Savings and Economic Development," *Bulletin of the Oxford University Institute of Economics and Statistics* (May 1970). Rahman, A. "Foreign Capital and Domestic Savings: A Test of Haavelmo's Hypothesis with Cross-Country Data," *Review of Economics and Statistics* (February 1968). Areskoug, K. *External Borrowing: Its Role in Economic Development* (New York: Praeger, 1969). Weisskopf, T. "The Impact of Foreign Capital Inflow on Domestic Savings in Underdeveloped Countries," *Journal of International Economics,* 2, 1 (February 1972). Chenery, H.B. "Development Alternatives for Latin America," (w/P. Eckstein) *Journal of Political Economy* (July/August 1970). Chenery, H.B. "A Uniform Analysis of Development Patterns," (w/H. Elkington and C. Aims), *Economic Development Reports*, Nos. 148, 158, Harvard University Center for International Affairs. Papanek, G.F. "Aid, Foreign Private Investment, Savings and Growth in Less Developed Countries," *Journal of Political Economy*, 81, 1 (January/February 1973). Clark, C. *Population Growth and Land Use* (New York: Macmillan, 1967).

and it is being postulated now that, while the recipient government indeed consumes $(1 - c)$ units out of unit inflow of capital, it also increases its domestic saving effort *via* taxation, and so on, so as to yield a higher parameter 'b'—the marginal propensity to save out of income. This formulation would appear to yield estimates that dampen the adverse effect of foreign capital on saving.

Next, we must also note that the adverse impact being discussed is only the primary impact. However, even if foreign capital substitutes for domestic saving, at given income, it will (as long as it adds net to investment) increase (future) income and hence saving on that account. Hence to evaluate fully the effect of foreign capital on the domestic saving ratio, the estimated saving functions need to be "fed" into a growth model. Grinols and Bhagwati have shown that, if we do this in a simple Harrod-Domar model, the impact effect *can* get reversed for a reasonable number of cases in simulation experiments using plausible parametric values.[85]

Among the studies in the NBER project containing an analysis of the issue of the impact of foreign inflows on domestic saving is that on India.[86] Its conclusions, even on the limited issue of the primary impact effect, are far less conclusive than the results of the more ambitious (in terms of countries covered) studies discussed so far. The authors of the India study begin with the equation:

$$C_t = \beta_0 + \beta_1 (Y_t + F_t) \tag{6.12}$$

where F_t is the foreign capital inflow, defined as the negative of the balance on current account. They then estimate the following form of the equation:

$$S_t = \alpha_0 + \alpha_1 Y_t + \alpha_2 F_t + u_t \tag{6.12a}$$

Clearly, when $\alpha_1 = (\alpha_2 + 1)$, this equation will correspond to Equation (6.12a). A positive (negative) value for α_2 would be consistent with the hypothesis that external resources complement (substitute) domestic resources.

The following version of Equation (6.12a) with F_t lagged by one year, is also estimated:

$$S_t = \alpha_0 + \alpha_1 Y_t + \alpha_2 F_{t-1} + u_t \tag{6.12b}$$

The idea underlying Equation (6.12b) is that if indeed consumption is related to expected volume of resources available, then it may be reasonable to presume that such expectations for any year are formed on the basis of the actual resources in the previous year. This would suggest that S_t should be related to Y_{t-1} and F_{t-1}. Given that the correlation between Y_t and Y_{t-1} is very high (while that between F_t and F_{t-1} is not), Equation 6.12b is assumed however to do just as well as one with Y_{t-1} instead of Y_t.

The results for both Equations 6.12a and 6.12b are shown in Table 6-8. It turns out that the explanatory power of contemporaneous external resource flow when used in conjunction with income in explaining saving is virtually nil: the coefficients on F are statistically insignificantly different from zero. The lagged response equations also perform uniformly badly; with one exception, the coefficients on F_{-1} are also not significantly different from zero. The authors thus infer that domestic saving does not seem to be influenced by external resources.

On the other hand, they also caution in favor of a mild skepticism relating to this conclusion. For one thing, the introduction of F_{-1} generally seems to lead to higher (*not* lower) coefficients on Y than, for comparable periods, in the other regressions that they have reported that do *not* use F as an explanatory variable at all. In contrast, a different test suggests an opposite in-

Table 6-8. Alternative Saving Regressions for India: 1951-1970

Period		Equation	R^2
1951-1952 to 1969-1970	(a)	$S_1^{II} = -1241 + \underset{(0.02)}{0.22\,Y} - \underset{(0.30)}{0.08\,F}$	$R^2 = 0.94$
	(b)	$s_1^{II} = -1487 + \underset{(0.02)}{0.24\,Y} - \underset{(0.33)}{0.57\,F_{-1}}$	$R^2 = 0.95$
1951-1952 to 1965-1966	(a)	$S_1^{II} = -1611 + \underset{(0.03)}{0.25\,Y} - \underset{(0.45)}{0.18\,F}$	$R^2 = 0.93$
	(b)[a]	$s_1^{II} = -1976 + \underset{(0.03)}{0.28\,Y} - \underset{(0.38)}{0.78\,F_{-1}}$	$R^2 = 0.95$
1951-1952 to 1959-1960	(a)	$S_1^{II} = \underset{(747)}{-553} + \underset{(0.06)}{0.16\,Y} - \underset{(0.49)}{0.02\,F}$	$R^2 = 0.63$
	(b)	$s_1^{II} = \underset{(665)}{-1262} + \underset{(0.06)}{0.22\,Y} - \underset{(0.42)}{0.70\,F_{-1}}$	$R^2 = 0.75$
1960-1961 to 1969-1970	(a)	$S_1^{II} = \underset{(741)}{-641} + \underset{(0.04)}{0.19\,Y} - \underset{(0.57)}{0.29\,F}$	$R^2 = 0.81$
	(b)	$s_1^{II} = \underset{(626)}{-862} + \underset{(0.04)}{0.21\,Y} - \underset{(0.62)}{0.49\,F_{-1}}$	$R^2 = 0.82$

Notes:

1. Figures in parentheses are standard errors.
2. To estimate (real) saving by the "residual" approach, investment was deflated by the Perspective Planning Division deflator. The entire current account surplus was deflated by the unit value index of imports to arrive at the real capital, inflow which, in turn, was subtracted from real investment to arrive at the estimated real saving used here.
3. The lower-case saving regressions refer to *per capita* saving.

[a]The coefficient on F_{-1} is significantly different from zero at 5 percent level; other coefficients on F_{-1} are not significantly different from zero, in this table.

Source: *India,* op. cit., Chapter 15, Table 15-3.

ference: that is, that domestic saving is a function of $(Y + F)$ rather than (Y). Thus, recall that if Equation (6.12) is rewritten as follows:

$$C = \beta_0 + \beta_1(Y + F) \tag{6.13}$$

and

$$S = Y - C \tag{6.14}$$

one then has:

$$S = \beta_0 + (1 - \beta_1)Y - \beta_1 F$$

so that one has the relationship that the coefficient on Y is equal to one plus the coefficient on F (or F_{-1}, if we put in lagged response). One can therefore test whether the coefficients on Y are indeed significantly different from one plus the coefficients on F and F_{-1} in Table 6-8. This test by the authors indicates that the hypothesis of Equation (6.12) is *not* rejected by the data in Table 6-8. Thus they cannot rule out *altogether* the possibility that external resources substitute for domestic saving. On balance, therefore, they conclude that there is not enough evidence, and at best conflicting evidence, on the issue as to whether the absorption of external resources has adversely affected India's domestic saving effort.

It is also worth noting here the argument, advanced by Bhagwati and Srinivasan in the India study, that the impact of external capital inflow in the form of aid may be felt primarily on public saving, rather than aggregate domestic saving.[87] This is because the pressure to reduce domestic effort in response to aid inflow is likely to be felt mainly in tax effort and hence in public saving. Table 6-9 sets out the relevant regressions that use national income (Y) rather than public revenues and private income as an explanatory variable because the latter are correlated with it. The authors then conclude that:[88]

> As in the case of total savings, the explanatory power of contemporaneous capital inflow is nil in explaining either public or private savings. The lagged capital inflow, however, has a significant negative coefficient in the case of private savings but the marginal propensity to save in the lagged relationship is higher than that in the unlagged one. These results, however, are diffficult to interpret, as we would normally have expected the external resource inflow to work primarily through the budget—in view of the larger component of foreign aid—by reducing *public* savings: the significance of the lagged foreign resource inflow in influencing private savings seems to us therefore to be mainly spurious.[89]

Table 6-9. Private and Government Saving Regressions for India: 1951-1952 to 1965-1966

$$S^{II}_{1p} = \underset{(304)}{-1135} + \underset{(0.03)}{0.19}\,Y - \underset{(0.36)}{0.28}\,F \qquad R^2 = 0.91$$

$$S^{II}_{1p} = \underset{(245)}{-1433} + \underset{(0.02)}{0.22}\,Y - \underset{(0.28)}{0.77}\,F_{-1} \qquad R^2 = 0.94$$

$$S^{II}_{1g} = \underset{(158)}{-476} + \underset{(0.01)}{0.06}\,Y - \underset{(0.19)}{0.10}\,F \qquad R^2 = 0.84$$

$$S^{II}_{1g} = \underset{(160)}{-543} + \underset{(0.01)}{0.06}\,Y - \underset{(0.18)}{0.01}\,F_{-1} \qquad R^2 = 0.84$$

Notes: Figures in parentheses are standard errors. S, Y, and F represent real savings, national income, and external inflow of capital. F_{-1} is a one-period lagged variable. The subscripts p and g denote, respectively, private and public savings. Refer to the source for further explanations.

Source: *India,* op. cit., Table 16-4.

Thus we conclude that our analysis contradicts the thesis that incoming foreign resources have seriously interfered with the domestic savings effort. This is probably not surprising since the planning mechanism has, by and large, served to make the domestic tax-and-savings effort keep in step with the aid flow, both because of internal clarity on this objective and external (aid-donor-induced) pressure-cum-ethos in this regard.

On the other hand, basing himself on econometric results (reported above in Table 6-3), Behrman concludes the opposite for Chile and, citing the evidence in support of the substitution hypothesis, he states:[90]

> In one sense, in fact, the support is too strong because the total of the relevant coefficients implies that a permanent increase in real net foreign savings of one unit *ceteris paribus* results in a decrease in real net domestic savings of at least the same order of magnitude. If it were not for the problem of multicollinearity, therefore, one might conclude that in the Chilean case there is support for a rather extreme version of the hypothesis. However, given that the relevant coefficient estimates for the real private domestic savings functions are probably biased upward in absolute value because part of the effects of price and possibly of real monetary balances are incorporated, any deduction about at least the size of the substitution must be qualified. Nevertheless, the conclusion seems warranted that the impact of net real foreign savings on Chilean real domestic savings may be quite significant.

V. CONCLUDING REMARKS

In conclusion, it would seem that the problem of the interrelationship between trade regimes and *domestic* saving generation is fairly complex, having numerous possible dimensions. And the evidence on these issues is also fairly diverse in the country studies in the Project and elsewhere. The matter becomes even more unclear if we consider the linkages between trade regimes and *foreign* saving so that the relationship between trade regimes and overall *investment* is, in turn, complex as well.

We *can*, however, argue that much of the theoretical argument and the relevant empirical evidence demonstrate persuasively that the proponents of restrictionist exchange control regimes are clearly in error when they assert that such regimes—while they are inefficient on static grounds (as discussed in Chapters 5 and 7)—will, or are likely to, contribute to increased domestic saving and/or to augmented capital formation. If anything, much of our evidence—at least on the domestic saving issue—suggests an opposite relationship.

In conclusion, we should also note of course that, *in theory* at least, more saving is not necessarily better than less saving. However, for policy purposes, in LDCs of the type studied in the Project, trade regimes that encourage greater domestic saving would surely be regarded by most analysts as better on that account.[91]

NOTES

1. It should also be emphasized that saving data are typically subject to wide margins of error and are often unavailable by broken-down components necessary for sophisticated analysis: all this handicaps the analysis greatly.

2. Cf. Bhagwati, *The Theory and Practice of Commercial Policy*, op.cit.; and P. Pattanaik, "Trade, Distribution and Saving," *Journal of International Economics* 4 (April 1974): 77-82. The possible link between the efficacy of a devaluation (requiring absorption) and its income distributional effect, which parallels in many ways the argument in the text, has also been noted by international trade economists: a particularly cogent contribution here is Carlos Díaz-Alejandro's analysis of Argentina: *Exchange Rate Devalution in a Semi-Industrialized Country* (Cambridge, Mass.: M.I.T. Press, 1965).

3. We should note that a problem with the Cambridge school's argument is that the theories of consumption developed by F. Modigliani and R. Brumberg "Utility Analysis and the Consumption Function: An Interpretation of Cross-section Data," in K. Kurihara, ed., *Post-Keynesian Economics* (New Brunswick, N.J.: Rutgers University Press, 1954) and M. Friedman (*A Theory of the Consumption Function*, Princeton, N.J.: Princeton University Press, 1957) suggest that the marginal propensity to consume might vary by income bracket but there is no suggestion that it will vary according to whether the income accrues in the form of interest, rent, or wages. One possible rationale for the Cambridge approach, however, may be that distribution by functional shares might be a proxy for the size distribution of income, so that an increase in wage

income may be equivalent to a distribution from higher to lower income brackets. As it happens A. Blinder's recent work ("Distribution Effects and the Aggregate Consumption Function," *Journal of Political Economy*, 83 June 1975): 447-476, shows that, for the United States at least, the distribution of national income between capital and labor bears only a loose relationship with size distribution; moreover, it is not clear whether wages or non-labor incomes are more unequally distributed.

4. Pattanaik, op.cit. Also see the extension of the theoretical analysis to a model incorporating one non-traded good by K. Okuguchi, "Trade, Savings and Non-traded Goods," *Journal of International Economics* 7 (November 1977): 379-384.

5. See, however, Chapter 2 where the limited character of this identification has been discussed at greater length.

6. *Chile*, op.cit., page 284; reference to columns 11 and 12 in Table 6-3 above.

7. At the same time, given the structure of Behrman's short-run modeling of Chile's economy, it follows that QRs, by increasing in the short and medium run the share of labor and agriculture in total income, would increase saving whereas devaluation has the counteracting effects of increasing the share of agriculture but reducing that of labor. Cf. ibid., pages 284-285.

8. Note, however, that several of these partially overlap with one another. For example, the urban sector propensity to save may be different from the rural sector's for the reason, among others, that it has a larger corporate sector, or it may be lower because it has a lower export sector, and so on. In each of the four sector-specific arguments, however, the macro-analyst is assuming that the particular sectoral saving propensities are stable and most fruitful for analysis and prediction.

9. Cf. A. Maizels, *Exports and Economic Growth of Developing Countries* (Cambridge: Cambridge University Press, 1968), pp. 58, 69, and 95, in particular; T. Weisskopf, "The Impact of Foreign Capital Inflow on Domestic Savings in Underdeveloped Countries," *Journal of International Economics*, 2, 1 (February 1972); and G. Papanek, "Aid, Foreign Private Investment, Savings and Growth in Less Developed Countries," *Journal of Political Economy*, 81, 1 (January/Februry 1973): 120-130.

10. Maizels, op.cit., p. 58. He carefully adds, however, that: "Equally, in other countries, in which relatively little revenue is derived from duties on foreign trade and in which the savings ratio does not differ markedly from one sector to another, a close relationship between exports and savings would not be expected to exist" (p. 58).

11. Cf. The model was discussed elegantly in an early classic paper by Trevor Swan, "Longer-Run Problems of the Balance of Payments," in *The Australian Economy: A Volume of Readings*, edited by H.W. Arndt and W.M. Corden, (Melbourne, 1963); and discussed rigorously in another classic paper by Ivor Pearce, "The Problem of the Balance of Payments," *International Economic Review* 2 (January 1961): 1-28. In her survey of balance of payments theory, in the *Journal of Economic Literature* (March 1969), Anne Krueger cites the conduct of balance of payments analysis in terms of models allowing for a non-traded good as one of the two important developments in the theory of devaluation.

12. It is assumed, of course, that outputs equal values added. If there are interindustrial transactions, one would have to adjust the argument in the text to ensure that expanding regional production also implies expanding value added.

13. As we will see below, this argument has some relevance to a discussion of Pakistan's experience, since clearly there were considerable income differentials among the two wings of Pakistan and the foreign trade regime can be argued to have favored the richer wing (which is presently Pakistan) at the expense of the poorer wing (which is now Bangladesh), the latter having been the exporting region.

14. Cf. J. Bhagwati, "The Case for Devaluation," *Economic Weekly* (June 6, 1965); and R.N. Cooper, "Devaluation and Aggregate Demand in Aid-Receiving Countries," in Bhagwati et al., eds., *Trade, Balance of Payments and Growth, Essays in Honor of C.P. Kindleberger* (Amsterdam: North-Holland Co., 1971). A systematic theoretical analysis of different factors that may lead to a deflationary impact is provided in the elegant paper of Paul Krugman and Lance Taylor, "Contractionary Effects of Devaluation," *Journal of International Economics* (August 1978).

15. Cf. Bhagwati, *The Theory and Practice of Commercial Policy*, op.cit.

16. This formulation is based on S. Chakravarty, *The Logic of Investment Planning, Contributions to Economic Analysis Series* (Amsterdam: North-Holland Co., 1956).

17. The time path of the average savings ratio I_t/Y_t is given by dividing the equation for I_t by the equation for Y_t in the text.

18. For further analysis of this simple model, see J. Bhagwati, "The Nature of Balance of Payments Difficulties in Developing Countries," in *Measures for Trade Expansion of Developing Countries*, Proceedings of a Japanese Economic Research Center Conference, Tokyo, October 1966; and the elegant piece by R.E. Findlay, "The 'Foreign Exchange Gap' and Growth in Developing Economies," in Bhagwati et al., eds., *Trade, Balance of Payments and Growth*, 1971, op.cit.

19. The case for foreign aid can also be made more effectively in this case since foreign aid, aside from supplementing any given domestic savings, would then help break the foreign exchange constraint.

20. Cf. Ronald McKinnon, *Money and Capital in Economic Development* (Washington, D.C.: The Brookings Institution, 1973).

21. There is some empirical evidence on this issue in Lester Taylor, "Price Expectations and Households' Demand for Financial Assets," *Explorations in Economic Research*, 1, 2 (Fall 1974), and David H. Howard, "Personal Saving Behavior in Five Major Industrialized Countries," International Finance Discussion Paper No. 90, Board of Governors of the Federal Reserve System, November 1976.

22. H.S. Houthakker, "On Some Determinants of Savings in Developed and Underdeveloped Countries," in E.A.G. Robinson, ed., *Problems in Economic Development* (London: Macmillan, 1965).

23. The figures in brackets are standard errors.

24. Jeffrey Williamson, "Personal Saving in Developing Nations: An Intertemporal Cross-Section from Asia," *Economic Record*, 44, 106 (June 1968): 194-210.

25. Ibid., p. 199.

26. *Turkey*, op.cit., p. 243. One footnote has been omitted.

27. J. Williamson, "Determinants of Personal Saving in Asia: Long-Run and Short-Run Effects," *Discussion Paper No. 67-11* (Department of Economics, University of the Philippines, September 15, 1967), Appendix B.

28. *Chile*, op.cit., Chapter 12, pp. 284-285. The anti-Kaldor effect has been noted for Chile in Chapter 5 as well.

29. Cf. *Exchange-Rate Devaluation in a Semi-Industrialized Country*, (Cambridge, Mass.: M.I.T. Press, 1965); especially Chapters 2 and 5.

30. Cf. T. Weisskopf, op.cit.

31. Cf. Papanek, op.cit., and Table 6-7 below.

32. *India*, op.cit., Chapter 15. The discussion below is almost a quote from that study, with minor stylistic changes to adapt it to the present context.

33. The *t* values were:

Form of Equation	*Degrees of Freedom*	*t*
3a	168	−5.23
3b	158	−0.84
3c	158	−0.19

34. The "*F*" values were:

	Traditional		*Non-Traditional*	
Form of Equation	*Degrees of Freedom*	*F*	*Degrees of Freedom*	*F*
3a	364	1.57	596	2.18
3b	360	5.92	590	2.26
3c	360	7.74	590	0.32

35. *Turkey*, op.cit., pp. 240-241.

36. *Chile*, op.cit., Chapter 12, p. 284. However, as Behrman notes, this conclusion probably did not hold under the Allende regime as the government did not remain a high, marginal saver: for example, in 1971, real saving became negative while real revenues rose!

37. *South Korea*, op.cit., Chapter 8, p. 137.

38. Ibid., Chapter 9.

39. *India*, op.cit., Chapter 16, pp 238-239; two footnotes are omitted from the quote.

40. However, they note that:

> . . . higher savings rates may still imply lower growth rates if the investment needed to sustain unit growth of income increases sufficiently in the process owing to inefficiencies or misallocation of resources. In particular, in relation to the urban expansion, note that such an outcome of the economic policies, even if it leads to an increase in the savings rate, may well require additional investments in high cpaital-output ratio activities such as housing and related infrastructure in the cities and thus slow down economic growth on that account (p. 239).

41. Agriculture-based exports from many other countries in the Project—for example, Colombia, Turkey, Philippines, Korea, and Egypt—were *not* significantly in oligopolistic markets, however.

42. Cf. A. Bergan, "Personal Income Distribution and Personal Savings in Pakistan," *Pakistan Development Review* 7 (Summer 1967). Also see T.M. Khan, "Some Reflections on Planning Experience in Pakistan," *Pakistan Development Review* 8 (Autumn 1968): 391-398.

43. The precise calculations of such income distributional shifts (discussed in Islam, *Pakistan*, op.cit., Chapter on "Mobilization of Domestic Resources") do not allow for impact on income itself of the shift to a liberalized regime and on the international prices themselves, given the lack of perfect competition internationally in markets for tea, cotton textiles, and jute, in particular. They should not be taken literally, therefore, but are useful in establishing directional changes.

44. *Chile*, op.cit., Chapter 12, page 284. We may note that the rural saving propensity may be a function of the extent to which a capital market is developed in the rural areas.

45. The estimates in Bergan, op. cit., however, refer to average, rather than marginal, saving propensities.

46. Ibid., p. 220.

47. However, we should not forget that the two sets of coefficients are for different data; and that Williamson uses only direct taxes.

48. *Chile*, op.cit., Chapter 11, page 261. Footnotes have been deleted from the quote.

49. Cf. *India*, op.cit., Chapter 16, p. 240.

50. However, the authors note also that, whenever these premiums were "cashed" in the market by *illegal* transactions, they escaped the tax net. Also, in contributing to the large amount of "black" money in circulation, the exchange control regime that made transfers of AU licenses illegal but not infrequent was itself a major force in making the tax effort of the Indian fiscal authorities less effective.

51. *Pakistan*, op.cit., Chapter on "Mobilization of Domestic Resources," pp. 2-3.

52. Turkey, op.cit., page 178. Note that this windfall gain is *net* of duties and surcharges, of course.

53. *Israel*, op.cit., pp. 155-56. Four footnotes from the original have been omitted in this quotation. Table 6-3 in the quote has been renumbered here as Table 6-5.

54. Michaely notes however that "a calculation such as that presented in Table 6-5 based as it is on arbitrary assumptions—could not yield more than a general impression. Moreover, even such a tentative conclusion must be hedged by recalling that it is based on a mechanistic assumption regarding the government's method of operation, namely, that changes in the government's receipts from abroad are fully reflected in the development budget without any offsetting, discretionary changes by the government. To what extent such a mechanistic view of the government's decision-making process in this matter is correct would not be easy to determine."

55. Or, as Krueger has noted for Turkey, shift the saving to investment in activities such as construction which have high incremental capital-output ratios, thus retarding growth.

56. Cf. Luis Landau, "Saving Functions for Latin America," in H. Chenery, ed., *Studies in Development Planning* (Cambridge, Mass.: Harvard University Press, 1971); and T. Weisskopf, "An Econometric Test of Alternative Constraints on the Growth of Underdeveloped Countries," *Review of Economics and Statistics*, 54, 1 (February 1972). The reader must consult these papers for details of the tests.

57. Op.cit., p. 217.

58. Op.cit., pp. 204, 208-209.

59. Other explanations can also be provided, as in Section I where the capital-markets hypothesis was discussed by us.

60. Leith, *Ghana*, op.cit., also cites some evidence relating to this issue, but it is less than persuasive because it relates to all, rather than personal, saving and to inflation rather than the real interest rate. He finds a negative coefficient on the inflation rate, indicating that the saving rate responds negatively to inflation: "an increase of 5 percentage points in the rate of inflation is met by a decrease of about 1.6 percentage points in the percentage of GNP saved. Cf. Leith, ibid., pp. 86-87, footnote 1.

61. For details, see *South Korea*, op.cit., Chapter 8, especially the estimates of Equations 8.14 and 8.15 therein.

62. Ronald McKinnon, "Saving Propensities and the Korean Monetary Reform in Retrospect," submitted to the Conference on *Money and Finance in Economic Growth and Development* (April 18-20, 1974), Stanford University, p. 3.

63. Cf. *South Korea*, op.cit., Table 11-4.

64. *India*, op.cit., Chapter 16, pp. 2-3.

65. The authors also note that if one believes that the marginal propensity to save rises with per capita income (e.g., Landau, op.cit.), its failure to do so in the 1960s, relative to the 1950s, may imply a failing of the QR regime on the saving front (p. 285).

66. Both the risks must be adjusted, of course, to allow for anticipated, endogenous changes in price level and profits.

67. *Israel* op.cit., Chapter 6, p. 151.

68. *Israel*, op.cit., page 153.

69. *South Korea*, op.cit., Chapter 7, pp. 106-108. Note that *public borrowing* has been the major element here rather than direct foreign investment.

70. *Chile*, op.cit., Chapter 8, pp. 209-211.

71. *Ibid*, p. 210. The single exception was the liberalization under President Frei.

72. Short-term flows are also discussed by Behrman but are more directly relevant to the short-run liberalization analysis of the type undertaken in the companion synthesis volume of Krueger.

73. Raymond Vernon's "product-cycle" hypothesis, which relates essentially to manufacturing abroad a differentiated product that was earlier exported, overlaps with "tariff-jumping" investment but Vernon also invokes other cost-reducing advantages abroad. In direct contrast to Vernon's product-cycle type of theory, Bhagwati has developed a theory of mutually penetrating investment (MPI) whereby, within an industry with differentiated products (e.g., radial tires and standard tires; compacts and large cars), the response to competition in each other's markets is for each country's industry to invest in the other's. Thus, if Dunlop is skilled in conventional cross-ply tires and Pirelli in radials, their response to competing with each other in both types of tires could be for Dunlop to go easy on radials but buy equity into the Pirelli radials and for Pirelli to give up on cross-ply tires and buy equity into the Dunlop cross-ply. This, in fact, has happened: For details, see J. Bhagwati's review of R. Vernon, *Sovereignty at Bay: The Multinational Spread of U.S. Enterprises* (New York: Basic Books, 1971), in *Journal of International Economics* (September 1972). Thus, whereas the firm goes abroad in the Vernon model to manufacture its own differentiated product, thus *de facto* "exporting" and investing in its research and development, in the Bhagwati model it goes abroad to invest in its competitor's organization, to take an equity interest in the production of the differentiated product where its *competitor* has an advantage and hence *de facto* the firm is "buying" and investing in the *competitor's* research and development. The Bhagwati theory of MPI (mutually penetrating investment) represents thus a radically new type of investment phenomenon, in contrast to the Vernon PC (product-cycle) investment model. However, the MPI model, more likely, applies to investment among countries with similar industrial structures and hence product-differentiated advantages in different products in the same industry group.

74. Chapter 4, Section III.

75. Chapter 4, Section II.

76. For obvious reasons, we have not considered here the interaction of foreign trade regimes with swings in trade credits. The classic analysis of this phenomenon is by Bent Hansen, *Foreign Trade Credits and Exchange Reserves, Contributions to Economic Analysis* (Amsterdam: North-Holland Co., 1963).

77. Cf. Franco Modigliani, "International Capital Movements, Fixed Parities and Monetary and Fiscal Policies," in J. Bhagwati and R.S. Eckaus, eds., *Development and Planning: Essays in Honor of P.N. Rosenstein-Rodan* (London: Allen and Unwin, 1973), p. 239: "There is a broad measure of agreement among professional economists on the proposition that the free movement of long-term international capital, just like the free movement of commodities, is highly desirable since it contributes to a more efficient use of resources. . . ."

78. For an account, somewhat favorable to capital inflows, see C.P. Kindleberger, "Restrictions on Direct Investment in Host Countries," in J. Bhagwati and R.S. Eckaus, eds., *Development and Planninng*, ibid. Also, for theoretical analysis of optimal tax-cum-subsidies on trade and capital flows, see the papers of R.W. Jones, "International Capital Movements and the Theory of Tariffs and Trade," *Quarterly Journal of Economics* 81 (February 1967): 1-38; and M.C. Kemp, "The Pure Theory of International Trade," 56 *American Economic Review*, (September 1966): 788-809.

79. The figure in this footnote illustrates such a relationship between domestic saving and foreign aid flows. The variable F/Y (foreign aid to income) can be replaced by F if the hypothesis is modified to refer to absolute aid flows.

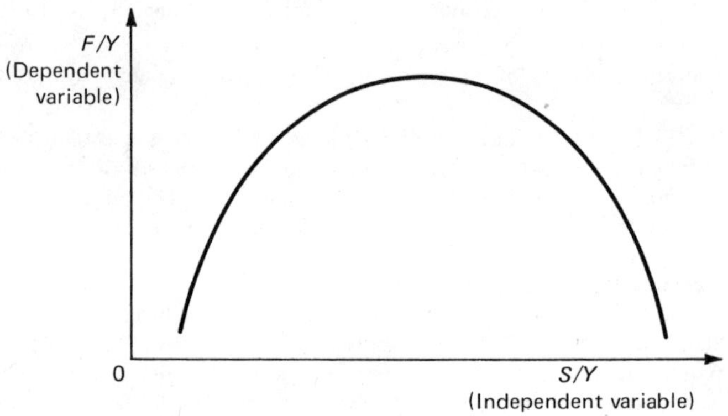

80. Nor, for that matter, has cross-sectional analysis of aid-flow distribution among recipients, using other variables such as per capital income, been notably successful. For a review of these analyses and regression estimates, see J. Bhagwati, *Amount and Sharing of Aid* (Washington D.C.: Overseas Development Council, 1970), Appendix II.

81. The relationship would be as in the illustration in this footnote.

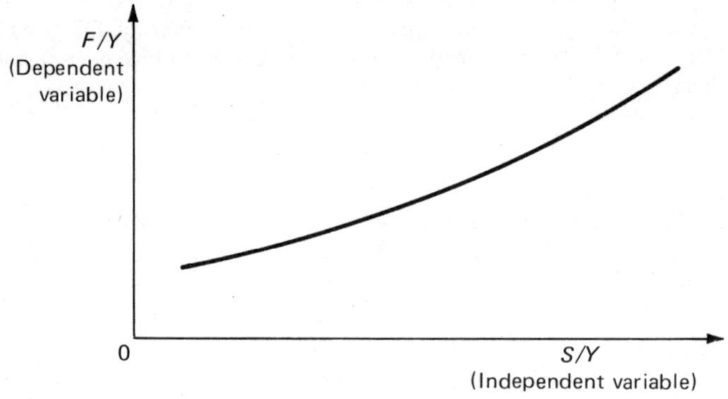

The net effect of merging the two capital flows, as is done in many of the empirical analyses shortly to be reviewed, would be to moderate (and could even reverse) the decline in F/Y at higher S/Y ratios where the aid curve turns down.

82. Thus, the figure in the preceding note modifies to the diagram (where, for simplicity, we assume a negligible 'a') in this footnote.

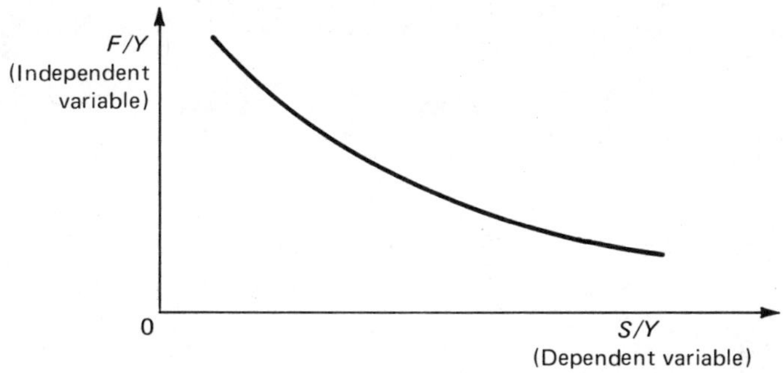

83. On the other hand, if we assume that the country decides on an optimal time path, given an intertemporal utility function, it is not necessarily true that aid will not be *more than offset* by current consumption. For such "counterintuitive" results, I am indebted to an unpublished paper of Richard Freeman.

84. Among the exceptions is G. Papanek, *Journal of Political Economy*, op.cit.

85. Cf. E. Grinols and J. Bhagwati, "Foreign Capital, Savings and Dependence," *Review of Economics and Statistics*, 58 (November 1976): 416-424. They do not make any adjustment for the assertion sometimes made that foreign inflows *reduce* the efficiency of factor use and thus increase the marginal capital-output ratio. There is no evidence of any value that indicates that aid is utilized any more or less well than average capital use in the developing countries.

86. Cf. *India*, op.cit., Chapter 15 on "Savings and the Foreign Trade Regime."

87. Cf. *India*, op.cit., Chapter 16, pp. 234-235. Note that public saving is usually measurable more reliably than aggregate saving.

88. *India*, ibid., Chapter 16, pp. 234-235; footnotes have been omitted but footnote 5 has been turned into a comment footnote to this quote.

89. In fact, the authors mention the possibility that the resource inflow could have improved investment opportunities—and, in India, the inflow of private foreign investment also leads to the same result as joint ventures are promoted actively by governmental policy—and led to increased private saving *a la* Hirschman to utilize these opportunities! The only "weak" argument in support of the negative coefficient on F_{-1} is that consumption is a function of available imports that, in turn, reflect foreign aid inflow: PL480 imports would sustain that argument somewhat.

90. *Chile*, op.cit., page 285.

91. Whether *foreign* inflows of aid or private (direct and portfolio) long-term investment are good or bad is however a complex issue that is rather more open to debate. Hence, arguing that restrictionist exchange control regimes, on balance, reduce such inflows is *not* the same as arguing that therefore such exchange control regimes are inefficient. The arguments for and against unrestricted (levelwise and compositionwise) inflows of private foreign capital are too well known to be recounted here; this is also the case for the debate on the productivity of foreign aid in recipient countries. However, the reader would do well to consult the South Korea study by Frank et al. that develops a rather novel argument on the suboptimality of foreign capital inflow into Korea along Fisherian lines.

Chapter 7

Export Performance and Other Effects

We now proceed to discuss a number of miscellaneous growth and distributional arguments regarding the effects of the foreign trade regimes. We start with the effects on export and then discuss economic performance. (This subject might have followed immediately on the analysis of allocative efficiency in Chapter 5 but has been relegated here as export performance seems to affect *growth* performance in diverse ways as discussed in Chapter 8.) We then consider rather more "greyish" areas such as the effects on innovation and technical change and on quality of labor and on entrepreneurship in general. Finally, the evidence in the Project studies on the effects of the foreign trade regimes on income distribution is reviewed.

EXPORT PERFORMANCE

Anne Krueger's companion volume reports on the results of the Project studies in regard to export performance in detail and analyzes the results in great depth.[1] Hence our treatment here will be extremely brief and addressed only to a few essential observations.

1. First, note that a principal result of overvaluation of the exchange rate, as in Phase II regimes, is that there is a *bias* against exports. The ratio of the effective exchange rate on exports (EER_x) to that on imports (EER_m) can be taken as an index of how far exports are profitable relative to import-competing production. Hence when EER_x/EER_m is less than unity for a commodity this may be described as the existence of a bias against its exportation.

This index of bias against exports dates back to the 1960s and was in vogue in India, for example, where it was used, taking into account the incentives on *both* outputs and inputs. For example, the incentive implicit in the availability of imported inputs at tariff-exclusive (i.e., international) prices would also be taken into account.[2] Furthermore, this definition of export bias (as the ratio of effective exchange rates in export and domestic markets) is identical with the later definition of export bias, used in the World Bank documents, for example, *for individual activities* as the ratio of effective rate of protection in foreign and in domestic markets.[3]

The export-bias index, EER_x/EER_m, basically seeks to capture the relative price change between exportables and importables on the presumption that (with the usual restrictions such as convexity and competitiveness of markets being satisfied) this would imply a corresponding production and hence export-level shift. However, it is readily possible to construct analytical exceptions to this conclusion so that, as with other indices that are used to "explain" reality, this index also has to be regarded with some caution.

In fact, the Project studies, attempting to take into account also the complications inevitably introduced by the presence of non-traded goods and of differential rates of overall inflation in different countries also utilized the concepts of domestic price-level-deflated *EERs* (i.e., *PLD-EERS*). These were deflated in turn for foreign price-level changes (i.e., *PPP-EERs*), which make them close to purchasing-power-parity notions, of course.[4]

2. As it happens, there are several different types of evidence available in the Project studies to suggest that restrictive foreign trade regimes, with high explicit or implicit tariffs and associated export-bias ($EER_x/EER_m < 1$), are associated with lower export performance, and that changing the overall foreign trade regimes successfully to Phases IV and/or V, with significantly reduced reliance on exchange controls and reduced export bias as well, pays handsome dividends in terms of higher exports.

First, there is the usual type of evidence that, after successful liberalization (normally accompanied by devaluation), export earnings may decline or be sluggish but later tend to show responsiveness. This phenomenon, known in the literature as the *J*-curve behavior (with initial decline and later rise), has been documented for a number (but by no means all) of the liberalization episodes that the Project countries experienced and that have been studied in depth. Thus, for example, the June 1966 Indian devaluation and liberalization policy package, once adjustment was made for the exogenous decline in exports brought about by two serious agricultural droughts, showed this pattern of export behavior.[5] In many cases, attention has been focused on the short-run export response so that the medium- and long-run response, which was more favorable, has been missed by earlier analysts.[6]

Next, the Project studies provide a considerable amount of statistical analysis of the responsiveness of minor exports in particular and manufactured exports in general, which (on the basis of regression analysis using mainly time-series estimates) suggests strongly that the exports of these developing countries are in general responsive to price changes. This evidence is at the micro-level for specific commodities (including sometimes even primary products) and also for broad aggregates by sectors. Table 7-1 contains several of the regressions produced by different authors in the Project on this question and which are broadly destructive of "elasticity pessimism."[7] It should be noted that the Project studies do deploy different indices for their price variable. There is indeed here some of the tendency among econometricians to keep shifting among alternative price variables until something "works." But, with this customary caveat in mind, we should note that the evidence broadly supports those who contend that prices do matter.

Finally, Krueger's cross-sectional analysis of the ten Project countries in her synthesis volume also underlines the significance of prices in improving or inhibiting the growth of exports. In her regressions, she uses dummies to represent Phases I, II, IV, and V. The Krueger regressions indicate that *PLDEERs* on exports seem to affect both traditional and non-traditional (otherwise described as "minor" in many of the studies) export values, and that Phases IV and V do seem to affect export performance favorably.[8]

In this regard, note the vastly more important point that the Project results indicate strongly that it is really a shift to successful liberalization and therefore *continuing* liberalization that is critical to improved export performance on a *sustained* basis; that is, a shift to Phase IV from Phase II will show such an improved performance, but not really occasional jabs at liberalization, each resulting in eventual relapse into Phase II (from Phase III liberalization attempts). Thus, it is the sustained transition during the 1960s from Phase II to Phase IV or Phase V by South Korea, Israel, and Brazil that was attended by high rates of export growth.[9]

Additionally, it is also worth noting that it is not just the price aspects of the restrictive Phase II regimes that inhibit export performance. As has been documented in the Indian case, for example, the whole framework of exchange controls in a Phase II situation militates against export performance. Thus, for instance, the ability to expand production to fill export orders requires access to import licenses for raw materials, and capacity expansion requires import (and industrial) licenses. In each case, red tape and uncertainty cloud the scene.[10]

Finally, drawing on other evidence, we may note that statistical analysis of the usual decomposition variety where the export performance of several LDCs is decomposed into that attributable to overall growth of demand, regional composition, commodity composition, and a residual "competitive factor" effect, contrasting the 1950s when most LDCs were in Phase II and the 1960s when some had successfully shifted to Phase IV, shows that the latter

Table 7-1. Principal Project Results on Time Series Regressions of Exports

Country	*Years*	*Equation*	*Y: Export Variable*	*X: Foreign Exchange Rate Variable*	*Estimate of Coefficient of X (t-Statistic)*
Chile	1947-1965	$Y = a + bX_1 + cX_2$ + standard deviations of relative prices + quantitative supply factors + quantitative demand factors	Agricultural real exports	X_1: Ratio of unit value of sectoral exports multiplied by the exchange rate to the sectoral labor price including employer social security contributions	*b:* 39.2 (9.1)
				X_2: Black-market PLD-nominal-exchange-rate *minus* national accounts PLD-NER	*c:* 6.72 (2.6)
Chile	1947-1965	$Y = a + bX_1 + cX_2$ + standard deviations of relative prices + quantitative supply factors + lagged exports	Large-scale mining real exports (I)	X_1: Ratio of U.S. producer price for copper adjusted for direct tax rate on mining to index of intermediate prices for mining adjusted for the nominal exchange rate for large-scale mining.	*b:* 6.83 (7.8)
				X_2: Ratio of U.S. producer price for copper adjusted for direct tax rate on mining to price of labor in mining including employer social security contributions.	*c:* 1.34 (6.2)

Table 7-1 (continued)

Country	Years	Equation	Y: Export Variable	X: Foreign Exchange Rate Variable	Estimate of Coefficient of X (t-Statistic)
Chile	1947-1965	$Y = a + bX_1 + cX_2$ + standard deviations of relative prices + (modified) quantitative supply factors + lagged exports	Large-scale mining real exports (II)	Same as above	*b:* 7.99 (5.6) *c:* 1.58 (4.4)
Chile	1947-1965	$Y = a + bX_1 + cX_2$ + quantitative supply factors + quantitative demand factors	Small- and medium-scale mining real exports	X_1: Same as for large-scale mining, but lagged one year	*b:* 0.99 (5.8)
				X_2: PLD-NER, lagged one year	*c:* 25.1 (1.5)
Chile	1947-1965	$Y = a + bX_1 + cX_2 + dX_3$ + standard deviations of relative prices + quantitative supply factors + lagged exports	Industry real exports	X_1: Ratio of unit value of sectoral exports multiplied by the exchange rate to domestic sectoral domestic product price	*b:* 5,271.0 (2.8)
				X_2: PLD NER, lagged one year	*c:* 117.1 (4.2)
				X_3: Black-market PLD-NER *minus* national accounts PLD-NER, lagged one year	*d:* 40.8 (5.1)
Colombia	1955-1972	$Y = a + bX + cZ_3$	Change in log of dollar value of recorded minor exports	Change in log of PPP-EER for recorded minor exports	.81 (2.50)

Colombia	1955-1972	$Y = a + bX + cZ_3 + dZ_4$	Change in log of dollar value of recorded minor	Change in log of PPP-EER for recorded minor exports	.87 (2.84)
Colombia	1955-1970	$Y = a + bX + cZ_3 + dZ_4$	Change in log of dollar value of exports of BCST	Change in log of PPP-EER for recorded minor exports	1.13 (2.54)
Colombia	1955-1970	$Y = a + b + cZ_3$	Change in log of dollar value of non-BCST recorded minor exports	Change in log of PPP-EER for recorded minor exports	.59 (1.38)
Colombia	1955-1972 quarterly	$Y = a + bX + cZ_3$	Change in log of dollar value of recorded minor exports	Change in log of PPP-EER for recorded minor exports	.95 (3.59)
Colombia	1955-1963 quarterly	$Y = a + bX + CZ_3$	Change in log of dollar value of recorded minor exports	Change in log of PPP-EER for recorded minor exports	.68 (2.02)
Colombia	1964-1972 quarterly	$Y = a + bX + cZ_3$	Change in log of dollar value of recorded minor exports	Change in log of PPP-EER for recorded minor exports	1.04 (2.07)
Ghana	1961-1962 to 1966-67	$Y_t = a + bX_{t-½}$	Log of value of non-cocoa exports in 1968-1969 prices in N¢ million	Log of PLD EER for non-cocoa exports	.44 (6.28)
Israel	1955-1969	$Y = a + bX + cZ_1$	Log of value added in exports of goods at constant prices	Log of PPP EER for exports of goods based on domestic prices of GNP	.50
Israel	1960-1969	$Y = a + bX + cZ_1$	Log of value added in exports of goods at constant prices	Log of PPP EER for exports of goods based on domestic prices of GNP	.65
Israel	1960-1969	$Y = a + bX + cZ_2$	Log of value added in industrial exports	Log of PPP EER for industrial exports based on domestic prices of GNP	1.19

Table 7-1 (continued)

Country	*Years*	*Equation*	*Y: Export Variable*	*X: Foreign Exchange Rate Variable*	*Estimate of Coefficient of X (t-Statistic)*
Israel	1960-1969	$Y = a + bX + cZ_2$	Log of value added in industrial exports	Log of PPP-EER for industrial exports based on industrial price level	.87
Philippines	1962-1968	$Y = a + bX + cZ_5 + dZ_6$	Copra exports in thousands of metric tons	Export price index of copra 1955 = 100	1.93 (2.11)
Philippines	1962-1968	$Y = a + bX + cZ_7 + dZ_6$	Coconut oil exports in thousands of metric tons	Export price index of coconut oil 1955 = 100	.87 (3.68)
Philippines	1950-1969	$Y = a + bX + cZ_8 + dZ_9$	Export supply of logs and lumber in millions of board feet	Export price index of logs and lumber 1955 = 100	16.18 (4.05)
Philippines	1955-1968	$Y = z + bX + cZ_{10} + d\tau$	Export supply of copper concentrates in thousands of metric tons	Sum of export price index of copper concentrates from $t = 0$ to $t = \tau - 1$	.72 (1.46)
South Korea	1957-1970	$Y = a + bX + cW_1 + dW_2$	Exports of manufactured goods	Official foreign exchange on a PPP basis	.26 (1.70)
South Korea	1963-1970	$Y = a + bX + cW_1 + dW_2$	Exports of manufactured goods	Official foreign exchange rate on a PPP basis	1.71 (13.80)

Country	*Number of Equations (Number of Years per Equation)*	*Equation*	*Y: Export Variable*	*X: Foreign Exchange Rate Variable*	*Estimate of Coefficient of X (Standard Error)*
Turkey	4 (18-19)	$Y = a + bX + cV_1$	Log of chrome or copper exports in million dollars or tons	Log of foreign price of commodity multiplied times EER for commodity	−.01 (.22) to

				divided by home goods price index	.57 (.21)
Turkey	6 (10-19)	$Y = a + bX + cV_2$	Log of cotton or hazelnut or mohair or olive oil or raisin or tobacco exports in tons	Log of foreign price of commodity multiplied times EER for commodity divided by home goods price index	–.01 (.17) to 5.39 (6.04)
Turkey	5 (10-19)	$Y = a + bX + cV_3$	Log of hazelnut or mohair or olive oil or raisin or tobacco exports in tons	Log of foreign price of commodity multiplied times EER for commodity divided by home goods	–.05 (.08) to 8.21 (6.37)
Turkey	1 (15)	$Y = a + bX + cV_2$	Log of cotton exports in million dollars from 4th quarter of one year to 3rd quarter of next year	Log of foreign price of commodity multiplied times EER for commodity divided by home goods price index	.99 (.60)
Turkey	2 (15-19)	$Y = a + bX + cV_2$	Log of minor exports in million dollars	Log of foreign price of commodity multiplied times EER for commodity divided by home goods price index	.81 (.40) to 1.34 (.26)

Abbreviations
PLD = Price-level-deflated.
EER = Effective exchange rate.
PPP = Purchasing-power-parity.
BCST = Bananas and cotton and sugar and tobacco.

Variables
Z_1 = Log of aggregate capital stock in economy.
Z_2 = Log of capital stock in industry.
Z_3 = Index of instability of PPP EER for recorded minor exports, which is annual average of quarterly percentage fluctuations.
Z_4 = Lagged percentage change in output of BCST.

Z_5 = Export price index of dessicated coconut 1955 = 100.
Z_6 = Domestic output of coconuts expressed in equivalent units of copra in thousands of metric tons.
Z_7 = Annual money wage rate in manufacturing in pesos divided by implicit price index for value added in manufacturing 1955 = 100.
Z_8 = Plywood export price index 1955 = 100.
Z_9 = Domestic output of logs in millions of board feet.
Z_{10} = Sum of annual money wage rates in mining from $t = 0$ to $t = \tau - 1$.
τ = Time variable such that $\tau = 0$ in 1956 and $\tau = 12$ in 1968.
W_1 = Non-agricultural output.
W_2 = Export incentives represented by combination of multiple foreign exchange rate premiums plus subsidies.
V_1 = Time.
V_2 = Log of index of total agricultural production.
V_3 = Log of index of total agricultural production lagged one year.

Notes

(1) Non-cocoa exports typically account for 35 to 40 percent of total Ghanaian merchandise export earnings.

(2) Diamonds are excluded from Israeli industrial exports.

(3) (a) Colombian minor exports are non-coffee and non-petroleum exports.
(b) Minor exports constituted 34 percent of total Colombian export revenues in 1970-1972.
(c) BCST constituted 38 percent of registered Colombian minor exports in 1968-1970.

(4) South Korean regressions were performed using Cochrane-Orcutt procedure.

(5) (a) Turkish minor exports are non-chrome, cotton, hazelnut, raisin, tobacco, or wheat exports.
(b) Turkish minor exports averaged about \$100 million in the 1950s and ranged from \$133 million to \$192 million in the 1960s while total Turkish exports were \$320 million in 1960 and \$523 million in 1967.

(6) (a) Israeli regressions have been run by Halevi and reported by Michaely.
(b) Philippines regressions have been run by Bautista and Encarnación and reported by Baldwin.

(7) The *India* study does not report econometric results in a form reproducible in this table. The *Egypt* study has no results to report in this area. The *Chile* study also has estimates of export response in a general equilibrium framework, as against the single-equation estimates reported in this table.

Sources: *Chile,* pp. 186-187. *Colombia,* p. 65. *Ghana,* p. 131. *Israel,* p. 140. *Philippines,* pp. 132-138. *South Korea,* p. 85. *Turkey,* p. 209.

group of Phase IV countries had dramatically improved export performance *and* that a sizeable share of it could be assigned to the residual "competitive" factor.[11] Such analysis of the competitive factor is not generally considered to be as persuasive as the time-series analyses of the type deployed in many of the Project studies. However, it has considerable suggestive value and is corroborative of the conclusions indicated by the Project.

II. EXPORT PERFORMANCE AND GROWTH PERFORMANCE

The interesting question, in turn, is whether the superior export performance associated with Phases IV and V also leads to superior economic performance in terms of growth.

There is little doubt that the Project countries that have managed to shift during Phases IV and V to sustained, improved export performance (i.e., Brazil, Israel, and South Korea) by reducing bias against exports have also managed to register acceleration in their growth rates whereas countries (such as India) with sustained Phase II regimes, and corresponding bias against exports, have generally continued their poor growth performance. This conclusion remains with us even when special contributory factors have been accounted for in the country studies.

Quite aside from the fact that transition to Phases IV and V is attended by *improved* growth rates, the cross-sectional contrasts among the Project countries indicate strongly that the countries that have shifted to Phases IV and V have *better* growth performance than those that have continued in Phase II-type restrictive regimes. This cross-sectional evidence is not merely apparent to casual scrutiny. Krueger's cross-sectional analysis of the Project countries in the companion synthesis volume also indicates a favorable relationship between Phases IV and V in particular, and export performance quite generally, and the observed growth rate.[12]

While the Project results are obviously based on Phase designation and hence on detailed and careful analysis of the ten countries involved, it may be noted that an important statistical analysis of Irving Kravis also supports our general results.[13] Using decomposition analysis to differentiate LDCs with high export performance based on domestic policies, and taking a thirty-nine-country sample, Kravis has noted a 0.51 Spearman coefficient between ranks with respect to the index of such export performance and ranks regarding the growth rate of real national product.

The possible *reasons* why this shift to Phases IV and V, and the associated improvement in export performance, leads to the observed improvement and superiority of growth performance are systematically taken up in Chapter 8 and lead to perhaps the most important "prescriptive" conclusions of the

Project insofar as the transition to Phases IV and V is then concluded to be a desirable policy objective. The analysis in Chapter 8 will naturally draw on the allocative efficiency and savings arguments of Chapters 5 and 6, respectively. But additional arguments will also be touched upon in regard to the links between foreign trade regimes and "growth" factors such as innovation and entrepreneurship formation. The evidence on these questions is therefore presented next.

III. OTHER GROWTH EFFECTS

Foreign trade regimes may influence growth *via* their effect on the growth and quality of entrepreneurship and the degree of innovativeness and technical change.

A. Entrepreneurship: Quantity and Quality

It is sometimes argued that a Phase II regime is necessary, coupled with automatic protection to domestic industry, in order to generate domestic entrepreneurship. Perhaps there are primitive economies where such an argument may be made with some plausibility. But the Project countries surely do not seem to qualify.

Thus, in regard to India, Bhagwati and Srinivasan argue:[14]

> The notion that India lacked an adequate supply of entrepreneurship and that a system of automatic protection conferred by the QR-regime was necessary to induce investment is impossible to reconcile with the facts of Indian history up to the time that planning began in the 1950s.
>
> The tradition of entrepreneurship in India has long been documented by economic historians. Furthermore, this historic supply of entrepreneurship was not merely for trade but also for industry. In fact, the industrialization of India started in the nineteenth century and proceeded with moderate, and even negligible, tariffs during the first part of the twentieth century. Furthermore, the leading industrial entrepreneurship tended to be economically rational and even "progressive." Thus, Jamshedji Tata, who set up in 1913 the first successful Indian steel mill, came from a background and fortune in cotton trade; and he built up an efficient and stable industrial force which was critical to performance in a steel mill. And Morris D. Morris has shown clearly how, in the cotton textile industry, where a stable and disciplined labor force was *not* critical to performance, the entrepreneurs were willing to accommodate quite different labor practices rather than invest time and money in changing them. In Tata's case, the entrepreneurial activity even extended to setting up, from the beginning, a school to train Indian technicians to take over from the foreign personnel at the earliest!

It would appear to us, therefore, that in the Indian context it is not persuasive to argue that a QR-regime, with its automatic protection for indigenously produced items, was necessary to induce industrial investment. Furthermore, in the Indian case, the public sector has been an important investor in industry, thus weakening still further the argument for a QR-regime to provide automatic and indiscriminate protection to induce investment.

There is therefore nothing in the Indian experience to suggest that India could not have sustained the desired *ex-ante* levels of investment in industry by using a suitable tariff policy, the standard instruments of monetary and fiscal policy and her public-sector investment programs.

For the Philippines, Baldwin notes the substantial growth of domestic entrepreneurship in manufacturing during Phase II. However, he regards this as a shift from previous entrepreneurship in other sectors and therefore does not consider Phase II as having been a necessary condition for the *emergence* of entrepreneurship.[15]

Next, in regard to the *quality* of the entrepreneurship, while the question has not been explicitly addressed in the Project studies, it has been observed that Phase II regimes, with automatic or semi-automatic protection, are likely to create a *rentier*, as against a Schumpeterian capitalist, entrepreneurial class. This is particularly so if domestic free entry by native entrepreneurs is also strictly regulated by industrial licensing as in Pakistan and India up to the present date.[16] This is clearly one of the truly "grey" areas of economic analysis but not, for that reason, a most important issue in judging foreign trade and, indeed economic, regimes.[17]

B. Innovation and Technical Change

Again, on the issue of whether Phase II-type restrictive regimes have any discernible effects on attention to quality, on innovation and technical change, on learning by doing, and so on, the Project studies have little evidence except for detailed treatment by Bhagwati and Srinivasan for India and much briefer judgments by other authors (e.g., Colombia, Chile, and the Philippines). The evidence, at least in the Indian case, would seem to suggest that Phase II regimes, when accompanied by excessively sheltered environments, do result in low quality and designing. But these conclusions do not necessarily carry over to technical change. Nor, for that matter, can one argue (at least on the basis of current evidence) that industries that are more involved in export markets, as against domestic markets, show greater attention to quality or to technical change and innovation.

Thus, in the Indian case, the authors consider four different arguments regarding the impact of the highly protective Indian Phase II regime on attention to quality and on technical progress. They then proceed to analyze the related, but distinct, question as to whether export orientation of industries makes them more technically progressive.[18]

First, they contend that in a regime that grossly reduces competition and creates a captive market for many products thanks to the doctrine of indigenous availability,[19] it would be "rational" and profitable for an entrepreneur not to pay attention to the quality of production. Thus, it is only the "quality-minded" entrepreneurs who are known to produce products that approximate international standards of performance for similar products. For the rest, the effects of the economic regime appear to be evident, though impossible to quantify. Products with faulty performance because of production defects or defects in the inputs of domestic manufacture are pertinent here.

Second, shading into the problem of innovation, is the well-documented phenomenon of "design deficiencies," which Mark Frankena[20] has studied in some depth for the engineering goods industry during the 1960s. Frankena carefully explains that he is not discussing design deficiencies in the sense that Indian producers do not produce the "latest," capital-intensive and automated designs, but rather that, even for designs that sell in the LDCs of Africa and Asia, the Indians are uncompetitive and "unpreferred" vis-à-vis those of rival producers. He also generally confines himself to examples that indicate that Indian designs are fully dominated by other designs, no matter what the shadow or actual prices of the factors of production.

Third, the authors state that they expect that the lack of competition in the Indian-type economic regime raises the possibility that firms may choose "leisure" rather than "profits." If this takes the form of being simply sloppy about reducing costs and increasing productivity from the plant by better management, this is equivalent to "technical regress" and to social disadvantage.

Finally, they attempt to examine whether estimation of technical progress for the Indian manufacturing sector shows any evidence of increase in productivity. They hypothesize that the result of a framework of sheltered markets would be the absence of any noticeable trend toward growth in productivity. They note initially that labor productivity did increase through the period of their study. However, they note that such estimates have little relationship to growth of overall productivity, and that the superior approach is to proceed by estimating production functions and "technical change" therewith. The results of proceeding by this alternative route are to generate an estimated positive *Hicks-neutral*, overall productivity change over the period 1946-1964 at 2.8 percent annually.[21] This "reasonably large" number would appear to suggest that Phase II did not retard "technical change" in the Indian manufacturing sector. However, the authors argue that this conclusion would be unwarranted because "new investments in the new industries already embody the growth of know-how abroad. The estimation of (Hicks-neutral) technical progress, using the 'disembodied' progress assumption, will thus tend to show positive, and even large, improvements in overall productivity even when there are no such improvements." They therefore conclude that "unless, therefore, the estimation of productivity change is adjusted for 'embodied' technical change—a factor of obvious importance for India which imported the bulk of its capital goods . . . [it is not possible to] reach a firm econometric conclusion on whether the framework of Indian policies retarded the growth of overall productivity in the economy."[22]

In regard to the differential effect of export orientation on technical change in specific industries, Bhagwati and Srinivasan noted that the cross-sectional test that might have been done, by comparing the technical change in the new import-substituting *versus* that in the old, exporting industries would not have made much sense because the former would necessarily show higher technical change insofar as they would embody the progress made abroad (as noted above). Ideally, therefore, the test would have required data on the new industries themselves, but testing whether the industries with larger export orientation were characterized by greater technical change, for example. But data for enough numbers of years to undertake the required time-series analysis were just not available. They turned therefore to the alternative route of finding out whether the export-oriented industries were characterized by greater research and development expenditures compared to the domestic-market-oriented industries. Here, the results were not encouraging to those who hypothesize that export orientation would lead to differentially higher technical change. Their conclusions may be quoted:

> We must note . . . the increasing evidence that research and development expenditures are finally beginning to emerge on the Indian scene, in a number of import-competing industries, that such expenditure is being undertaken by the very large firms, and that it is undertaken in the process of import substitution itself and reflects a quasi-Kennedy-Weizsacker process of search for processes that would avoid the use of scarce, imported materials and develop the use of cheaper, indigenous inputs. Of course, as stated earlier, this research and development activity may be expensive in relation to results: but it is certainly there now and is adding to the technological maturity and expertise that the country seeks as an objective in itself. Historically, one has only to recall Japan's transition from shoddy manufacture under bad imitation to decent manufacture under good imitation to excellent manufacture under outstanding imitation to innovative manufacture in recent years. In such a historical perspective, it would appear logical to entertain the strong possibility that at least *some* of the inadequacies noted earlier may be due to the difficulties of "*first-stage*" manufacture

in a number of modern industries and that the growth of research and development in recent years may represent a growing transition to decent manufacture.[23]

Next, basing themselves on a specially commissioned survey of research and development expenditures and policies of chemical and engineering firms, they conclude:

(a) that the import substitution strategy does *not* eliminate the incentive to conduct research and development but merely imparts a bias toward conducting it in a different direction, so that the really important question then is not whether it is eliminated by the import substitution strategy but rather whether the kind induced by such a strategy reduces or increases welfare in relation to the research and development that would otherwise be conducted; and (b) that orientation toward export markets does not in itself seem to increase the incentive to conduct research and development, so that it is difficult to sustain the argument that an export promotion strategy is superior to an import substitution strategy because it will lead to greater (and presumably welfare-increasing) research and development in the economy.[24]

The argumentation and evidence from the other studies, while not detailed, is also somewhat mixed. Thus, Carlos Díaz-Alejandro writes for Colombia:[25]

Leonard Dudley, in a study of 25 import-substituting industries in the Colombian metal products sector during 1959-66, found important learning effects, explaining half of substantial productivity gains, particularly in casting, forging, and stamping. Whether or not import-substituting activities generated larger learning effects than exporting ones, however, is a moot point. There is anecdotal evidence showing that some firms (e.g., in textiles) are remarkably X-efficient and innovative whether they devote themselves to import substitution *or* to exporting, as are Germans with alternative socioeconomic systems. It will be recalled from Chapter 6 that as of 1971 major exporting firms still relied heavily on domestic sales. When the exporting experience becomes longer, and more differentiated from domestic sales, greater possibilities for exploring contrasts in behavior between exporting and import-substituting firms may become possible.

On the other hand, for Chile, Jere Behrman writes:[26]

Some advocates of more restrictive regimes claim that these barriers will permit development of native entrepreneurs and increases in labor productivities through learning by doing. Evidence to support these claims is difficult to find. The relatively low and stagnant productivities in the traditional import-substitution subsectors alluded to in Chapter 10, for example, if anything suggest the opposite conclusion. Restrictive barriers may have primarily lessened pressures for increased efficiency and productivity that the international market otherwise would have provided.

For the Philippines, the evidence cited by Robert Baldwin on technical change and its relationship to the Phases distinguished in the study is not decisive either. Thus, he cites the statistical exercise of Jeffrey Williamson where growth sources are broken down in the usual manner among input changes and technical change as the residual.[27] During Phase I, more or less spanning Williamson's period 1947-1955, technical change contributed 4.08 percent in an overall 7.3 percent growth rate. Williamson's second period, 1955-1965, unfortunately spans *both* Phase II initially and then Phase IV so that it is not possible to say anything contrasting about these two Phases. The technical change contribution for this period turns out to be 0.53 percent in an overall growth rate of 4.5 percent. Williamson cites the revival from wartime destruction as the possible cause of the unusually higher contribution of technical change in Phase I. And the low, almost negligible contribution of technical change in the later period may be cited as evidence of Phase II, continuing perhaps into Phase IV with a lag, being detrimental to technical change. But one is well advised to withhold final judgment on the issue.

IV. INCOME DISTRIBUTIONAL EFFECTS

Finally, the effects of the foreign trade regimes on income distribution, whether size or functional or in other classifications of political and sociological interest, must be noted. Evidence on these issues, now of great interest, is to be found in varying degrees in some of the Project studies.

A. Equality of Access by Small-scale Entrepreneurs

Note first that a principal defense of Phase II regimes appears to have been that the liberalized regime implied by Phases IV and V would favor the large-scale producers, produce regional imbalances, and be therefore inequitable. Chapter 2 has already discussed these matters, with evidence from countries such as India, Pakistan, and Colombia, and the conclusions are not supportive of these assertions in favor of restrictive regimes.[28] This conclusion is not surprising at all once one realizes that the rents implied by the restrictive regimes are unlikely, in the end, to be frittered away on those that do not matter, no matter what the politicians and bureaucrats say.

On the other hand, it does not follow that liberalized regimes, with greater export orientation, will have necessarily less inequality either. For, while such regimes would permit freer access to scarce imports, and hence greater scope for the smaller-scale and ill-connected entrepreneurs to get at these imports, it is possible that the basic inequality that is manifested in the unequal distribution of import licenses in Phase II regimes would merely be transferred to other areas such as imperfect access to investible capital funds. Thus, one may well hypothesize that unequal opportunities arise from basic, unequal distribution of wealth and status and that, whether the foreign trade regime is Phase II or Phase IV, the inequalities of access by the small-scale and underprivileged will persist and only their outward manifestation will change. But even this conclusion is destructive of the oft-repeated claim that restrictive regimes would produce greater equality of access by, say, the small-scale entrepreneurs.

Carlos Díaz-Alejandro has made this point in a broader context, arguing that unequal size distribution of income (to which we will presently turn) is also unlikely therefore to be sensitive to changes from import-substitution (Phase II) to export-promotion (Phases IV and V). Thus, he says:

> In earlier chapters, I argued that Colombian import controls and the protective system in general do appear to reinforce income inequality, regional disparities, and industrial concentration. The protective system has also encouraged a large number of capital-intensive projects. . . the elimination of import controls would still leave a multitude of similar mechanisms through which the rich and powerful could take advantage of state power to buttress and further their position. Imperfections in domestic capital markets, to give one fashionable example, are as large a source of inequality as import controls. Thus, focusing just on the protective system can give a misleading impression of the true sources of inequality, confusing a symptom for the cause of the disease, which, as noted by many Colombians, lies in the excessive economic and political power held by privileged minorities. It is debatable whether the economic and political power such minorities may lose from the abolition of import controls is greater than the power gains that would accrue to, say, cattle, cotton, and sugar landowners from their expanding exports.[29]

B. Distribution of Income by Class

The functional distribution of income, while it can be strongly related to foreign trade regimes in theoretical analysis (e.g., the familiar Stolper-Samuelson theorem),[30] does not appear to show anything like a strong and predictable relationship in the Project studies.

Thus, for Chile, Behrman finds that Phases and mean shares of labor income in GDP in Chile are not strongly associated.[31] On the other hand, Behrman notes that there are significant non-zero correlation coefficients among levels and rates of change of ERPs and implicit tariffs and levels and rates of change of nominal wages and wage shares. The nominal and effective structures of protection created by the international trade regime thus were associated with low but relatively rapidly rising wages, the wage increases in turn being associated with the changes in protection.[32] At the same time, the short-run effect of devaluation appeared in Behrman's econometrics to show a negative impact on the real wages of labor.[33]

For Colombia, again, there is no *strong* association between labor share in GDP and the Phases. Instead, there is, as in Chile, an upward secular trend in labor's share.[34] Díaz-Alejandro notes however the *slight* downturn in this share (from 40.4 percent in 1967-1970 to 40.1 in 1971-1972) and the fact of this being Phase IV as against the earlier Phase II (with occasional Phase III episodes) when the share rose steadily (from 35.9 percent in 1950-1954). Whether this "end or reversal of the upward trend in the manufacturing and overall wage shares that had started after 1955-1958"[35] warrants the conclusion that liberalization of the foreign trade regime in Colombia had an unfavorable impact on the wage share in GDP may however be open to disagreement in view of the wide margins of error that attend the income-share data in developing countries.

For Turkey, Anne Krueger considers the impact of the foreign trade regime to have been felt, *not* on the division of income between broad groups such as capital and labor, but rather *within* these categories.[36] Thus she argues that probably the largest effect of the trade regime was on the distribution of labor income. This was because the import-substitution industries generally paid higher wages and required skilled workers so that an increase in demand for skilled workers raised the wages of those men relative to those of the unskilled. Moreover, the fact that demand for unskilled labor rose more slowly than under an alternative trade regime probably meant fewer employment opportunities, rather than lower wages, in the presence of minimum wage legislation.[37]

> The incidence of fewer employment opportunities for unskilled workers was on the urban unemployed and those in rural areas who would have migrated if employment had been available. Insofar as there would have been more migration, per capita incomes in the agricultural sector might have been higher had urban employment increased more rapidly. Regardless of whether it was the urban unemployed or potential migrants who were adversely affected, the income-distributional effect was to increase the labor income accruing to one group and reduce the labor income going to another. Without quantitative evidence to estimate the magnitude of the increase in skilled workers' incomes and the elasticity of demand for unskilled workers, it is not possible to estimate whether labor income increased or decreased. *With the two changes in offsetting direction, however, it is likely that any change in aggregate labor income was relatively small.*

C. Other Types of Distributional Effects

There is little else in the Project studies that is conclusive on issues such as the links of Phases with the size distribution of income or the distribution between different sectors. On size distribution, the evidence itself is very fragile and probably treacherous to compare across countries when available. However, it appears that a Phase IV country such as South Korea has had, *a la* Gini coefficients, a better income distribution both initially and trendwise than a Phase II country such as India. But this contrast may be rooted, not in the foreign trade regime, but rather in the wealth structure of the countries in question, in particular, in the land reform that the Japanese successfully imposed on Korea but which has escaped effective implementation in large parts of India. One might hypothesize, however, that Phase II regimes, by leading to more sluggish growth performance relative to Phase IV regimes, would *ceteris paribus* reduce the rate at which growing labor force may be employed gainfully and hence in "overpopulated" countries such as India may have contributed to greater poverty *via* increasing underemployment and thus to a deterioration in the income distribution, possibly in the Gini coefficient measure, and certainly in terms of the rather more telling index represented by the share of income going to the bottom three deciles.

On sectoral distribution of income, the Phase II regimes presumably would favor the import-substituting sectors vis-à-vis the exporting sectors. Here, however, the evidence suggests that the outcome is not inevitable in practice. Thus, as noted in the preceding chapter,[38] Anne Krueger notes that in Turkey the major exporting interests are in agriculture and mining. The effect for agriculture of any redistribution away from exporting interests that might have resulted from currency overvaluation was largely offset by the government's price policies toward agriculture, with price intervention by the various state agencies and cooperatives resulting in severing the relations between the real exchange rate and the price received by farmers for wheat, tobacco, figs, raisins, and hazelnuts. For those commodities, which constitute the bulk of agricultural exports, the chief determinant of prices was therefore the nature of the price support program and not the real exchange rate. As for the mining sector, mining activity was stagnant and even declining in response to the erosion of the real exchange rate. However, most mining enterprises are state-owned, and during the 1950s Central Bank credits covered most of their deficits, with the result that the incidence of the losses was spread over the entire community.

On the other hand, for Chile, Jere Behrman argues that the restrictive foreign trade regimes did "shift income and resources toward government, manufacturing and services"[39] and, additionally, that industries with presumably greater political clout did manage to secure higher levels and greater increases in the degree of protection. The latter conclusion is based on significantly non-zero correlation coefficients between the degree of concentration in 1957 and the levels and rates of change of implicit tariffs and of effective rates of protection (for industries entering the manufacturing census).[40] Behrman also notes a discernible *regional* shift, linked with the sectoral shift in distribution:[41]

> In the Chilean case, questions of regional distribution are tied quite closely to sectoral ones. Increased quantitative restrictions generally have caused shifts from the north (mining) and south (agriculture) to the center (manufacturing, commerce, and government). Most government revenues have been spent in the center, most imports are made to the center, and most expenses of operating the regime have been incurred in the center. The attempts to offset these movements. . . have only partially balanced the flows to the center induced by the other aspects of foreign-sector policy.

Perhaps the most dramatic regional impact of the foreign trade regime that has been noted in the Project is that in Pakistan where the export sector, predominantly based in East Pakistan (now Bangladesh), lost relative to the import-substituting sector located primarily in West Pakistan.[42] Given the regional imbalance in power, with the military rule reflecting mainly West Pakistani interests, the question must again be raised: Would a less restrictive regime not have led to the use of alternative means to divert resources from East to West Pakistan?

On balance, therefore, the Project evidence on the income distributional and egalitarian effects of the foreign trade regimes is somewhat sketchy and mixed. However, it seems to suggest that the income distributional outcome may reflect more basic underlying distribution of wealth and power. Therefore *either* the foreign trade regime is deliberately chosen (as perhaps in Pakistan and Colombia) so as to reflect the aims following from such distribution of power *or* the inadvertent or unavoidable effects of the foreign trade regime are offset (as in Turkey) by the adoption of other policies.

Moreover, insofar as the equality of access to scarce imports and industrial activities is concerned, the evidence on the *actual* working of import controls in some Project countries (e.g., India, Pakistan, Colombia) is hardly encouraging to those who would consider restrictive regimes to be egalitarian, thus casting doubt on the occasional assertion in Phase II countries that such a foreign trade regime, even if inefficient on allocational grounds, is superior on the distributional dimension.

NOTES

1. Cf. Krueger, *Liberalization Attempts*, Chapter 8, for the short-term response of exports to Phase III episodes and Chapter 9, for the long-term response.

2. This definition of bias against exports is explicitly used in J. Bhagwati, *The Theory and Practice of Commercial Policy*, Frank Graham Memorial Lecture (1967), Princeton (International Finance Section), 1968. Also see V.K. Ramaswami's "Export Subsidy and Implicit Exchange Rates when Intermediate Goods are Traded," in his *Trade and Development*, J. Bhagwati, H.G. Johnson, and T.N. Srinivasan, eds. (London: Allen and Unwin, 1971). The concept of the bias against exports, familiar to trade theorists who study overvaluation, was developed independently in the OECD synthesis volume of Little, Scitovsky, and Scott, op.cit., as well, but not precisely as defined above.

The effective exchange rate on exports is thus defined as the units of domestic currency that can be obtained for a dollar's worth of exports, taking into account export duties, subsidies and surcharges, special exchange rates, input subsidies related to exports, and so on. The effective exchange rate on imports (EER_m) is correspondingly defined as the units of domestic currency that would be paid for a dollar's worth of imports, taking into account tariffs, surcharges, interest on advance deposits, and so on. In principle, the EER_m should include premiums on import licenses; however, in the NBER studies, the EER_m was defined exclusive of them for the simple reason that, for many countries, no reliable data on import premiums could be obtained either directly or via suitable surveys of c.i.f. and retail prices.

3. This has to be because any *differential* in the effective rate of protection between domestic and foreign markets for an industry, for example, must necessarily reflect fully the differential returns that accrue from exporting and domestic sales when full account is taken of the subsidies and taxes attaching to sales in the two markets. It should be emphasized that the equation of the two measures of export bias exists for *individual* activities.

4. Refer to the appendix giving the definitions of these concepts.

5. For a full discussion of the cross-country evidence, see Krueger's *Liberalization Attempts,* op.cit., Chapter 8

6. For a notable exception, see Richard Cooper, *Currency Devaluations in Developing Countries* (Princeton, N.J.: International Finance Section, Princeton University, 1971). Cooper also notes the response of exports to devaluations in developing countries.

7. The responsiveness of minor, "new" exports suggests strongly that, while the 2×2 trade-theoretic model where both goods are traded is unrealistic, the augmentation of this model with a *preassigned* non-traded good is also incapable of capturing reality adequately. What one really needs therefore is a model where goods may be traded or cease to be traded, depending on the policy equilibrium. Such a model, on Ricardian lines, was considered by P.A. Samuelson many years ago ("Theoretical Notes on Trade Problems," *Review of Economics and Statistics*, May 1964) and has been elegantly developed further by R. Dornbusch, S. Fischer, and P.A. Samuelson, "Comparative Advantage, Trade and Payments in a Ricardian Model with a Continuum of Goods," *American Economic Review* 67 (December 1977): 823-839.

8. Cf. Krueger's *Liberalization Attempts*, op.cit.

9. The role of expectations ensuring that export incentives are seen to have been made favorable over continued periods is obviously critical to this result: for that is when entrepreneurs will wish to make investments in export markets. See the extended discussion of the Brazil, South Korea, and Israel experience in Krueger, *Liberalization Attempts*, op.cit., Chapter 9.

10. Again, this is the kind of effect on exports that only Phase-change analysis can pick up statistically, if at all.

11. Cf. Hossein Askari and Vittorio Corbo, "Export Promotion: Its Rationale and Feasibility," 1975. (Mimeo.) This statistical study was commissioned under the Project originally and also distinguished between "minor" and other exports, defining minor as all those exports that were below 10 percent of the total value in the initial year.

12. Cf. Krueger, *Liberalization Attempts*, op.cit., Chapter 11, Table 11-2.

13. Cf. Irving Kravis, "Trade as a Handmaiden of Growth: Similarities Between the Nineteenth and Twentieth Centuries," *Economic Journal* 80 (December 1970): 850-872 in particular. Also see the interesting study by C. Michalopoulos and K. Jay, "Growth of Exports and Income in the Developing World: A Neoclassical View," AID Discussion Paper No. 28, November 1973.

14. *India*, op.cit., page 213; all footnotes have been omitted.

15. *Philippines*, op.cit., pp. 141-142: ". . .a vigorous and economically bold group quickly moved into manufacturing from such activities as commerce, finance, and traditional exports," (p. 142).

16. Cf. J. Bhagwati, *India in the International Economy*, Lal Bahadur Shastri Lectures (1973), Osmania University Press, Hyderabad, India, 1974.

17. It is reminiscent of the nineteenth-century controversy over the British permanent settlement in Bengal where Francis, arguing on the basis of physiocratic doctrine, wished to vest rights in land in those who were hiterto tax collectors for the Mughals in Delhi, with fixed-rent obligations to the British, thinking that this would create the physiocrat-theoretic capitalist class on land that would accumulate and lead to economic progress, while Warren Hastings argued that the resulting landed class would instead become a rentier class. As it happened, Hastings turned out to be right!

18. *India*, op.cit., pp. 213-222.

19. See the discussion of this Indian rule of automatic protection in Chapter 2 above.

20. *India*, op.cit., pp. 213-222.

21. Ibid., pp. 216-217.

22. Ibid., p. 217.

23. Ibid., pp. 218-219.

24. Ibid., pp. 221-222. For further analysis and discussion of the survey results, see pp. 222-226.

25. *Colombia*, op.cit., p. 239; footnote omitted.

26. *Chile*, op.cit., p. 274; footnote omitted.

27. *Philippines*, op.cit., p. 142.

28. Cf. Chapter 2, Sections C(2)-(a) and C(2)-(b).

29. *Colombia*, op.cit., pp. 239-240.

30. Such models were discussed at length in Chapter 5.

31. "The largest decline was recorded in the Phase IV period of 1957-61, but the only other fall was for Phase II of 1952-55. Otherwise, an upward secular trend dominated. The same secular trend also predominated in the average real wage-again with little indication of Phase-associated fluctuations"; *Chile*, op.cit., p. 257.

32. Ibid., pp. 257-258.

33. Ibid., pp. 258-259.

34. Cf. *Colombia*, op.cit., p. 245; Table 8-10 on labor share in GDP and the corresponding Phases in Chart 1-1, for example, on p. 3.

35. Ibid., p. 245.

36. *Turkey*, op.cit., p. 243.

37. Ibid., p. 243. See full quote on pages 140-141.

38. *Turkey*, op. cit., p. 241; quoted in full on pages 146-147.

39. *Chile*, op.cit., pp. 263-264.

40. For detailed results, see ibid., Tables A.5 and A.6 on pp. 329-333.

41. Ibid., p. 264.

42. Cf. *Pakistan*, op.cit.

PART IV
Conclusions

Chapter 8

Foreign Trade Regimes: Overall Conclusions

What prescriptive conclusions may then be drawn regarding the optimal foreign trade strategy to be followed by developing countries? The issue of the appropriate foreign trade strategy was posed as early as the 1950s by some of the leading international economists of the day, with Ragnar Nurkse arguing for what would be described today as the import-substituting strategy on the grounds of elasticity pessimism and Gottfried Haberler, Jacob Viner, and others arrayed on the other side in favor of what might be described currently as the export-promoting strategy.[1]

Interestingly, Alex Cairncross, in reviewing the relative arguments of Nurkse and Haberler had ended on a somewhat neutral note between these two strategies, appealing for a verdict from empirical evidence in the following terms:

> At the end of it all, the reader may still feel that neither Nurkse nor Haberler has settled the primary issue: how far a shortage of foreign exchange (contrasted with capital, skilled labour, land, etc.) is a limiting factor in economic development. The majority of the under-developed countries are monocultures, dependent for their earnings of foreign exchange on a single commodity (or at most two or three). These earnings are highly inelastic except when exports of the principal commodity form a small fraction of the world's consumption. At the same time, nearly all the plant and machinery that they require has to be imported, so that the scale of industrial investment is limited by the foreign exchange available to pay for it. In those circumstances, what should be the policy of a country seeking to accelerate its development? We know what most countries have done; it would be interesting if we could be told, by an economist of the standing of Nurkse or Haberler, what the results have been and what they should have done.[2]

As it happens, the results of the present Project, as also the earlier analysis in the well-known OECD Project directed by I.M.D. Little, Tibor Scitovsky, and Maurice Scott,[3] do contain an answer to Cairncross's celebrated query. It seems to come down in favor of the export-promoting trade strategy—in the manner and for reasons, and with nuances and reservations, to be discussed in the rest of this concluding chapter.

I. EXPORT-PROMOTING VS. IMPORT-SUBSTITUTING STRATEGY AND RELATIONSHIP TO PHASE ANALYSIS

The import-substituting (IS) and export-promoting (EP) trade strategies need to be defined carefully. This is particularly important as the phrase "import substitution" is often used "somewhat loosely" (as indeed in Chapter 5 in this volume) as a decline in the ratio of imports in total supply of individual activities. This definition then is a purely statistical artifact without any theoretical meaning or underpinning.[4]

The meanings that we will impart here to the two rival trade strategies are best illustrated by reference to an idealized theoretical model as follows. Thus consider the traditional model of international trade theory where primary factors produce two traded goods, *X* and *Y*; and with the customary restrictions on production functions, we generate a production possibility curve such as *AB* in Figure 8-1. If *CD* is the given international price ratio, a free trade policy that equates domestic to foreign prices of the commodities will bring production to P^* in a perfectly competitive situation. (Note that, under these assumptions, the free trade policy is also socially optimal, an implication to which we will return later.)[5] It is evident then that a trade regime that equates EER_x with EER_m in this model happens to be one that also implies the choice of such a free trade policy and will lead to production at P^*. Consider, however, the presence of a foreign trade regime that leads to $EER_x < EER_m$. This will imply a shift in equilibrium production to a ("distorted") point such as *P* where the relative production of the importable commodity *Y* has moved *up* from what it was at P^*.

We therefore may *define* a policy of import substitution (IS) as one where the effect of the foreign trade regime is to make $EER_x/EER_m < 1$, implicitly comparing it with the free-trade position that makes $EER_x/EER_m = 1$ and eschewing any welfare connotations from the definition. Asymmetrically, however, we will define the export promoting (EP) policy as one where, by contrast with the IS policy, EER_x/EER_m is restored to unity. This elimates the bias against the exportables and in favor of the importables that the IS policy (with $EER_x/EER_m < 1$) implies, rather than reversing it in the other direction

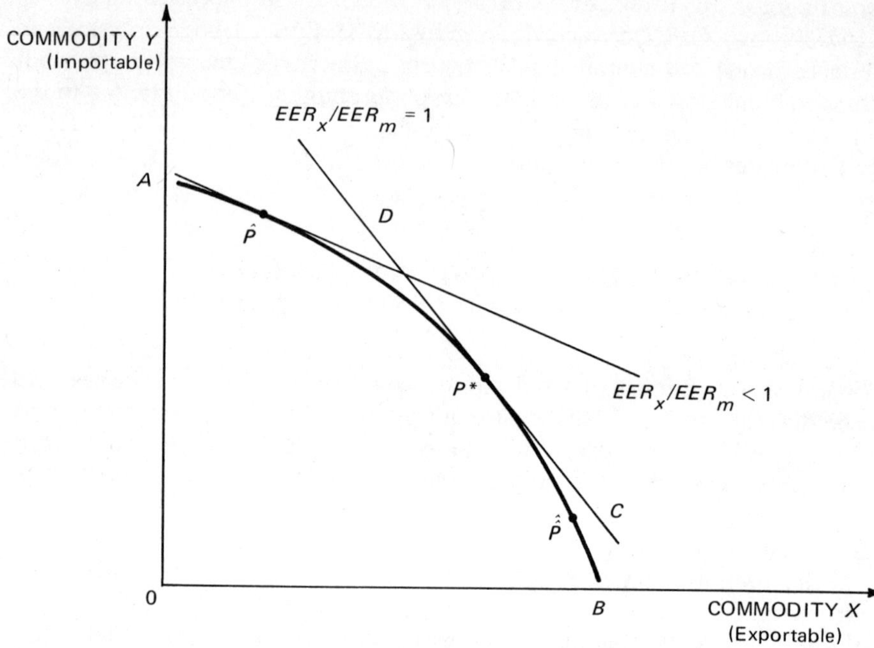

Figure 8-1. Definition of Import-Substituting and Export-Promoting Strategies.

such that $EER_x/EER_m > 1$, which would lead, for example, to production in Figure 8-1 at a point such as $\hat{\hat{P}}$ to the right of P^*.

The reason for this asymmetrical choice of definition of the EP strategy is that the countries that are popularly regarded as "export promoting" because of their successful export performance happen to offset, rather than turn on its head, the export bias implied by $EER_x < EER_m$. This is possibly one of the important reasons, as we shall presently see, for their successful *economic* performance.[6]

The link of these definitions with the Phases utilized in the Project studies is relatively straightforward since Phase II, which represents the restrictive foreign trade regime, is essentially one characterized by $EER_x/EER_m < 1$ and therefore by the IS strategy whereas the liberalized trade regimes of Phases IV and V evidently bring this ratio significantly closer to unity and hence are characterized by the EP strategy.

These "neutral" definitions leave open the question whether the *degree* of import substitution that is implied by the IS strategy is optimal or not. They also do not address the related question as to whether the *pattern* of interindustrial import substitution under the Phase II regimes, as observed in the Project studies, is also suboptimal and, if so, whether the *pattern* of interindustrial export composition under the Phase IV and V regimes, as actually studied in the Project, is economically more mindful of costs and benefits and hence superior under the EP than under the IS strategy. The answers to both these questions, among others, are pertinent to the explanation of the superior economic performance that, as already noted in the preceding chapter, attends on the EP strategy in Phases IV and V.

II. REASONS FOR SUPERIORITY OF EXPORT-PROMOTING STRATEGY: SOME HYPOTHESES

Drawing in a stylized fashion on the evidence in the Project studies on the many issues already alluded to in this volume, we may now note that the evidence suggests that, while one source of the economic superiority of the EP strategy is the possible "neutrality" of the incentives that define the pattern of industrial and export composition under this strategy as against the "chaotic" non-neutrality of the incentives that arise in the IS strategy, almost certainly the more important source of superiority comes from the mere fact of the improved economic performance that follows from the removal of the bias against exports under the EP strategy.

A. Pattern of Import Substitution vs. Pattern of Export Composition

We have already noted in depth in Chapter 5 the chaotic pattern of import substitution that emerges under the IS strategy implied by Phase II. In large part, it should be noted, this is a consequence of the fact that the foreign trade regime leads to indiscriminate import-substituting incentives as a result of overvalued exchange rates. In principle, import-substituting incentives could be far less chaotic and more neutral across different industries if tariffs were utilized instead on an across-the-board basis, for example.

It would appear that, by contrast, the calculations of EER_x for different industries in South Korea during Phase IV suggest a less chaotic pattern of interindustrial incentives.[7] Whether this contrast is regarded as sufficiently large depends, to a considerable degree, on the significance that is attached to the calculations of *EERs*, which are the *ad valorem* equivalents of a number of incentives that contain the usual share of "indirect" incentives such as the link-up of domestic profitability to export sales. It also depends, to some degree, on the significance that is attached to the presence of export *targeting,* which, if it acts as a "stick" as it definitely did in South Korea in the mid-1960s,[8] would seem to be a counterpart of the physical targeting that attends on import substitution in Phase II economies.

As it happens, there is also some statistical argumentation to suggest that the export promotional policies in a Phase IV country such as South Korea may have led to some wasteful export promotion, rather similar to the wasteful import substitution noted for Phase II countries. Thus, Wontack Hong has produced estimates recently of social losses from certain exports from South Korea.[9]

But when all this is noted, it still seems reasonable to conclude that the EP strategy under Phases IV and V does appear, in practice, to be characterized by a less chaotic and more neutral pattern of interindustrial incentives than does the IS strategy under Phase II. Whether this contrast is truly large and, in turn, makes for a substantial impact on the returns to overall investment is difficult to judge, however.[10] That it should go *some* way toward explaining the superior growth performance of the EP strategy countries, on the other hand, should not be open to serious dispute.

B. The Degree of Import Substitution and Effects of Superior Export Performance

The more important source of superior economic performance of the EP economies would seem to lie, however, not in the efficiency of the export-composition pattern vis-à-vis that of the import-substitution pattern, but rather in the indisputable fact of the vastly improved export performance. The interesting and important question is: why? A number of links between superior export and improved economic performance can be suggested and their importance assessed.

First, it should be noted, in conformity with the observation above regarding the relatively greater neutrality of export incentives across different exportables under the EP strategy, that the EP trade regime does not equally tend to carry the export subsidization, on the average, to such lengths as actually to make the ratio EER_x/EER_m substantially *greater* than unity, that is, the EP strategy amounts by and large to, and is therefore in fact defined here to be characterized by, having the ratio EER_x/EER_m fairly close to unity.[11]

It would thus appear plausible to conclude that the EP strategy tends generally to be less given to overall excesses than the IS strategy and that, in practice, this may be the source of its asymmetrical economic advantage. If so, we must ask again why this asymmetry exists in practice. The reasons would seem partly to consist in the fact that the successful shift to export-promoting strategy (or Phase IV) generally takes place within the overall context of continuing exchange controls but that the QR-caused bias against exports is offset by giving the import premiums to exporters through schemes such as supply of imported materials at international prices, and so on,[12] and by using exchange rate adjustment more freely and thereby directly reducing import premiums and hence the bias against exports. The result is *generally* (not always) to eliminate or reduce the bias against exports rather than to create excessive bias *for* exports. Because of budgetary considerations, cash subsidies that could conceivably create massive bias for exports are usually not substantial (though not unknown). On the other hand, the import-substituting strategy, especially via the mechanisms of import premiums from QRs, could and did typically cause the EER_m to get way out of line with EER_x (which was then determined almost exclusively by the exchange rate). The costs of such a *substantial* fall in EER_x/EER_m below unit are generally not understood and, in any case, do not fall directly on the budget.

Second, equally important might be the sheer fact that a more comfortable balance of payments position, resulting from improved export incentives and earnings, generally eases up the excesses of the IS strategy. This should be obvious from the well-known demonstration that, under a foreign exchange bottleneck (in the sense of Chenery), additional foreign exchange is more productive than under a savings bottleneck. But it is also apparent from the fact that a comfortable external payments situation eases up excess capacity (generated largely by the QR regime in the first place), may reduce the need to hold excess inventories, and leads often to elimination of critical bottlenecks, and so on.[13] It is perhaps remarkable that these kinds of problems, attendant on economies in Phase II, are rarely to be found in Phase IV and V economies that have successfully transited to the EP strategy on a continuing basis.

Third, in regard to the general easing of the balance of payments (and hence of the losses that attend restrictive payments policies) under the EP strategy, it is also worth noting that this effect has been reinforced in the Project countries by the substantial inflow of foreign capital that seems to attend such a strategy.[14] While different political factors help to explain the substantial inflows of foreign funds in South Korea, Brazil, and Israel, these are undoubtedly to be supplemented by economic factors in the case of the former two countries. For South Korea, in particular, the proportion of gross investment coming from foreign saving has run at well over a third on the average and, as a proportion of GNP, foreign saving has run at an average of as much as around 10 percent during 1960-1971.[15]

This inflow is *not* exogenous to the EP strategy, as is sometimes assumed, but can be seriously argued to be a result in large part of the EP strategy itself. Thus, while the bulk of the Korean and Brazilian influx of foreign funds is through public *borrowing* rather than through inflow of direct investment, this borrowing would not have been possible were it not for an export performance that was perceived to be truly remarkable and as a sign of the ability of the country to avoid the "transfer problem" difficulties that could otherwise be expected to follow from sizeable external borrowing. It is of course well known that private bankers (and the IBRD, Asian Development Bank, etc., which are included under "private" in at least some statistics) look at debt-service/export ratios, so that loans are rather directly linked, in some fashion, to export performance. Hence, it may even be legitimate to regard Brazil's "export-led" growth as merging, *via* this link between export performance and foreign borrowings, into what Fishlow calls the "debt-led" model of economic growth.

Besides, it can be argued that the large-scale inflow of *direct investment*, which has also been more sizeable in South Korea (as a percent of GNP) than in the other countries in the Project, reflects the EP strategy.[16] In fact, it may be argued that, under the EP strategy, both the magnitude of the private (direct) investment inflow *and* its efficacy in promoting economic growth will be greater over the long haul than under the IS strategy. This contrast may be explained as follows. Regarding *magnitude*, an EP strategy, with its lack of discrimination against foreign markets, is likely to attract foreign firms essentially on the nineteenth-century pattern of "factor endowment" advantages. Whereas in the nineteenth century, this meant natural resources, today it means exploiting Heckscher-Ohlin style low wages. On the other hand, by creating "artificial" inducement to invest *via* tariffs and/or QRs, so that one gets "tariff-jumping" investments oriented to the domestic market alone, the IS strategy provides an artificially limited incentive to invest in the country. The lack of complete time-series data on direct investment magnitudes in the countries in the Project and elsewhere prevents a statistical examination of this hypothesis. But it seems reasonable enough, with due adjustments being made for differences among countries on account particularly of their economic size, political attitudes to foreign investment, and political stability more generally.

As regards the *efficiency* of foreign direct investment under the EP strategy, it can again be argued that "tariff-jumping" investments, induced by the IS strategy, are more likely to imply social losses or (at minimum) reduced gains than investments attracted by Heckscher-Ohlinesque factors. Thus, following a long line of theoretical writings by Uzawa, Hamada, Minabe, and Bhagwati, and independently thereof, Brecher and Díaz-Alejandro have recently argued succinctly that tariff-induced investment in a 2 × 2 trade-theoretic model of a small open economy that imports capital-intensive goods will, for small changes, *worsen* the welfare loss that the tariff itself implies.[17] In this model, it can be shown that successive imports of foreign capital will lead to welfare changes as illustrated in Figure 8-2. Thus the tariff leads to decline in social utility from *F* to *T*; successive inflows of capital thereafter reduce welfare until autarky is reached at *A*; then welfare starts improving as the domestic price ratio moves toward the international price ratio; with M_l, the two price ratios are equal, as in Mundell,[18] and further inflows will leave welfare at this, free-trade-equivalent, level until complete specialization is

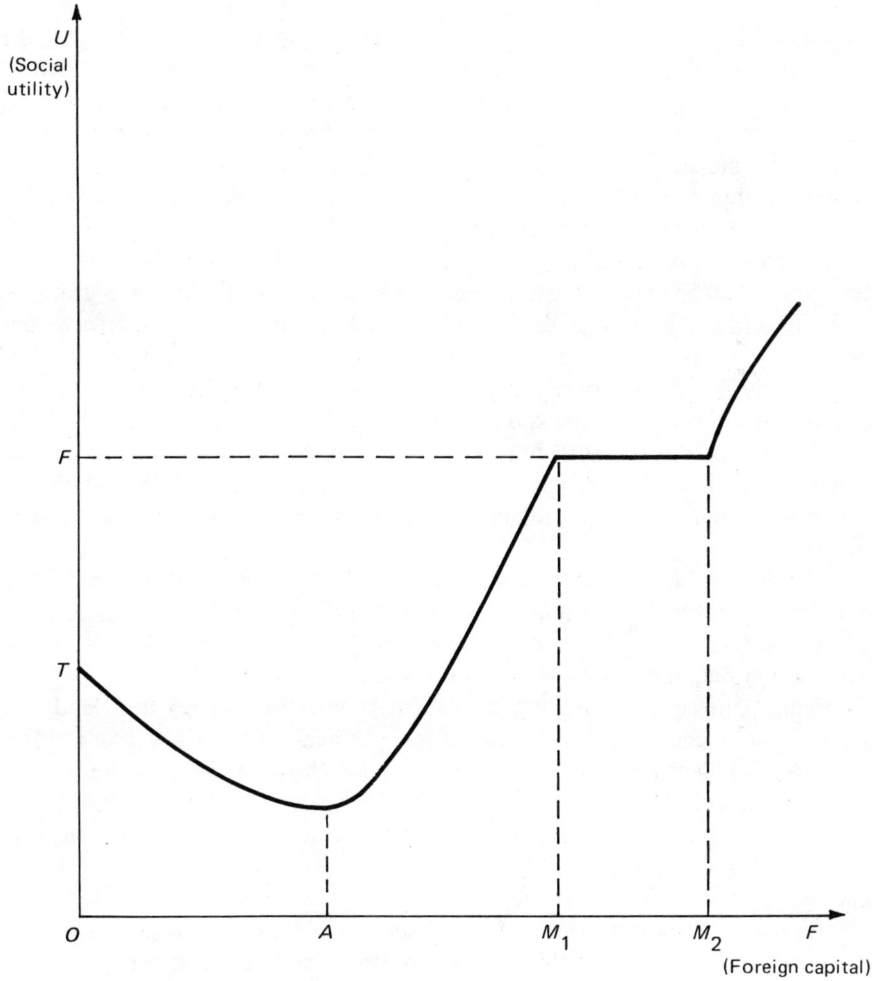

Figure 8-2. Welfare Effect of Successive Inflows of Capital in Presence of Tariff Distortion.

reached and then the MacDougall-type[19] gains will follow from diminishing returns to inflowing capital. As long, therefore, as the IS strategy leads to inflows within the range OA (short of autarky), which seems reasonable, the inflow of foreign capital will be immiserizing rather than welfare improving.

Finally, there is some statistical argumentation in the Project studies to indicate that the IS strategy may be sometimes growth reducing because the import-substituting industries happen (empirically) to be capital intensive relative to the exportable industries. Systematic evidence on this possibility is found in Chile by Behrman[20] and for Turkey, in particular, by Krueger who presents a detailed statistical exercise of the incremental income that would then have followed from a reallocation of investments within the manufacturing sector so as to reflect a "moderate import-substitution" strategy and alternatively a "balanced export promotion and import substitution" strategy. She concludes that the latter alternative would have resulted in a "considerably higher rate of growth of manufacturing output."[21]

It may also be noted here that a more complex programming exercise by Bhagwati and Srinivasan, using the well-known Eckaus-Parikh optimizing planning model for India, also shows that an improved export performance would have resulted in a greater value of the objective function. However, the critical role in this outcome seems to be played, not by the relative capital-output requirements of the exportables and the importables but rather by the fact that the planning model builds into itself the foreign exchange constraint possibility and the "better-export-performance" alternative enables the planner to get around this with greater benefit as evaluated by the specified objective function.[22]

While the factors just noted are probably the ones that are critical in defining the asymmetrical outcomes under the IS and the EP strategies, some additional factors may be cited that might contribute to the asymmetry but for which no systematic evidence is yet available.

Thus, one could argue that the export-promoting strategy may lead to a *generally* reduced reliance on direct or physical, as distinct from price, measures.[23] Direct controls have been argued with plausibility, in the Project studies as also in the earlier OECD work, to be very costly in practice. It is possible that the general incidence of such direct controls may be significantly less under export promotion because price, distribution, and other controls may make little sense to bureaucrats when firms' outputs are mainly addressed to overseas, rather than domestic, markets. A different, and perhaps more perceptive, formulation of this kind of contrast was well put by an economist familiar with both the Indian (Phase II) and the South Korean (Phase IV) trade regimes. The Indian regime consists mainly of "don'ts" whereas the Korean regime consists mainly of "do's." Whether these contrasts are, in a basic political sense, endemic to the two strategies being contrasted is not clear; but the Project studies do suggest that they exist currently.

In the still more grey area, one may argue that the EP strategy must produce, through international competition, greater efficiency than the IS strategy with its sheltered markets. While this argument is plausible *a priori*, there is as yet no real evidence at all on the subject. The issue besides is complex as the domestic competition may be sufficient to provide the incentive to efficiency under import substitution whereas exports may be to imperfectly competitive foreign markets or may simply be subsidized to the point necessary to offset any possible inefficiency-raised cost disadvantage. As already noted in Chapter 7, there is little convincing evidence on these questions yet.

Then, there is the factor of economies of scale, long recognized in international trade theory and policy discussions relating to customs unions, free trade areas, and similar cases where the size of the market is critical to the analysis of economic efficiency. In relation to the EP strategy, it seems plausible to argue that the creation of incentives (or rather, the elimination of the disincentives) to enter the foreign markets augments the size of the market and hence will lead to greater exploitation of economies of scale. Again, however, the issue is more complex insofar as the growth of firm size may be constrained by other policies and objectives (as in India) so that export promotion may take place from firms with constrained sizes by diversion from domestic production and/or by growth of new licensed firms of small size. Again, therefore, the statistical evidence and analysis of this possible cause of asymmetrical advantage of the EP strategy is not yet available in anything like the degree that would be reasonably compelling; but it does remain a plausible hypothesis.

Finally, it should be noted that, as stated in Chapters 6 and 7, there is little evidence that the EP countries are technically more progressive or that they have higher savings ratios because of a larger export sector. The superior economic performance of the EP strategy therefore cannot be additionally explained, at least on current evidence, by these "dynamic" considerations.

III. CONCLUDING OBSERVATIONS

Thus, on the basis of substantially more detailed and systematic analysis of growth effects than before and on the Phasewise classification of the country experiences, the present Project studies have managed to provide fairly persuasive support to the proponents of the EP strategy, as defined here. The results also point carefully in the direction of a number of unsettled hypotheses that might assist in explaining this superiority of the EP strategy and therefore suggest further areas for systematic investigation.

At the same time, as is evident from the companion synthesis volume of Professor Krueger, the Project throws considrable light on the question as to how the transition to the EP strategy might be successfully made, starting from the restrictive foreign trade regimes associated with the IS strategy. Thus the Project manages to go a substantial way in the direction of filling a lacuna in the previous studies of the trade and payments policies of developing countries.

While however, the Project underlines the developmental advantages that have accrued to the countries utilizing the EP strategy and also illuminates the manner in which restrictive foreign trade regimes may be successfully reshaped toward this end, a corollary to such a prescription for more than just a handful of developing countries is that the world trading system be reasonably open and accommodating to the trade needs of such a strategy. In fact, the problems that Japan has run into in regard to her international economic policy-making illustrate this point to advantage. It is thus not merely that Japan has often had an undervalued yen but also that, even if she was not building up exaggerated reserves and was instead spending all her export earnings, she would create waves because her growth rate, and the associated trade expansion, are just too great for the more sluggish rest of the world to accommodate without serious disruptions of *sectoral* markets that lead to unceasing calls for VERs (voluntary export restrictions) and other trade restrictions against Japanese exports.

Ragnar Nurkse, writing in the 1950s, was quite aware of this problem for the EP strategy. The OECD Project authors took the precaution also of stressing this when recommending against the IS strategy.[24] In fact, one cannot suppress the thought that the success stories of South Korea, Taiwan, Brazil, Singapore, and Hong Kong would not have been quite so impressive if they had not been built partly on the failures of the countries sticking overly long to the IS strategy and their consequent export (and associated economic) lag.

Nonetheless, as the Project results have made clear, even if the growth of protectionism in the international economic system prevents the world markets from accommodating the exports that would ensue if all or many developing countries followed the EP strategy, and therefore they would have to be import substituting in response to this external situation, it does not follow that the Phase II type policies of chaotic import substitution *pattern* have also to be accepted. The latter are, in principle, avoidable by the pursuit of Phase IV and V type liberalized trade regimes, while utilizing relatively neutral across-the-board tariffs so as to achieve *both* the required degree of import substitution *and* a rational pattern of it as well. A policy of exchange rate overvaluation, resulting in Phase II, is empirically a typically more expensive way to undertake the import substitution that may be required by an unfavorable external environment.

NOTES

1. Cf. Jacob Viner, *International Trade and Economic Development* (Oxford: Clarendon Press, 1953); Ragnar Nurkse, *Patterns of Trade and Development*, Wicksell Lectures (Stockholm: Almquist and Wicksell, 1959); and Gottfried Haberler, *International Trade and Economic Development* (Cairo: National Bank of Egypt, 1959). Raul Prebisch has also been identified generally with the import-substituting position.

2. Alex Cairncross, *Factors in Economic Development* (London: 1970), p. 208.

3. Cf. I. Little, T. Scitovsky, and M. Scott, *Industry and Trade in Some Developing Countries: A Comparative Study* (London: Oxford University Press, 1970).

4. For a systematic analysis of the measures of import substitution, as used in the statistical literature by economists such as Hollis Chenery, and for a clear statement of the need to define the concept analytically, rather than as a departure from initial import to supply ratio, see Padma Desai, "Alternative Measures of Import Substitution," *Oxford Economic Papers* 21 (November 1969): 312-324.

5. The conditions under which such optimality of free trade may break down have been analyzed in depth in the literature on trade and distortions. For a synthesis of these results, see J. Bhagwati, *The Theory and Practice of Commercial Policy*, 1968, op.cit.; H.G. Johnson, "Optimal Trade Intervention in the Presence of Domestic Distortions," in R.E. Caves, H.G. Johnson, and P.B. Kenen, eds., *Trade, Growth, and the Balance of Payments* (Amsterdam: North Holland Co., 1965); and J. Bhagwati, "The Generalized Theory of Distortions and Welfare," in J. Bhagwati, R.W. Jones, R. Mundell, and J. Vanek, eds., *Trade, Balance of Payments, and Growth* (Amsterdam: North Holland Co., 1970). A recent, book-length review of these results is also available in W.M. Corden, *Trade Policy and Economic Welfare* (London: Oxford University Press, 1974).

6. Note that all definitions are essentially arbitrary and must be chosen so as to reflect analytical convenience.

7. *South Korea*, op.cit., Chapter 6, p. 84.

8. Ibid., pp. 46-47.

9. Wontack Hong, "Distortions and Static, Negative Marginal Gains from Trade," *Journal of International Economics* (May 1976). The Hong study utilizes input-output techniques rather than the technique of valuing inputs and outputs at international prices, which is more appropriate to the problem at hand and which was used to demonstrate the "extreme" example of wasteful export promotion represented by value subtraction at international prices for exported items in earlier studies of India and Pakistan. For a theoretical examination of the value subtraction phenomenon, see J. Bhagwati, T.N. Srinivasan, and H. Wan, Jr., "Value Subtracted, Negative Shadow Prices of Factors in Project Evaluation, and Immiserizing Growth: Three Paradoxes in the Presence of Trade Distortions," *Economic Journal* 88 (March 1978): 121-125.

10. Skepticism about the size of the impact may stem from the somewhat tenuous nature of the effective incentive calculations (as noted); it may also follow from a Harberger-type notional calculation suggesting that the allocative losses tend to be excessively small fractions of national income anyway. The latter argument, however, is conditional on a rather static view of reallocation of given resources: once growing resources are taken into account, as they should be for our present purposes, the estimated losses may be much larger. See the extended discussion of this point in J. Bhagwati, *The Theory and Practice of Commercial Policy*, 1968, op.cit., pp. 51-52.

11. For evidence on this, see *South Korea*, op.cit., Table 5-10 which uses PPPEERs rather than EERs and also see Krueger, *Liberalization Attempts*, op.cit., Table X-2, where the EERs for Israel and South Korea are given for 1955-1971 and 1961-1970, respectively. Needless to say, there are exceptions on several specific commodities where export subsidization does get carried beyond

to EER_x/EER_m being greater than unity in varying degrees: this being part of the chaotic policy incentives commented on earlier; and in the South Korean case the average EER_x/EER_m ratio has also often tended to be higher than unity, while remaining fairly close to it.

12. A great deal of evidence on such schemes is to be found in the Project studies; also see Chapter 2 above.

13. See the discussion in Chapter 5 on these points.

14. The general easing of the balance of payments in Brazil was also aided, as Fishlow has reminded the author, by the fact that, from the mid-1960s, the Brazilian terms of trade changed quite favorably. Thus, while exports in nominal terms were increasing at rates of more than 30 percent, the volume increase was a much more modest (though impressive) 10 percent approximately.

15. Cf. *South Korea*, op.cit., pp. 106-107 for details.

16. Ian Little has pointed out to the author that, in the case of Taiwan, which is not included in the Project but is a successful example of the EP strategy, foreign direct investment has not been important. In Taiwan, according to his estimates, private foreign investment was negligible in the 1950s, and from 1960-1966 it still only averaged about US $4 mn. per annum. From 1967 through 1975 it has averaged US $47 mn. (including overseas Chinese investment which may be about 30 percent of the total). This represented 6½ percent of average fixed capital formation in manufacturing. Judging by approvals, 43 percent of the cumulative total had gone into electrical machinery and electronics, followed by chemicals, non-electrical machinery and instruments, and the rest nowhere. It is also notable that the multi-national company making goods for export to itself or its own sales organization was important only in electronics (and this is also true of South Korea). Another fact which helps to put foreign investment in perspective is that, in 1976, 21 out of the 321 largest industrial corporations were foreign.

17. Cf. R. Brecher and Carlos Díaz-Alejandro, "Tariffs, Foreign Capital and Immiserizing Growth," *Journal of International Economics* 7 (November 1977): 317-322.

18. R.A. Mundell, "International Trade and Factor Mobility," *American Economic Review* 49 (June 1967): 321-325.

19. G.D.A. MacDougall, "The Benefits and Costs of Private Investment from Abroad: A Theoretical Approach" *Economic Record* 36 (1960): 13-35.

20. *Chile*, op.cit., pp. 275-280 and p. 286: "Finally, the foreign-sector regime also might alter the aggregate capital-output ratio through changes in the allocation of investment by destination among production sectors with different capital intensities. . . above, in fact, evidence is reported of more restrictive regimes leading to greater investment in more capital-intensive subsectors."

21. *Turkey*, op.cit., p. 261 and pp. 255-263. Krueger is careful to take into account possible objections regarding the marketability of the resulting increases in exportable production. She also explores the import content and employment implications of the alternative allocational strategies.

22. *India*, op.cit., Chapter 14. The authors emphasize the illustrative nature of their exercise but conclude that: "On balance, we still consider the present exercise to be instructive in its illustration of the growth potentiality of additional exports (in the manner precisely set out at the outset of this chapter), simply because any unhappy features of the model will affect both the simulation and the reference runs; and there seems to us to be no clear presumption that the *difference* between the two runs, attributable to the change in the export vector, will be significantly affected. We should also note, to avoid unnecessary confusion, that the Eckaus-Parikh model is a *planning* model and *not* an econometric (behavioral-predictive) model so that the reader should not be surprised by discrepancies between the model's simulation runs and actual developments in the Indian economy" (p. 198).

23. The points in this paragraph and the next two were made, with slight differences in emphasis, in J. Bhagwati and A. Krueger, "Exchange Control, Liberalization and Economic Development," *American Economic Review, Papers and Proceedings* 63 (May 1973): 419-427.

24. Cf. Nurkse, op.cit., and Little, Scitovsky, and Scott, op.cit., Chapter 8.

Appendix

DEFINITION OF CONCEPTS USED IN THE PROJECT

Exchange Rates.

1. *Nominal exchange rate:* The official parity for a transaction. For countries maintaining a single exchange rate registered with the International Monetary Fund, the nominal exchange rate is the registered rate.

2. *Effective exchange rate (EER):* The number of units of local currency actually paid or received for a one-dollar international transaction. Surcharges, tariffs, the implicit interest foregone on guarantee deposits, and any other charges against purchases of goods and services abroad are included, as are rebates, the value of import replenishment rights, and other incentives to earn foreign exchange for sales of goods and services abroad.

3. *Price-level-deflated (PLD) nominal exchange rates:* The nominal exchange rate deflated in relation to some base period by the price level index of the country.

4. *Price-level-deflated EER (PLD-EER):* The EER deflated by the price level index of the country.

5. *Purchasing-power-parity adjusted exchange rates:* The relevant (nominal or effective) exchange rate multiplied by the ratio of the foreign price level to the domestic price level.

Devaluation.

1. *Gross devaluation:* The change in the parity registered with the IMF (or, synonymously in most cases, de jure devaluation).

2. *Net devaluation:* The weighted average of changes in EERs by classes of transactions (or, synonymously in most cases, de facto devaluation).

3. *Real gross devaluation:* The gross devaluation adjusted for the increase in the domestic price level over the relevant period.

4. *Real net devaluation:* The net devaluation similarly adjusted.

Protection Concepts.

1. *Explicit tariff:* The amount of tariff charged against the import of a good as a percentage of the import price (in local currency at the nominal exchange rate) of the good.

2. *Implicit tariff:*(or, synonymously, tariff equivalent): The ratio of the domestic price (net of normal distribution costs) minus the c.i.f. import price to the c.i.f. import price in local currency.

3. *Premium:* The windfall profit accruing to the recipient of an import license per dollar of imports. It is the difference between the domestic selling price (net of normal distribution costs) and the landed cost of the item (including tariffs and other charges). The premium is thus the difference between the implicit and the explicit tariff (including other charges) multiplied by the nominal exchange rate.

4. *Nominal tariff:* The tariff—either explicit or implicit as specified—on a commodity.

5. *Effective tariff:* The explicit or implicit tariff on value added as distinct from the nominal tariff on a commodity. This concept is also expressed as the effective rate of protection (ERP) or as the effective protective rate (EPR).

6. *Domestic resources costs (DRC):* The value of domestic resources (evaluated at "shadow" or opportunity cost prices) employed in earning or saving a dollar of foreign exchange (in the value-added sense) when producing domestic goods.

DELINEATION OF PHASES USED IN TRACING THE EVOLUTION OF EXCHANGE CONTROL REGIMES

To achieve comparability of analysis among different countries, each author of a country study was asked to identify the chronological development of his country's payments regime through the following phases. There was no presumption that a country would necessarily pass through all the phases in chronological sequence.

Phase I: During this period, quantitative restrictions on international transactions are imposed and then intensified. They generally are initiated in response to an unsustainable payments deficit and then, for a period, are intensified. During the period when reliance upon quantitative restrictions as a means of controlling the balance of payments is increasing, the country is said to be in Phase I.

Phase II: During this phase, quantitative restrictions are still intense, but various price measures are taken to offset some of the undesired results of the system. Heightened tariffs, surcharges on imports, rebates for exports, special tourist exchange rates, and other price interventions are used in this phase. However, primary reliance continues to be placed on quantitative restrictions.

Phase III: This phase is characterized by an attempt to systematize the changes which take place during Phase II. It generally starts with a formal exchange-rate change and may be accompanied by removal of some of the surcharges, etc., imposed during Phase II and by reduced reliance upon quantitative restrictions. Phase III may be little more than a tidying-up operation (in which case the likelihood is that the country will re-enter Phase II), or it may signal the beginning of withdrawal from reliance upon quantitative restrictions.

Phase IV: If the changes in Phase III result in adjustments within the country, so that liberalization can continue, the country is said to enter Phase IV. The necessary adjustments generally include increased foreign-exchange earnings and gradual relaxation of quantitative restrictions. The latter relaxation may take the form of changes in the nature of quantitative restrictions or of increased foreign-exchange allocations, and thus reduced premiums, under the same administrative system.

Phase V: This is a period during which an exchange regime is fully liberalized. There is full convertibility on current account, and quantitative restrictions are not employed as a means of regulating the ex ante balance of payments.

Author Index

Subject Index

About the Author

Jagdish Bhagwati is Ford International Professor of Economics at MIT. Born in 1934, he was educated at Bombay, Cambridge, MIT, and Oxford. He has been Professor at the Indian Statistical Institute, the Delhi School of Economics, and Ford Visiting Research Professor at Berkeley. He has authored and edited 18 books on the theory and policy of international economics and on developmental problems including aid and migration. His numerous papers on virtually every aspect of the theory of international trade have established him as a leading trade theorist. He is Editor of the *Journal of International Economics,* has served on the editorial board of the *American Economic Review,* and is on the board of editors of *World Development* and the *Journal of Development Economics* and of advisers of the *Journal of Policy Modeling.* He has been a consultant and member of expert groups at several international agencies, including the UNCTAD, OECD, UNIDO and ILO, and was a Senior Research Associate of the National Bureau of Economic Research. In 1967, he gave the Frank Graham Memorial Lecture and in 1973 the Shastri Lectures. He is a Fellow of the Econometric Society and was the recipient of the Mahalanobis Memorial Medal of the Indian Econometric Society in 1974.